BOARDS
THAT MAKE A
DIFFERENCE

John Carver

BOARDS THAT MAKE A DIFFERENCE

A New Design for Leadership in Nonprofit and Public Organizations

Jossey-Bass Publishers · San Francisco

BOARDS THAT MAKE A DIFFERENCE
A New Design for Leadership in Nonprofit and Public Organizations
   by John Carver

Copyright © 1990 by Jossey-Bass, Inc., Publishers, 350 Sansome Street, San Francisco, California 94104.

Substantial discounts on bulk quantities of Jossey-Bass books are available to corporations, professional associations, and other organizations. For details and discount information, contact the special sales department at Jossey-Bass Inc., Publishers (415) 433–1740; Fax (800) 605–2665.

For sales outside the United States, please contact your local Simon & Schuster International Office.

Jossey-Bass Web address: http://www.josseybass.com

Manufactured in the United States of America on Lyons Falls Turin Book.
This paper is acid-free and 100 percent totally chlorine-free.

Library of Congress Cataloging-in-Publication Data

Carver, John
      Boards that make a difference : a new design for leadership in nonprofit and public
organizations / John Carver.
         p.   cm. — (The Jossey-Bass nonprofit sector series) (The Jossey-Bass public
administration series)
      Includes bibliographic references (p.   ).
      ISBN 1–55542–231–4
      1. Directors of corporations.   2. Associations, institutions, etc.—Management.
3. Corporations, Nonprofit—Management.   I. Title.   II. Series.   III. Series: The
Jossey-Bass public administration series.
      HD2745.c37   1990
      658.4'22 — dc20   89–77419
                                                                                                                  CIP

JACKET DESIGN BY WILLI BAUM

HB Printing   20 19 18 17 16 15 14 13 12   FIRST EDITION

A joint publication of
The Jossey-Bass
Nonprofit Sector Series
and
The Jossey-Bass
Public Administration Series

CONTENTS

Preface   xi

The Author   xxi

1. A New Vision for Governing Boards   1

2. Policy as a Leadership Tool   24

3. Designing Policies That Make a Difference   40

4. Focusing on Results: Clarifying and Sustaining   56
    the Organization's Mission

5. Setting Limits: Standards of Ethics   82
    and Prudence

6. Strong Boards Need Strong Executives: 109
    The Board-Executive Relationship

7. The Board's Responsibility for Itself   130

8. Officers and Committees   149

9. Making Meetings Work   167

10. Redefining Excellence in Governance: 193
    Strategies for Board Leadership

Resource A: Varieties of Applications   213

Resource B: Bylaws   221

Resource C: Policy Contributors   225

    References   229

    Index   235

PREFACE

This is a book about boards, particularly boards of nonprofit
and public organizations. But rather than describe nonprofit
and public boards, councils, and commissions as they are,
Boards That Make a Difference prescribes how they can be.

This is a hopeful book. Boards can be the forward-
thinking, value-oriented, leading bodies we claim them to be.
In my consulting work with a multitude of boards and chief
executives, I have found a great deal of cynicism and resig-
nation. Knowledgeable skeptics think boards can never get
beyond being spoon fed by their executives and that, because
of their nature, boards must remain fundamentally reactive.
With good evidence, many people believe that boards will
always stumble from rubber stamping to meddling and back
again. They believe the realities of group decision making
forever destine boards to be incompetent groups of competent
people. My impressions, too, are just as dismal, but I believe
the cynicism is justified *only so long as boards continue to be
trapped in an inadequate design of their jobs.*

Board members are as conscientious and giving a group
as one could ever find. Members of volunteer boards and

underpaid public boards interrupt their personal and occupational lives to support something in which they believe. Space is not adequate to give sufficient credit to the works wrought by board members in any given community in one year. Personal drive of board members has accomplished formidable tasks. Perseverance of board members has surmounted seemingly intractable barriers. Patience of board members has outlasted drudgery. Generosity of board members has made the impossible possible.

Board members arrive at the table with dreams. They have vision and values. In many cases, their fervently held beliefs and sincere desire to make a difference impel them to board membership in the first place. Symphony board members want to improve community culture. City councilpersons want to increase the benefits gained for the costs of citizenship. A trade association board wants to augment the opportunities to do business. School board members want to prepare children better for life. Boards of hospitals, port authorities, social agencies, chambers of commerce, credit unions and other organizations want to offer their constituents a better life.

Yet, by and large, board members do not spend their time exploring, debating, and defining these dreams. Instead, they expend their energy on a host of demonstrably less important, even trivial, items. Instead of impassioned discussion about the changes to be produced in their world, board members are ordinarily found passively listening to staff reports or dealing with personnel procedures and the budget line for out-of-state travel. Committee agendas are likely to be filled with staff material masquerading as board work. Even when programs and services are on the agenda, discussion is almost always focused on activities rather than intended results. Boards are less incisive, goal directed, and farsighted than their average members.

Much as board members and executives unintentionally conspire to water down the powerful work of genuine governance, they often have a nagging awareness that something is not quite right. Usually, however, their recognition is focused on a specific aspect of board folly. It is rarely the basic design, the system of thought. Concern is often expressed through complaints over time spent on trivial items, time spent reading reams of documents, meetings that run for hours and accomplish little, committees that are window dressing for what staff wants to do, meddling in administration, staff that are more in control of board agendas than is the board, reactivity rather than proactivity, an executive committee becoming the de facto board, not knowing what is going on, rubber stamping staff recommendations, and lack of an incisive way to evaluate the executive.

Some of the preceding complaints apply to all non-profit and public boards. In my experience, *most* of what the majority of boards do either does not need to be done or is a waste of time when done by the board. Conversely, most of what boards need to do for strategic leadership is not done. This sweeping indictment is not true of all boards all the time, of course, but I contend that it is startlingly true enough of the time to signal a major dysfunction in what we accept as normal.

In these pages I argue for dissatisfaction with what we now accept as ordinary and outline a path that boards can follow to become extraordinary. For the failures of governance are not a problem of people, but of *process*. The problems lie squarely in our widely accepted approach to governance, including its treatment of board job design, board–staff relationships, the chief executive role, performance monitoring, and virtually all aspects of the board–management partnership. This book is a strong indictment of what is, but it is intended to make a compelling case for what can be.

The model presented here originated in the mid 1970s. Like many managers, my own training was in a professional discipline rather than in management. As a CEO, I worked for years learning how to do what I was already paid to do. Those who worked for this manager-in-training endured that travesty far beyond what I can ever now appreciate. As my skills as a manager grew, I became increasingly aware of the shaky foundation upon which management rests: the determination of purpose, which is largely a product of governance. Increasingly schooled as administrators, we worked toward ends haphazardly established as if we were introducing computer guidance into a Conestoga wagon. I was driven to discover what could bring governance into the new age. Out of that quest, an approach to governance developed that severely departed from much of conventional wisdom. Boards here and there wanted to hear more about it, so a consulting practice grew that subsequently made regular employment impossible.

I have for the past several years been engaged with boards and their executives somewhere in the United States or Canada twice in the average week. These clients have annual revenues ranging from a low of near zero to a high of over $3 billion. In the course of this work, I have written articles on governance and executive management for such organizations as the U.S. Department of Health and Human Services (1979b), the Canadian Hospital Association (1989a), the Association of Mental Health Administrators (1979a, 1981b), the Human Interaction Research Institute (1984a), the National Association of Corporate Directors (1980a), the Non-Profit Administrator's Guide (1982), the University of Wisconsin (1981a), the Florida League of Cities (1984c), the Non-profit Management Association (1984b), the Indiana Library Association (1981c), the National Association of Community Leadership Organizations (1983), the Center for Community Futures (1986b), and others (1988a, 1988b). My work has been featured in audiotapes for Family Service America (1985a) and the Public Management Institute (1985b) and in videotapes for the Georgia Power Company (1986c), the National Recreation and Park Association (1987), and the University of Georgia (1989d). Other writings have been circulated unpublished (1980b, 1985c, 1986a) or are submitted for publication (1989b, 1989c; Carver and Clemow, 1990).

I have run hundreds of governance and chief executive workshops for communitywide groups, for state and national conferences, for trade associations, and for political bodies. The attraction for these clients was a model or framework that enabled them to see their roles and gifts in a new light. They were not always able to implement the model in full, but they had a new standard to shoot for.

So the past couple of decades have provided rich relationships with members and chief executives of literally thousands of boards located in every state of the United States and in several provinces of Canada. The probing and challenging of these insightful clients contributed to the widespread applicability of my governance model. The governance model that emerged is generic, capable of whatever tailoring is necessary to fit any type of organization. And while I do adapt the model to business board settings, particularly to parent–subsidiary systems, the exclusive focus of this text is on nonprofit and public organizations. This extensive dialogue in which generic application of the model for nonprofit and public governance was forged included a wide array of endeavors:

public schools
private schools
liquid waste disposal
Third World development
YWCA
hospitals
mental health centers
poverty agencies
mental retardation
junior league
airport authorities
parks and recreation
women's centers
national church bodies
housing authorities
arts guilds
pest control districts
chambers of commerce
dental societies
county fairs
community theaters
agriculture cooperatives
wilderness programs
alcoholism treatment

city councils
county commissioners
libraries
architects' societies
boards of Realtors
sports facilities
industrial associations
local churches
family service
family planning
adult learning
credit unions
regional planning
zoos
postrelease programs
economic development
women's shelters
retirement funds
rehabilitation centers
national associations
state boards of education
state mental health systems
medical specialty societies
national family planning
  associations

private industry councils   planning and zoning commissions
League of Women Voters   health maintenance organizations
child protective services   community leadership training
health departments   golf course superintendents
Hispanic leadership   vocational centers
holding companies   extension services
employment services

I cannot begin to describe the personal and professional
sustenance that these many boards and their executives continue to provide me. Working routinely with organizations
whose pursuits are beyond my understanding or beyond my
dedication is humbling even to a consultant's robust ego.
Their boards have educated me about topics such as waste
disposal, international relief, public housing, and the ravages
of racism. Their work and their determination have awed me
time and time again. Not infrequently have I been literally
moved to tears by their perseverance and commitment to make
a difference in the world. Their contribution to me is not
only one of the mind, in helping forge an approach to governance, but one of the spirit as well.

Out of that profound appreciation and respect, my
counsel to boards minces few words. I am hard on boards
simply because *I know how good they can be.* Out of what is,
frankly, a love affair with boards, I have written this book for
board members who want to make a difference. I have written
it for board leaders who wish to guide deliberation toward
the big questions. I have written it for executives who want a
strong rather than a weak board, one that demands a strong
executive as well. I have written for executives who know
that management can be only as good as its governing foundation. I have written for the long-term benefit of taxpayers
and donors, as well as the clients, patients, students, and other
beneficiaries whose needs are to be served.

So come with me on an adventure into what board strategic leadership might be. Let us consider how a board can
do in the boardroom what it came to do in the first place:
project a vision, infuse an organization with mission, bid a
staff to be all it can be, and itself grow a little in the process.

Organization of the Book

Chapter One, "A New Vision for Governing Boards," recounts the varieties of boards, their predictable difficulties, and the need for more precise principles of governance. I seek to establish not only that individual boards need to function better, but that our ideal of what "better" means is sorely in need of revision. Chapter Two, "Policy as a Leadership Tool," makes a case for a new approach to policy-making and what boards should make policy about. Even though there is more to the board job than policy-making, I argue that it is in reconceiving the nature of policy that the possibility for a new level of leadership is born. Rather than use the traditional categories of board policies borrowed from administration, I develop four new categories tailored for the governing role. In Chapter Three, "Designing Policies That Make a Difference," I deal with the depth and breadth of board policy in a way that frees boards from staff details and even from the endless stream of approvals. Chapter Four, "Focusing on Results: Clarifying and Sustaining the Organization's Mission," deals with policies about organizational results and initiates the next five chapters, which explain the four categories of board policy. These policies engage the board in governing outcomes rather than activities and resolve such issues as mission, priorities, and target recipient groups. Chapter Five, "Setting Limits: Standards of Ethics and Prudence," covers those policies that allow board control over administrative and programmatic action. These policies enable the board to fulfill its fiduciary responsibilities and to control the prudence and ethics of organizational practice without resorting to "meddling." Chapter Six, "Strong Boards Need Strong Executives: The Board-Executive Relationship," deals with policies that establish an effective relationship between board and staff through a chief executive officer. We explore the meaning of the CEO's role and the board's approach to delegation and to evaluation of the performance of this important person. Chapter Seven, "The Board's Responsibility for Itself," addresses the board's relationship to its stockholder-equivalents and its primary accountability to that trust. Policies covered by this chapter address the board's governing process and its job description. Chapter Eight, "Officers and Committees," extends the same discussion of board role to subgroups of the board. We explore minimizing committees and officers and making certain they do not interfere with either CEO or whole board roles. Chapter Nine, "Making Meetings Work," focuses on keeping the board on track with structured discipline and agendas built on the long view. Finally, the importance of thinking big, keeping the dream out front, and other ingredients of strategic leadership are discussed in Chapter Ten, "Redefining Excellence in Governance: Strategies for Board Leadership."

My promise to readers is the inability ever to see governance in quite the same way again. In the midst of the great quality revolution in American management, I submit a new standard of what quality means in the work of a board. This book redefines excellence in governance. And because we have so far to go, it is an urgent argument for revolution in the boardroom.

Consequently, however gentle my intent, *Boards That Make a Difference* is a presumptuous book. It is presumptuous in broadly lumping together such apparently different organizations as governmental bodies, social agencies, quasi-public entities, private clubs, and foundations. It is presumptuous in claiming that virtually all such boards, councils, and commissions, *even those that are not perceived to be in trouble,* are currently performing at a distressingly low percentage of their leadership potential. It is presumptuous in depreciating finance and personnel committees; in belittling financial reports, budget approvals, and the office of treasurer; and in exhorting boards to get out of long-range planning. And it is presumptuous in claiming that time-honored, virtually unquestioned beliefs and practices of nonprofit and public boards are the major impediments to boards' being the strategic leaders they could be. "The whole industry," to borrow an unidentified observer from Waterman (1988, p. 9), "seems trapped in a disastrous set of habits."

I propose a sweeping revision, a new conceptual framework in order to conduct our engagement with purpose and performance. This is not a book of helpful hints nor is it written to address incremental improvements in current board operation. The need I see is not so much to make boards better at the work they are doing, but to reinvent that work and its fundamental precepts, to design from the ground up a general theory—or at least a technology—of governance. My commitment is that boards and managers, impelled by a new comprehension of what governance is all about, will do no less than transform how we conceive and proclaim leadership in the boardroom.

Acknowledgments

For the intellectual spark that led to my questioning of the conventional wisdom and thereby the creation of a new model, I am indebted to Wolfgang S. (Bill) Price, whose work in program policy planning (later published in 1977) was, when I discovered it in 1975, the most refreshing approach to governance I had ever come across. Bill's acceptance of me as co-consultant changed the direction of my career.

Second, the board members of Quinco Consulting Center in Columbus, Indiana, boldly accepted the challenge to adopt an untested governance method in 1976. In my eight-year association with that board, it faithfully behaved consistently with its commitment. In doing so, it helped fine-tune a new approach, a contribution for which thousands of nonprofit and public boards are unknowingly in Quinco's debt.

Third, the extensive support I have received from persons close to me had much to do with my completing this work. Ronald P. Myers brought my board model to the attention of Jossey-Bass Publishers. Ken and Melanie Campbell, Rob and Kathy Kenner, Tom Lane, and Mary D. Shahan made their homes available for getaway writing. Carolyn Bailey, Sandra Meicher, Ronald and Sue Myers, David Mueller, and Sally Jo Vasicko offered priceless commentary on the manuscript. My secretary, Virginia Haag, chased references and made the painstaking transfers from one word processor to another. Lynn D. W. Luckow and Alan Shrader, my long-suffering editors at Jossey-Bass, offered more support and patience with my intermittent writing schedule than I had any right to expect. I am also grateful to the many former clients who allowed me to use their policies for illustration and quote their words to make my points.

Carmel, Indiana   John Carver
                                                         February 1990

THE AUTHOR

John Carver has consulted with boards and CEOs on five continents. He is arguably the world's most published author on the board role and the board-CEO relationship. Carver received his B.S. degree (1964) in business and economics, M.Ed. degree in educational psychology (1965) from the University of Tennessee at Chattanooga, and his Ph.D. degree (1968) in clinical psychology from Emory University. He served four years active duty with the U.S. Air Force Electronic Security Command (1956-1960).

After working several years in administration of a small manufacturing company, the bulk of Carver's activities were first in the management of public mental health and mental retardation services, then in the development and application of governance and management concepts. Most of his model building and consulting has been with nonprofit, governmental, and other public boards, councils and commissions in the United States and Canada. Some of his work has been with governance in business corporations.

Carver incorporated the National Council of Community Mental Health Centers in 1970 and served as its first chairperson. He presented testimony to U.S. House and Joint Conference committees in 1969, 1970, and 1971. He has served as adjunct and visiting faculty with the University of Tennessee Space Institute, Tulane University, the University of Texas, and the University of Minnesota.

BOARDS THAT MAKE A DIFFERENCE

Chapter 1

A NEW VISION
FOR GOVERNING BOARDS

It is virtually impossible to escape contact with boards. We either are on boards, work for them, or are affected by their decisions. Boards sit atop almost all corporate forms of organization—profit and nonprofit—and often over governmental agencies as well. The elected forums of our political jurisdictions are boardlike structures: Congress, state legislatures, city councils, and county commissions. In all kinds of human activity, we find formally constituted, empowered groups deciding courses of action and future conditions toward which some body of people will aspire.

This chapter claims that great opportunities exist for leadership because of the sheer number of boards and their relative ineffectiveness. First, I look at ways of classifying boards and then limit the scope of the book to *governing* boards. Second, I describe the peculiar market circumstances that justify grouping nonprofit and public organizations together. I then step back to view the difficulty all boards—business, nonprofit, and public boards—have in fulfilling their opportunities. I summarize the normal prescriptions for board ills along with reasons why the existing answers are insufficient. Next, I make the case that governance deserves special attention apart from other elements of management. The chapter concludes with an argument for a new model of governance and the contributions this model should make to strategic leadership by boards.

1

Varieties of Boards

At the one end of the scale, decisions are made by individuals and by small groups of family or associates. At the other end, decisions are made in plebiscites and elections. In between, decisions are made by empowered bodies called boards.

Houle (1989, p. 195) cites the existence of approximately 4.5 million boards in this country. This number includes nonprofit, governmental (including local legislative), and business boards. The argument in these pages for new principles of governance is not directed to every entity that calls itself a board. But it is meant for almost 1.4 million of them in the United States alone. Drucker estimated that nonprofit organizations "may now employ more people than federal, state and local government put together" (1978) and that "half the personal income of the United States (and of most other developed countries) is spent on public service institutions (including those operated by government)" (1977, p. 17). Two considerations enable us to delineate those bodies for whom this commentary has direct application: (1) the organizational position occupied by the board and (2) the economic nature of the organization.

Boards Considered by Organizational Position

Governing Board. The most important kind of board is the board of ultimate corporate accountability, the governing board. The governing board is always positioned at the top of the organization. "Corporate board," "board of directors," "board of trustees," "board of regents," and similar titles denote groups that have authority exceeded only by owners and the state. The governing board is as high in the structure as one can go and still be within the organizational framework. Its total authority is matched by its total accountability for all corporate activity.

Advisory Board. There also exist boards whose function is to give counsel, not to govern. Advisory boards can advise the governing board, the chief executive officer (CEO), or other staff. They can be positioned anywhere in the organization as long as they formally attach to some "proper" organizational element. Advisory boards are optional and have only as much authority as the authorizing point within the legitimate organization chooses to grant. In some fields it is common to find advisory boards that have been given extensive authority and whose advice is virtually ensured to have an effect. As long as some position within the organization can, even potentially, retract that authority, the group is not a governing board. For its authority can be curtailed only by the governing board itself, by law or—in the case of membership organizations— by the membership.

Line Board. Considerably more rare is the line board. "Line" describes a heretofore unlabeled board type. I know of no treatment of this category in the literature except the modified form discussed by Ackoff (1981). The line board is not advisory, for it wields definite authority over subordinate positions. But it is not at the top of the organization and does not, therefore, qualify as a governing board. It is merely a group inserted where a single manager might have been.

Workgroup Board. Sometimes people speak of a "working board" when they simply mean a board that stays busy. Hence, a governing, advisory, or line board might be a working board rather than a figurehead. My term *workgroup,* however, denotes a governing board with little or no staff. It must govern and be the workforce as well.

Very small organizations, such as civic clubs, are often in this dual position. The group is incorporated, so a corporate governing board exists. Yet, absent enough funds to pay a staff, board members become the only workforce in sight. This kind of board is not a true type in the way that governing, advisory, and line boards are. It is merely a governing board with another set of responsibilities. The organizational position of a workgroup board is not only at the top, but everywhere else as well. It is most important that such boards remember that they have two different, simultaneous roles and those roles are best served by keeping them clearly separate.

Boards Considered by Economic Nature of the Organization

The power and responsibilities of advisory and line boards are determined by the specific organization rather than by a commanding generic principle. The foregoing discussion serves only to distinguish governing boards as the sole subject of this text. Throughout this book I deal only with *governing* boards.

It has long been common practice to differentiate the vast and disparate array of organizations governed by boards into three groups: profit ("business"), nonprofit, and government. Further characteristics distinguish subgroups of each. For example, businesses are grouped as "public" (publicly traded equity) and "private" (no public trading). Nonprofits are also divided into "public" (directly related to government) and "private" (not as related). "Government" includes the jurisdictional governance of cities, townships, counties, and states, but it also covers districts for water supply, schools, pollution control, and a host of other authorities. I ignore the subgroups and concentrate on the three major types: profit, nonprofit, and government.

For-Profit Boards. Business corporations engage in trade in order to produce a return for stockholders. These companies ordinarily compete in a market that is more or less free. Governing boards in business range from the obligatory, figurehead board of an entrepreneurial business to a highly formalized, paid group representing diverse stockholders.

Nonprofit Boards. Corporations chartered for charitable or interest purposes have no stock ownership, though state statutes may require a formal membership as a stockholder-equivalent. Abroad, such organizations are often referred to as nongovernmental organizations (NGOs). In the United States, the term *private voluntary organization* (PVO) is frequently used to describe international nonprofits. NGOs and

PVOs, though not terms used in this text, are included among nonprofit agencies.

Although nonprofit corporations may accumulate surpluses, their accounting systems have no place for profit. They differ from other corporations in that they are exempt from certain taxes and are unable to distribute their surpluses to holders of equity. Nonprofit corporations ordinarily receive a large proportion of their revenues from "funding" and donations rather than from sales of a product. Nonprofit governing board obligations under the law, however, are similar to those for other corporations.

Governmental Boards. Governmental boards, elected or appointed, are more bound by legal requirements on both composition and process than are the foregoing types. They are like nonprofit boards with respect to profit and distribution of earnings. Governmental boards may be quasi governmental (such as water systems or airport authorities) or fully governmental (such as city councils). They may or may not have taxing authority. Governmental boards, like nonprofit boards, ordinarily do not derive their revenues from sales but from taxation and user fees.

Profit, nonprofit, and governmental governing boards have much in common. They are alike in that they all bear ultimate accountability for organizational activity and accomplishment. They are unlike in how they are situated in the larger context of political–economic life. They differ in how much public scrutiny they receive, a factor that produces differences in the amount of posturing involved in board dynamics. They differ in the degree to which the procedures of governance are prescribed by law. They differ greatly in the strength of the traditions that drive their methods. Many governmental boards have traditions that were established long before twentieth-century management appeared on the scene. Powerful precedents make it difficult for state legislatures and county commissioners, for example, to behave as though modern management principles were ever developed.

This book focuses specifically on governmental and nonprofit governing boards. From here on I use the word *public* to refer to the various types of governmental entities, because in common perception, it bridges the gray area between special-purpose governmental groups and quasi-public nonprofits. This focus has utility in exploring governance even though there is nothing inherent in the nonprofit or public organization per se that causes governance to be different than it is in profit companies. Then why address public and nonprofit governance, particularly in view of the extremely disparate array of organization types included under that rubric? After all, are they not more different than they are alike? The Ford Foundation, a community arts guild, and a credit union may little appreciate membership in this mixed club. The justification for classifying them together is that the boards of most nonprofit and public organizations share a compelling job factor: the peculiar nature of their markets.

Life in the Muted Market

Companies organized for profit receive money through sales. Sales revenues are the result of a free exchange between the company and consumers. Consumers judge whether the good or service is worth the exchange demanded. If it is not, they do not buy; if it is, they buy.

Nonprofit organizations and government ordinarily receive money from sources other than those persons receiving their products. Direct consumers may pay a discounted price or even nothing. A subsidy is received from donors and tax sources to make up the deficit. There is no consumer judgment of product in the light of its rightful price, because the consumer is not confronted with that choice. Consequently, although nonprofit and public organizations may be buffeted about by budget pressures and funding squeezes, there is no direct market force bearing on the relationship between product and price.

The relevant variable that separates the governance of *most* public and nonprofit enterprises from *most* profit orga-

nizations is the automatic market test of product worth. I
define a market test as the free decisions of consumers whether
a given product, among alternatives, is worth the cost of its
production. If alternatives are unavailable because of artifi-
cially blocked competition, there is no clean market test. If
the consumer does not pay the entire price, there is no clean
market test. This definition focuses on the *automatic consumer judgment* aspect of market. Lack of this automatic
judgment does not deny other uses of the word *market*. For
example, public schools and family planning centers operate
in some identifiable *market* and may fare better if their staffs
do a good job of *marketing*. This use of market and marketing, however, is unrelated to the integrity of the market test I
have described.

Without a market to summarize consumer judgment,
an organization literally does not know what its product is
worth. It may know what the product costs to produce and
what the staff thinks about product quality. It may know that
consumers are raving with delight. It may even know precisely how effective the product is. But the organization still
does not know what its product is worth.

From a governance perspective, then, the relevant factor
that sets most nonprofit and public organizations apart from
profit organizations is not in the essence of managing, for the
principles of management are the same in each setting. The
difference is not in distribution of earnings, for this is a matter of accounting rather than substance. What is different—
with profound effects—is the lack of a behavioral process to
aggregate the many individual evaluations of product and
cost. The organization is adrift from the foundation that
would enable it to define success and failure, to know what is
worth doing, and in the largest sense, even to recognize good
performance.

So the typical public or nonprofit board is faced with a
challenge business boards never have to face. "In the nonprofit organization," observed Anthony (1977), "the objectives
are difficult to define and there is no automatic danger signal
comparable to the profit measure." In the absence of a market

test, *the board must stand for that function.* The board must bear this peculiar, additional burden if it is to perform responsibly. It is not enough to be efficient, nor is it enough even to produce fine products. Any reasonable definition of productive excellence must relate chiefly to whether a good or service is worth the full economic cost of its production.

From this point on, I refer to public and nonprofit organizations as if they all suffer from lack of a rigorous market test. That will prove sufficiently true to justify the simplification, though exceptions exist. Nonprofit hospitals, for example, operate in a harsh market environment, albeit one of great artificiality imposed by regulation and insurers. For those nonprofit and public organizations that are truly subject to an unsubsidized market judgment, the peculiarity discussed here is not true. In these cases, the board's task is easier, though the concepts and principles in the model presented here will still contribute to their governance. Among the vast array of public and nonprofit organizations, however, such truly market-tested instances are in the minority. With this proviso, I consider public and nonprofit boards to be, by and large, engaged in serving a muted market.

The Flaws of Governance

Yet, even boards that are free of this added "market surrogate" burden have shown that the challenges of governing are almost too much. Governing boards have not been vessels of exemplary efficiency in the best of situations. Drucker (1974, p. 628), writing of corporate boards, said "there is one thing all boards have in common, regardless of their legal position. *They do not function.* The decline of the board is a universal phenomenon of this century" [emphasis added]. Neu and Sumek (1983) found it "evident that the governance process is not working well . . . New approaches need to be developed."

Geneen (1984) of ITT complained that boards are unable to protect the interests of stockholders whom they represent: "Among the boards of directors of Fortune 500 companies, I estimate that 95 percent are not fully doing what they are legally, morally, and ethically supposed to do. And they couldn't, even if they wanted to" (p. 28). Worried that hospital board effectiveness is "getting critical," John A. Witt (1987, p. xiii) decried, "untrained boards instructing, or at least controlling, untrained subordinate boards . . . ineffectualness of boards and their members permeates several layers and often multiplies itself."

Smith (1958, p. 52) found it to be "ironic . . . that we in the United States have so neglected this most vital area." While every other management function has been exhaustively studied and analyzed, "the responsibilities of the board and the distinction between board and management have been sorely neglected. Management literature on the subject is pitifully brief and strikingly devoid of any real depth or new ideas."

Juran and Louden (1966, p. 7) pointed to the same root for the problem. "It is an astonishing fact that the job of the board of directors is, in proportion to its intrinsic importance, one of the least studied in the entire spectrum of industrial activities . . . As a consequence, the job of the board of directors has received neither the benefit of the broad exchange of practical experience nor the intensity of study which has been available to other corporate activities."

Though possessed of ultimate organizational power, the governing board is understudied and underdeveloped. Here we confront a flagrant irony in management literature: *Where opportunity for leadership is greatest, job design for leadership is poorest.*

It is against this uninspiring backdrop of governing boards in general that we deal here specifically with boards of public and nonprofit organizations. It is little wonder that such boards have difficulty, for their faults include those of profit boards plus those peculiarly contributed by their artificial market situation. For if the governing of supposedly rational, modern business corporations is not without underlying weaknesses, it should not be surprising that governance of nonprofit and public enterprise presents an extensive array of blemishes.

What Goes Wrong

It takes no scholar to find the problems. Simple, random observation of a few nonprofit and public boards will expose many of the normal shortcomings. Nonprofit and public boards stumble regularly and visibly. Individual board members and executives have often felt that one specific act or another is silly or empty. They rarely say so, however, for the charade has a commanding history, eliciting an almost conspiratorial agreement not to notice organizational fatuousness. Robert Gale, president of the Association of Governing Boards of Universities and Colleges, reported that "of the some 35 nonprofit boards I have served on, only one was truly effective" (personal communication, 1989).

The problem is not that a group or an individual *occasionally* slips into poor practice, but that intelligent, caring individuals regularly exhibit procedures of governance that are so deeply flawed. Common practices are such obvious drains on board effectiveness that a sophisticated model is not needed to recognize them. Although some boards may avoid a few of the following conditions, rarely does any one board avoid them all.

Time on the Trivial. Items of trivial scope or import get disproportionate attention compared with matters of greater scope or importance. Richard J. Peckham of Kansas, on joining a major public board, found it so lost in trivia that "I thought I'd been banished to outer darkness" (personal communication). Major program issues go unresolved while boards conscientiously grapple with some small detail. An Illinois school board proudly proclaimed the "active role the members of our board take in purchasing decisions . . . The administration [to replace desks in two classrooms] were directed to select three chairs from different companies and have them available for the next board meeting. The board then made the decision on warranty, durability, price and color." A national survey found almost half of America's school boards made the purchasing decisions for tape recorders, cameras, and television sets (National School Boards Association, undated).

Short-Term Bias. The "time horizon" over which concern and planning should take place is more distant at the governing level than anywhere else in the organization. Yet we find boards dealing far more with the near term and, even more dysfunctionally, with the past. Last month's financial statement gets more attention than an agency's strategic position.

Reactive Stance. Boards consistently find themselves reacting to staff initiatives rather than acting proactively. Proposals for staff action and recommendations for board action so often come from staff that some boards would cease to function if called upon to create their own agendas.

Reviewing, Rehashing, Redoing. Some boards spend most of their time going over what their staffs have already done. "Eighty-five percent of our time was spent monitoring staff work," says Glendora Putnam, Boston, of a prominent national board. "We can't afford that. We have too much wisdom [to be put to use]" (personal communication). Just keeping up with a large staff can take prodigious hours and even then can never be done fully. But the salient point is that reviewing, rehashing, and redoing staff work—no matter how well accomplished—do not constitute leadership.

Leaky Accountability. Boards often allow accountability to "leak" around the chief executive. Having established a CEO position, the board continues to relate officially with other staff, either giving them directions or judging their performance.

Diffuse Authority. It is rare to find a board–executive partnership wherein each party's authority has been clarified. A vast gray area exists. When a matter lies in this uncertain area, the safe executive response is to take it to the board. Instead of using this opportunity to clarify to whom the decision belongs, the board simply approves or disapproves. The event has been settled, but authority is left as unclear as it was before.

Many board flaws are cosmetic blemishes, indicative of more fundamental errors. "These are just symptoms of a problem," says Barry Romanko of the Alberta Ministry of Parks and Recreation, St. Paul, Alberta. "The problem is that we are giving boards the wrong job" (personal communication). Attacking the superficial flaws would in itself be a worthy undertaking. Similarly, it might be useful to invoke the usual admonitions: "Stick to policy!" "Let your CEO manage!" "Don't rubber stamp!" But it would be even more instructive to build a healthier infrastructure of governance concepts. More effective framing of the governance challenge can go far beyond the mere elimination of common problems; it can provide a clearing in which boards can be strategic leaders.

Inadequate Prescriptions

At some level, boards and executives are well aware of the historical deficiencies. An explosion of popular interest in management issues beginning in the 1970s sharpened the perception that governance is not all it can be. Board training has received more attention because of this awareness. Many board members, executives, and observers have offered counsel for ailing board practices all along. But somehow the prescriptions, quite rational in themselves, have fallen short. At best, they have cleaned up some of the clutter and more striking inefficiencies in board operation. But because few previous efforts have been based in a complete conceptual model, prescriptions have largely been piecemeal, anecdotal wisdom. Most prescriptions have concerned the level of board activity, the board–staff relationship, or the nature of board work. The appeal of each is that it accurately assesses one part of the elephant.

Prescriptions About Activity and Involvement

More Involvement. One solution to the problems of governance is that boards should be more involved. They should participate directly in the work of the organization, volunteering time and energy to become physically involved in doing things. A board operating at a distance is a board too detached to understand, much less to make a difference. Board membership means access to the good works of an organization without having to go through the hiring process to get there. Persons who espouse greater board activity have a great need to "know what is going on" in the organization. The board agenda is likely to be drawn out. Committee work may be heavy.

Less Involvement. Boards should be less involved. By participating directly in the work of the organization, the board tends to become lost in the trees and to lose sight of the forest. Board members are better as governors around a board table than as a prestigious auxiliary staff. The board's job is "to choose a CEO, then stay out of the way," confided a hospital trustee in Wisconsin. Persons who call for less involvement often propose keeping up with relevant facts through reports, particularly financial ones. Agendas are likely to be crisp and "businesslike." Committee work may be light.

Prescriptions About Board–Staff Relations

Board as Watchdog. The board, as the ultimately accountable agent, should keep a sharp eye on staff activities. This close oversight limits the degree of power delegated, requiring many board approvals and close questioning of staff. A utility commissioner in Minnesota claimed that the commission's main function is to "keep a wary eye on the staff." Boards acting as watchdogs become heavily involved in administration, often in busy committees relating to staff activities. Tight control is seen as the road to accountability or, at least, to safety. Some boards take the watchdog posture so far that they develop an adversarial relationship with staff; anything brought before the board becomes a trial. In an alternate watchdog role, the board allies itself with lower echelon staff members and perceives issues—as stated by a poverty agency board member in

Ohio—in terms of protecting staff from administrators. At their best, such boards are constructive skeptics.

Board as Cheerleader. Staff members are basically honest and capable, so the best board role is to be supportive and cheer them on. The hallmark is trust. After all, the key to governing well is choosing a chief executive in whom you can believe and then standing behind him or her. Cheerleader boards stay out of administration because it is none of their business. They may even refrain from asking the hard questions, because to do so would show a lack of faith. Rubber stamping executive requests is an expression of gratitude that things are going so smoothly. Often, the governing board role is seen as advisory after a CEO is installed. Loose control is the best approach ("after all, we are *just* volunteers"). A part-time board should not get in the way; its role is not so much to govern staff as to be its apologist and champion.

Prescriptions About Board Work and Skills

Board as Manager. Boards, though one step removed from daily operation, should become more proficient in management skills to act as managers. Board members are chosen in part because of their skills in personnel, finance, program leadership, and so forth. The board is likely to pore over financial statements, staffing patterns, and maintenance reports. It engages staff in the intricacies of management. Committees are structured along the lines of staff departments, such as personnel and public relations. The board, more or less autocratic, is seen as the supermanager or, at least, a partner in management with its top staff.

Board as Planner. As planning is an integral part of managing, boards should predominantly plan. Boards plan the elements of personnel, finance, and so forth rather than engaging in current implementation. Boards develop long-range plans and, with their committees, spend long hours to create a plan document.

Board as Communicator. The board should communicate better within itself and with staff. If board and staff could only hear each other better, the organization would have more satisfying process and, hence, a more satisfactory product. Particularly in multiethnic community boards, cultural barriers to communication lend great support to this approach. The path to better governance lies in better human relations.

Why the Prescriptions Disappoint

These are not the only prescriptions, nor are they really distinct types. They illustrate the range and divergence of solutions to board ineffectiveness. And, from the standpoint of slight improvements, they do not all fail. What is confusing is that each prescription contains just enough truth to be on track. At one time or another, they are all good approaches.

The problem with anecdotal wisdom, however, is its spotty applicability. A formerly rubber stamp-type board that has been duped by its CEO will surely improve by greater involvement, tighter control, or the board's acting as supermanager. A board fatigued by interminably long meetings may be wise to move toward shorter meetings with more "businesslike" agendas. In slightly different circumstances, however, these solutions would themselves be the problems.

Problem-based prescriptions sow the seed for the next difficulty, because the solution often outlives the problem that justified it. Soon the board that shifted to shorter meetings finds it cannot keep up as well as it desired. Or a good CEO is lost because he or she will not tolerate the tight control and suspiciousness left over from the previous pendulum swing.

Prescriptions for board improvement are often based on current problems or problems that board members have experienced elsewhere. Problem-based improvements may be absolutely sensible and still miss the mark. They may cure the present difficulties, yet not reduce vulnerability to a wide range of potential future problems. Correcting insufficiencies by looking backward to see what they have been simply invites the next, perhaps opposite, error.

Governance as Unique Management

A paradigm tailored to the special circumstances of governance would enable us to apply wisdom more coherently. When a function has been *assembled* from bits of historical practice more than it has been *designed,* it cannot so gracefully incorporate wisdom, but must patch it on here and there. Tailoring management principles for governance, however, assumes that boards call for special treatment. This section argues that governance certainly is special, though not for the reason most frequently cited.

The Red Herring of Voluntarism

Boards of nonprofit and some public organizations think of themselves primarily as volunteers. This identity as volunteers adds little and potentially costs a great deal. Responsibility, authority, job design, and demands of a board are not affected by being paid or unpaid. Except that it strengthens the sense of public service, being a *voluntary* board is irrelevant to governance and its attendant burden of accountability. On the other hand, some connotations of voluntarism can *detract* from the board's job, severely reducing its ability to lead.

Volunteers are a tradition of American life, offering many skills, insights, and hours in a commendable expression of helpfulness. Volunteers help get a job done without compensation. For a going organization, that usually means helping the staff, inasmuch as staff is engaged in the actual work. Governing boards, however, do not exist to help staff, but to own the business—often in trust for some larger ownership. If anyone is helping, it is the staff. Volunteers on governing boards are expressing an *ownership interest* rather than a *helpfulness interest.* Owning the business conveys a power that cannot be responsibly grasped so long as we think we are there to help, not to own. Power not used is power defaulted on and, ultimately, power irresponsibly used. It is destructive to confuse helpfulness with ownership. By emphasizing the volunteer status, boards risk weakening their effectiveness.

Because the same person can wear two different hats, board members may also be volunteers at a staff level. It is important that the hats be kept distinct in everyone's mind. The board as an official body (as opposed to individual members) is well advised to limit its role to owner only.

Boards as Trustees

Unlike other managers who work for a well-defined superior, boards ordinarily work for either a vaguely defined group or a well-defined though difficult-to-communicate-with group. The former is illustrated by a public radio station board, the latter by a city council. There is someone out here for whom the board acts in trust, but it is difficult to tell who that someone is. Consequently, boards have more difficulty than other managers in getting their marching orders and their evaluations.

This book promotes the concept of "moral ownership" to isolate the various stakeholders to whom the board owes its primary allegiance. For community boards, this ownership is the community at large. A board cannot carry out its responsibilities without determining exactly whom the ownership includes and how they can be heard.

Boards as Special Managers

Governing boards would do better to think of themselves as a special kind of management, not as volunteers. Consequently, what is known about the managing process, particularly "general" management, is relevant to boards. Boards need a grasp of some of the same skills a chief executive officer needs. These skills are of "overview" management as opposed to specialized management, such as purchasing, marketing, and personnel administration. In fact, some would strongly argue that sufficient information about governing is already available in management texts, workshops, academic degree programs, and journals. To these persons, governance is simply management at the board level and, indeed, for them the word *governance* serves no useful conceptual distinction.

This point of view is that management is management is management, even when it is governance. But the governance task *is* different from other management positions. In dealing with thousands of board members, I find that structural and interpersonal factors cause governance to be a unique kind of management. Certainly, the same basic management principles apply, but the form must be adjusted to deal with several features found in no other manager but the governing body:

- Boards are at the extreme end of the accountability chain. Other managers must deal with persons both above and below their stations. The buck stops with the board. It has no supervisor to carve out what portion of a given topic is its to oversee.
- The board acts, in a moral sense and sometimes a legal one, as agent of a largely unseen and often undecided principal, an entity that expresses itself in curious ways if at all.
- The board is a set of individuals operating as a single entity. Melding multiple peer viewpoints and values into a single resolution is peculiar to a group manager.
- The discipline of individuals tends to suffer when they are members of groups. A board is likely to have less discipline than has any one of its members operating alone.
- Boards are ordinarily more than the usual managerial arm's length from the next lower organizational level. They are not only part-time, but physically removed.

Mueller (1981) argued that governance in its essence differs from management. It is, he claims, an unfolding, always incomplete phenomenon driven by "soft realms of thought and deportment. They are value-laden, subjective, intuitive and characteristic of the art forms dealing with social interaction" (p. xii).

For all these reasons I have translated principles of modern management to address the peculiar circumstance of governing boards. The adaptation goes beyond a collection of helpful suggestions; it is a fundamentally reordered paradigm for governance.

Toward a New Governance

A model of governance is a framework within which to organize the thoughts, activities, structure, and relationships of governing boards. A designed model yields a new nature of governance, quite unlike a collection of even wise responses to specific governance problems. What should we expect from a model? What conditions should be better if there were a better framework within which to build governance actions? I think we have a right to expect a good model of governance to:

1. *"Cradle" vision:* A useful framework for governance must hold and support vision in the primary position. Administrative systems cause us to devote great attention to the specifics. Such rigor, itself commendable, can overshadow the broader matter of purpose. There must be systematic encouragement to think the unthinkable and to dream.

2. *Explicitly address fundamental values:* The governing board is a guardian of organizational values. The framework must ensure that the board focuses on values. Endless decisions about events cannot substitute for deliberations and explicit pronouncements on values.

3. *Force an external focus:* Because organizations tend to focus inward, a governance model must intervene to guarantee a marketlike, external responsiveness. A board would thus be more concerned with needs and markets than with the internal issues of organizational mechanics.

4. *Enable an outcome-driven organizing system:* All functions and decisions are to be made rigorously against the standard of purpose. A powerful model would have

the board not only establish a mission in outcome terms, but procedurally enforce mission as the central organizing focus.

5. *Separate large issues from small:* Board members usually agree that large issues deserve first claim on their time, but they have no common way to discern a big item. A model should help differentiate sizes of issues.

6. *Force forward thinking:* A governance scheme should help a board to thrust the majority of its thinking into the future. Strategic leadership demands the long-term viewpoint.

7. *Enable proactivity:* So that boards do not merely preside over momentum, a model of governance should press boards toward leading, not toward reacting. Such a model would engage boards more in *creating* than in *approving.*

8. *Facilitate diversity and unity:* It is important to optimize the richness of diversity in board composition and opinion, yet still assimilate the variety into one voice. A model must address the need to speak with one voice without squelching dissent or pretending unanimity.

9. *Describe relationships to relevant constituencies:* In either a legal or a moral sense, boards are usually trustees. They are also, to some extent, accountable to consumers, neighbors, and staff. A model of governance should define where these various constituencies fit into the scheme.

10. *Define a common basis for discipline:* Boards have a tough time sticking to a job description, being decisive without being impulsive, and keeping discussion to the point. A model of governance should provide a rational basis for the discipline a board enforces on itself.

11. *Delineate the board's role in common topics:* A model of governance should enable articulation of roles without isolation of any, so the specific contribution of the board on any topic is clear.

12. *Determine what information is needed:* A model of governance would introduce more precise distinctions

about the nature of information needed to govern, avoiding too much, too little, too late, and simply wrong information.

13. *Balance overcontrol and undercontrol:* It is easy to control too much or too little and, ironically, to do both at the same time. The same board can be both a "rubber stamper" and a "meddler." A model of governance would clarify those aspects of management that need tight versus loose control.   ⑬

14. *Use board time efficiently:* Members of nonprofit and public boards receive token pay or none in exchange for their time. Though they willingly make this contribution, few have time to waste. By sorting out what really needs to be done, a model should enable boards to use the precious gift of time more productively.   ⑭

A conceptually coherent way to approach governance would be strong medicine for nonprofit and public organizations. It would also have application in business corporations. In fact, a business breakthrough originating in the nonprofit sector was foreshadowed by McConkey (1975, p. 1) when he predicted that "the next major breakthrough in management will not occur . . . in the world of business. The breakthrough will, and must, take place in the so-called nonprofit sector."

Whether, as he indicates, the breakthrough "must" take place, it certainly *should* take place, given the serious flaws that exist. The most significant management breakthrough that could come to pass would be in the highest leverage element of organization: the governing board. Both the leverage and the room for improvement scream urgently for attention.

But boards have been around so long it is hard to see that the emperor has no clothes. We have grown accustomed to mediocrity in nonprofit and public board process, in the empty rituals and often meaningless words of conventional practice. We have watched intelligent people tied up in trivia so long that neither we nor they notice the discrepancy. We have observed the ostensible strategic leaders consumed by the exigencies of next month. Mindful people regularly carry out mindless activity and appear to be, as Phillip T. Jenkins, Bryn Mawr Associates of Birmingham, Michigan, put it, "the well intentioned in full pursuit of the irrelevant" (personal communication). Inexplicably, effective people have a different standard of excellence for public and nonprofit boards than for other pursuits, "often [tossing] aside the principles of good management, and sometimes even common sense, when they put on trustee hats" (Chait and Taylor, 1989). The forum where *vision* could be the chief order of business is mired so chronically in details that, growing weary, we come to see nothing amiss. Boards, after all, will be boards!

We need strong boards and we need strong executives as well. "One of the key problems," observed Robert Gale, "is that many boards are either too weak to accomplish anything or so strong they wind up managing the organization" (personal communication). When increased strength is dysfunctional, the solution is not, of course, to weaken the strong. It is better that the blessing of a strong engine be augmented by a better chassis, not "solved" by shorting out a few sparkplugs. When their strength causes boards not to do their own job better, but to intrude into the jobs of others, something is awry in the design. We must take a fresh look at governance concepts and the board–management partnership. The stark truth of Gale's comment is reason enough for a new model of governance.

It need not bespeak paranoia to observe along with Louden (1975, p. 117) that "if we do not concern ourselves with how we can rule organizations, the organizations will rule us." But the paradigm with which we traditionally "rule" is worthy neither of the people who give their time and talent nor of the missions they serve. Governance is overdue for a rebirth. Though much has been written over the past several decades about governing boards, with rare exceptions the efforts offer incremental improvement to an inadequate vehicle by new paint and tires. The purpose of this book is not to indict previous efforts or current performance so much as to prescribe a better way. Its message is that strategic leadership is exciting and accessible.

Next Chapter

The chapters that follow lay out a new vehicle for governing, a model whose promise is not incremental improvement in the capacity to govern, but transformation. Seeing policies in a more exacting light is the first step toward a new model of governance. So I begin in Chapter Two by arguing that the opportunity for greater strategic leadership lies first in the redefinition of policy and policy-making.

Chapter 2

POLICY AS A
LEADERSHIP TOOL

Public and nonprofit managers have incorporated much of modern management into their operations. Boards that would provide strategic leadership to increasingly sophisticated management require an equally modern governance. Modern governance is not simply modern management practiced by a governing board. To be sure, the principles of management and governance are closely related. But governance is more than management writ large. And it is more than a quality control board of expert managers and technicians running inspections and approvals to maintain order.

The pressure toward better management has created an awkward gap between the sophistication of management and the sophistication of the board. Although public and nonprofit management is not known for its rigor, it has advanced considerably in the past two decades. Governance, on the other hand, has scarcely moved at all. When chief executives are increasingly skilled as managers while their boards are not increasingly skilled as governors, leadership becomes a brittle commodity or, at worst, a mockery. Executives may end up patronizing the board in order to manage well. Boards can be led to busy pursuits that interfere as little as possible with management. The resulting scenario is not unlike that of a very mature child dealing skillfully with an immature parent. Most public and nonprofit CEOs expect, as part of their job obligation, to "stage manage" board meetings so their boards will not wander aimlessly or go out of control.

24

Such a game of seemingly necessary manipulation carries a cost that the fragile balance of leadership can ill afford. For this reason alone, governing boards must modernize the process of governance.

A modern approach to governing will enable a part-time, possibly inexpert group of persons *to lead.* They have neither the time nor the ability to control every action, circumstance, goal, and decision. And if perchance they did have both time and ability, the organization would slow to a halt as they carried out their task. The most expensive resource of public and nonprofit organizations, the staff, would be significantly wasted as the official second-guessing process ground on. Boards caught in the trap of being staff better than staff, as well as boards bewildered by unending details or confused by technical complexities, cannot lead. A modern approach to governance must enable a board to cut quickly to the heart of organization, being neither seduced into action nor paralyzed into inaction by trappings along the way.

This chapter argues that the secret to the new governance lies in policy-making, but policy-making of a more finely crafted sort. I begin by defining policy as it is used throughout this text. After making a case that policy clarification is the central feature of board leadership, I consider how a board might get a handle on policy in real board life. I end the chapter by describing the four new categories of board policy to be used throughout the text.

Policies as Values and Perspectives

The essence of any organization lies in what it believes, what it stands for, and what and how it values. An organization's works, rather than its words, are the telling assessment of its beliefs. Studies of corporate culture (such as Davis, 1984) look at the way people deal with problems, differences, customers, decision making, and each other as a way to penetrate the essence of organization. These values and perspectives form the bedrock on which the more mechanical and visible aspects of an organization are based.

I use the word *value* in its common meaning of "belief" or "relative importance," as when we speak of our "values" of right and wrong, prudent and imprudent, ethical and unethical, proper and improper, worthy and worthless, acceptable and unacceptable, tolerable and intolerable, and so forth. I use the word *perspective* to mean "way of looking at," "guiding principle," "approach," or "conceptual point of view." A board value might be that "Cost of living raises should be consistent with other organizations in our county." But what do we call the board position that "CEO evaluation will be based on total agency performance"? Though there is surely valuing to be found in the latter, we would be strained to call the statement a value. It can easily be called an "approach" to CEO performance, a "way of looking at" the nature of delegation, or a "perspective" on the CEO role.

Consider an organization's goals, compensation, inventory procedures, cash management, plant maintenance, paint scheme, promotion practices, market penetration plans, and innumerable other factors. With enough patience and inference, we could construct from these concrete realities a picture of the organization's values and perspectives. The organization likely was not designed by starting with explicitly considered values and perspectives and carrying through to the event-specific and concrete. Consequently, values and perspectives across the organization may be inconsistent. In this case we have uncovered a value—always unwritten—that the organization does not place great importance on consistency of values and perspectives!

As individuals, our behavior grows out of our perspectives and values as we confront external realities. Under a certain condition, our values or perspectives lead us to act in a certain manner. We are valuing, conceptualizing beings who constantly seek to make sense out of our world and ourselves by linking sense data with frameworks. The sense data are our more or less reliable measures of "reality"; the frameworks are our values and perspectives. Moreover, our sense data (what we think are "facts") are affected by the conceptual frameworks we have adopted. Even if the "facts" were wholly objective, our frameworks would lead us to say that a certain phenomenon is best looked at in this way or that this result is more important than that. External realities vary beyond our control, but ostensibly we are captains of our perspectives and values. And those values and perspectives compel us to develop certain competencies, to make certain choices, and, generally, to behave with some measure of continuity.

Organizations are similar to individuals in these respects. Their frameworks of values and perspectives determine specific decisions and behaviors in the face of specific facts. And their choices of what to regard as relevant facts about the environment are themselves determined by the same frameworks. So subtle is this effect that boards often do not regard their selection of facts as choices; after all, facts are facts. Organizations, like individual persons, are caught in a self-perpetuating, circular phenomenon that does untold damage to vision and to possibility thinking. Values and perspectives are thus powerful, often invisible forces that determine not only organizational circumstances, activities, and goals, but even the data that organizations admit into their assessment of reality.

Excellence in governance begins by recognizing this central, determining feature of organizations. Setting goals, deploying staff, writing procedures, formulating plans, developing strategy, establishing budgets, and *all other board and staff activity* depend on values and perspectives, whether resulting from debate or default. Decisions of all sorts, as so clearly argued by Drucker (1967, pp. 113–141), rest on principles and generic understandings. Unrecognized, this dependence can produce pernicious disparities, difficulties, and unfulfilled potential. For goals and plans may be developed unmindful of their underlying meaning, the binding glue that transforms disjointed parts into a whole. But recognized and properly used, these values and perspectives offer leaders the key to effectiveness.

It has been my experience with boards that a simple shift away from detailed and event-specific governance to values and valuing produces a powerful shift in board leadership. In focusing *directly* on perspectives and values, a board moves closer to the underpinnings of organizational behavior.

In the language of this text, values and perspectives are blended in the concept of *policy,* so in most contexts henceforth I refer to them in undifferentiated fashion simply as policies. Values dominate policies that are instructive to staff, that is, policies that tell staff what to do or not do. Perspectives dominate the policies which codify the board's own process and relationships. I have found no utility in belaboring the distinction between values and perspectives, so any differences between them are of no significant interest in subsequent discussion. It is only important to remember that "policy" as used here can express values, perspectives, or both.

Policy is an apt and familiar word for us to employ when referring to organizational values and perspectives, but the strength of familiarity is also a weakness. We must avoid the looser definitions currently attached to the word *policy* if we are to build a more exacting framework for policy-based governance. Conventionally, policy has referred to any board utterance. Policy sometimes means procedures, as in personnel "policies." Policy can refer to unstated as well as explicit values and perspectives. If this same word is to be used for more precise governance, we will have to keep in mind that what once passed for policy may not any longer.

To get to the core of organizational meaning, governing boards must concern themselves with policies. But because the central challenge is to lead rather than to analyze, governance must pronounce rather than merely educe policies. Inasmuch as sophisticated management processes use board policies as the point of departure, these documents must be conceived with care.

Leadership through Policies

Because policies permeate and dominate all aspects of organizational life, they present the most powerful lever for the exercise of leadership. Peters and Waterman (1982, p. 291) wrote that "Clarifying the value system and breathing life

into it are the greatest contributions a leader can make."
Leadership through explicit policies offers the opportunity
to think big and to lead others to think big. Leaders acutely
aware of the value aspect of life's events continually link day-
to-day exigencies with the underlying importances of life.
They tap something deeper, perhaps more uniquely human,
than the accountant, supervisor, or technician in all of us.
Work becomes not so much a series of structured mechanical
activities as a process of creating and becoming. Policy leadership clarifies, inspires, and sets a tone of discourse that
stimulates leadership in followers.

POLICY LEADERSHIP

There are four reasons why policy-focused leadership is
a hallmark of governance:

1. *Leverage and efficiency:* By getting hold of the most fundamental elements of organization, the board can affect
   many issues with less effort. However high-flown their
   intentions, boards have only so much time available,
   often measurable in hours per year.
2. *Expertise:* Board members do not ordinarily have all the
   skills required to operate their organization. To compensate, some boards focus their recruiting more on skills
   that match those of staff than those of governance. Governing by policies requires none of the specialties and
   can often be done better without them.
3. *Fundamentals:* When all the material a board might deal
   with is sifted and sorted, the real heart of the matter is
   the body of policies those materials represent. Boards that
   govern by attending directly to policies are more certain
   to address that which has enduring importance. Dealing so directly with the fundamentals has a compelling
   legitimacy.
4. *Vision and inspiration:* Dreaming is not only permissible
   for leaders, it is obligatory. Dealing meticulously with
   the trees rather than the forest can be satisfying, but it
   neither fuels vision nor inspires.

Directing an organization can be like rearing a child.
Controlling every behavior is a fatiguing and ultimately

impossible charge. Inculcating the policies of life is far more effective and, even if some slippage occurs on individual behaviors, it is the only serviceable approach in the long run. So whether a board wishes narrowly to control or more expansively to lead, governing through policies is the efficient way to operate.

To the extent a board wishes to provide strategic leadership, it must clarify policies and expect organizational activities to give them life. Clarifying calls for making policies explicit, making policies consistent, consciously choosing policies from among alternatives, and obsessively keeping the spotlight on the policies chosen never allows the governing focus to waiver from constant attention to policies, and the organization's fidelity to them.

Getting a Handle on Policies

We are not well equipped with language or useful conceptual categories to discuss policies. Even though we are accustomed to speaking of policies and even though boards claim to be "policy boards," the promising idea of policy governance is handicapped by our nascent skill in managing policies. Which policies must be addressed? What does a board policy look like? Are there inherent differences among types of policies? If a board addresses policies, what are the nonpolicy issues that it stops addressing? In preparation for proposing a classification system for board policies, I first look at the relationship between policy and the unending stream of organizational decisions. Second, I look at the relationship between policy and whole documents. Finally, I note the proactive possibilities in policy control.

Let us consider how boards ordinarily see their reality. Organizations present themselves to boards as a collection or sequence of concrete decisions, documents, arrangements (for example, staffing patterns or plans), and persons. Boards are accustomed to dealing with specific decisions and with resolving specific problems about this unending list. In fact, they pride themselves on being decision makers and problem solvers. They gauge their performance by such decisions and solutions, *not by the clarity of the policies that led to them.*

A board decision to increase a specific staff salary by $500 might really represent a board policy that would allow any salary to be adjusted up to 15 percent so long as budget balance is maintained. A board decision to establish mileage reimbursement at 24 cents might flow from the board's belief that the rate should be consistent with that of local governments. A board, presented with a staff plan for clinic hours, might approve the extension of operating time to 8 P.M. if its own value is merely that service hours not penalize patients who hold daytime jobs. A board's only policy concern, when asked to approve purchase of certain insurance coverage, may be that equipment is insured to 80 percent of replacement cost.

A board would do well to examine the policy implications of any initiative it is asked to approve. It can rise above the technical complexities by being a guardian of values rather than superstaff. "What policies are represented here?" should be a constant board query. "How do these actions relate to previous policies adopted by the board?" "What resolution of competing policies does this program, budget, or plan embody?"

(handwritten margin note: (SMALL GROUP DISCUSSION))

For example, in many service agencies, a "sliding fee" schedule adjusts the price of services or products on the basis of recipients' financial condition. Such schedules are ordinarily developed by staff, then inspected and approved by the board with great attention to form and content. Not uncommonly, the policies it represents get no systematic—much less rigorous—airing at all. Above all, fee markdowns in a public agency are implicitly based on how the economic nature of the organization is conceived. If, to put it simply, the agency is to plug holes in the market mechanism (provide for those whom the market price system would leave behind), there are many value choices to be made about which holes are plugged more than others. In other words, if we are to subsidize some persons or some needs more than others, on what basis will differential subsidy be established? These values will, at some level, be decided within the bounds drawn by a

(handwritten margin note: Eg)

mission statement. In fact, the policies relevant to this issue could be seen as "subsidiary" to mission. Were these policies to be clearly stated, administrative writing of the specifics of a fee adjustment schedule could proceed without board involvement.

To use another example, budgets are adopted with exhaustive attention to detail but with only cursory review of the important policies inherent in the array of numbers. Zero-based budgeting (ZBB) arose primarily in response to the unstated value in conventional budgeting that ongoing activity has the benefit of the doubt over marginal additions. That value had gone largely unnoticed in millions of annual budget approvals. Budgets make powerful, albeit nonverbal, commentary on policies regarding fiscal risk, conservatism in projection of revenues, and apportionment of resources among competing intentions. Budgets are often cited as the most important policy statement. And so they may be, but they are poorly conceived policies. The policies represented are buried so well in numbers that few boards get past the numbers to any rigorous debate about the underlying policies. If anything, the numbers seduce board members into a myriad of interesting but peripheral details.

We pore over the many pages of personnel "policies" (a misnomer), even though there are a mere handful of important policies underlying—and usually hidden in—the myriad specifics. Similarly, boards often overinvolve themselves in the many aspects of a long-range plan rather than isolate and resolutely deal with the very small number of large value issues on which a staff planning process can proceed.

In other words, because of the allure and handy concreteness of specifics, boards are no more accustomed to dealing directly with policies than are their staffs. Individual board members do hold values, of course, and sometimes state them clearly. The problem is that the board job design and process do not focus on the policy aspect of organization; nor do they provide a systematic way of collecting, deliberating, and enunciating those policies. Indeed, boards occasionally make a clear value pronouncement about an encompassing issue, only to "lose" the statement by burying it in a far longer document or in the minutes. Wisdom expressed but uncodified slips away.

By attending to policy content, a board can gain far more control over what matters in the organization and be at less risk of getting lost in the details. Even then, it can still be reactive if it confines its policy deliberation to what it is given by staff. James P. Weeks, member of the Naperville, Illinois, park commission, captured this thought when he said, "My *philosophy* will affect a process rather than react to a function already underway" (personal communication). There is no proactivity in inspecting what is already developed. Moreover, by that time the organization already has a sizable investment in the document or the staff recommendation. Beyond being reactive, this after-the-fact value inspection is shaped by staff interests, initiative, pace, and categories of work. Further, there is a great deal of executive prerogative about what to bring to the board and what not to bring. Inasmuch as boards often answer only what they have been asked, the resulting board response is hardly leadership.

To lead instead of follow, boards must get to the other end of the parade. Instead of following agendas driven by what staff wants approved, boards should initiate the agendas. Of course, no board knows what is going on in the staff domain well enough to do this. I am not suggesting that boards try to connect in a real-time sense to staff activity. I am saying that boards can know what is going on—and what should go on next—*in the board job*. The board is not responsible for managing, but it can surely be responsible for governing.

The objective is not to bring the board more knowledgeably into an ongoing administrative process, as if staff operations is the train to be caught. The point is to establish the board's policy-making process as both preliminary and predominant. If boards are truly governing, then board members are not obliged to tag along behind management. And they need not become superstaff in a conscientious attempt to tag along more professionally. They need only tend to their job of proactively establishing organizational policies.

Categories of Board Policy

Boards can scarcely lead the parade if their categories of work are derived from staff work. Normally, when a board addresses matters of policy, it is likely to do so within categories that mimic the administrative realm. Administrators are accustomed to breaking their domains down into certain areas: financial, personnel, service, data processing, and so on. Our tradition of board work encourages boards to derive their agendas from staff-based divisions of work. That these are sensible divisions of labor within a paid staff does not make them optimal divisions of thought at the board level.

This common board practice is tantamount to classifying a manager's functions on the basis of his or her secretary's job areas. Consider a new manager who inquires of his or her secretary just what categories of work have been successful in the clerical position. The manager finds that the secretary divides the job into typing, filing, telephone answering, and scheduling. So informed, the manager proceeds to divide the managerial job into managing about typing, managing about filing, managing about telephone answering, and managing about scheduling. Such a course of action would be ludicrous. We would think that such a manager had given little thought to the design of his or her own job, preferring thoughtlessly to mimic the concrete, handily available arrangement of a subordinate's. In fact, it is hard to conceive of any manager behaving in this way, *unless the "manager" is a board!* This error is so routine that we fail to see there is another way. Thus is conventional governance subtly managed by management, a far cry from management governed by governance.

In constructing a new wisdom of governance, I begin by creating categories to guide a board's debate and pronouncements, *groupings not derived from administration but from an inquiry into governance.* These categories also serve as vessels to contain board policies as they accumulate, and thereby become divisions of the board policy manual. The categories embrace board policies about (1) ends to be

achieved, (2) means to those ends, (3) the board–staff relationship, and (4) the process of governance itself. Policy-making
is not all of a board's job; linkage with the external environment, assessment of executive performance, and, in many
cases, fund-raising must be mastered as well. Policy-making,
however, is the *central* role and one that verbally contains
board positions and intentions about the other activities.
Well-considered and well-ordered policy-making fashions all
other board tasks into a coherent whole. Let us consider each
of the four categories.

Ends to Be Achieved

What should the results be? How will our being in business
affect the world? Our choices range from the broad (effects on
whole populations) to the specific (outcomes for a particular
client, student, patient, or other beneficiary). They relate to
both the long and the short term. It is this set of values about
intended impact on the world that is at the root of an organization's reason for existence.

 Both the cost and the benefit to the world must be taken
into account in considering an organization's transaction
with its environment. This most critical of all policy areas
concerns itself with what human needs are satisfied, for
whom, and at what cost. The governing board's highest calling is to ensure that the organization produces economically
justifiable, properly chosen, well-targeted results.

 Strategic leadership is proclaimed more through wisely
developed organizational ends than through any other aspect
of governance. This policy category could be called results,
impacts, goals, or outcomes as well as ends, each title having
its connotations. Governance of ends is specifically addressed
in Chapter Four.

Means to the Ends

If we isolate all values about organizational ends, the only
remaining values concern means. When we have dealt with

where we want to go, we are left with how we can get there. Speaking for myself, keeping ends and means separate is important, particularly because I have a pernicious habit of confusing means for ends. But suppose I supervise a team, to the members of which I delegate portions of the intended results. To maintain clarity in our communications, it is even more important that I differentiate between the activities (means) and the results (ends) to which the activities lead.

Beyond the need for clear communication, however, there is another important reason to keep ends and means separate. As a delegator, I am dealing with not only my own means but those of others as well. And what we know about managing people draws a sharp distinction between my means and theirs. I must tell myself how to do my part, but telling my subordinates how to do their jobs (rather than simply the expected results) has unintended effects. Unless they are unable or unwilling to make decisions, people do not like to be told how to do things. Their creativity is thwarted; they feel more like machines. If left free to choose the methods and held accountable only for results, people make the best of their hierarchical burden.

When this phenomenon is applied to an organization larger than a team, controlling methods at the top becomes a major source of organizational stress and even pathology. Bottlenecks develop because the part-time board cannot keep up with staff activities fast enough to prescribe them. The CEO cannot empower staff by decentralizing decision making because the board has withheld the power to make decisions. Having chosen to control a wide range of methods, boards look like amateurs trying in vain to play a professional game. Moreover, when organizational dialogue is so heavily invested in the "how," the "why" receives less attention. And issues of "why" are those most in need of board involvement.

As policies concerning one's own means and policies concerning the means of subordinates are such different topics, they must be kept separate. Policies about board means are addressed in the two categories yet to be introduced. Policies about staff means comprise those board values that guide the methods employed to achieve organizational ends. What expression is proper for board values in the domain of staff means? As we examine this question, remember that the most effective governing controls what needs to be controlled, yet sets free what can be free.

At the outset, the board's *only* interest in staff means is that they be effective, prudent, and ethical. I have never found any other legitimate reason to interfere with a subordinate's means. The main check on means, of course, is not on means at all, but on ends. The board's concern about effectiveness manifests in the degree to which the board's policies about ends are met. That leaves only one *direct* board interest in staff means: that they be prudent and ethical. This category of board values concerning the "how" of achieving results is composed, then, of policy statements defining prudence and ethics. Chapter Five explores the governance of staff means.

Board-Staff Relationship

The only remaining area is the board's own means. It is with regard to board means that policy is more likely to embody a perspective than, strictly speaking, a value. For mechanical ease rather than conceptual purposes, I divide the board's means into two parts: how the board relates to staff and how the board goes about the job of governing.

Policies about relating to staff include the board's approach to delegation, its view of the CEO role, and its manner of assessing performance. We deal directly with the board-staff or, more accurately, the board-CEO relationship in Chapter Six.

Process of Governance

It is in policies about the process of governance that the board addresses the nature of its trusteeship and its own job process and products. Nonprofit and public boards ordinarily govern on behalf of someone else, an often undefined group tantamount to stockholders of equity corporations. Board effectiveness can be sensibly assessed only if we know *in whose behalf* the board acts. For whom is it in trust?

In carrying out the top job in the organization, the board—like any manager—makes specific contributions beyond just a summation of what subordinates do. What are those contributions or, to put it another way, what is the board's job description? What principles or ground rules are used to discipline the process of leadership? What are and what are not legitimate board topics? What is the board's approach to its own discipline? How can the board structurally organize itself?

The issues are many, but the question in this category is simple: How do we approach the process and products of governance itself? These subjects form the content of chapters Seven and Eight.

Summary of the New Policy Categories

Values and perspectives that govern an organization can be divided into four categories, whether or not the board recognizes or uses them. It is my thesis that *explicit* use of these categories will profoundly alter the nature of board dialogue, documents, accountability, and, ultimately, the capacity for strategic leadership. These categories of policy, as further explained in subsequent chapters, can replace *all* other board documents except bylaws, minutes, and pronouncements of the state (articles of incorporation or enabling statutes). They are designed to be the centrally available, exhaustive repository of board wisdom.

Categories of board policies are printed in upper- and lowercase as shown here throughout the remainder of this text. When, for example, "board–executive relationship" appears in lowercase, the reader may assume it to denote exactly what it says rather than the policy category of the same name. As construed by the governance model presented, then, all policies of the board fall into these groups:

1. *Ends:* The organizational "swap" with the world. What human needs are to be met, for whom, and at what cost.

2. *Executive Limitations:* Those principles of prudence and ethics that limit the choice of staff means (practices, activities, circumstances, methods).
3. *Board–Executive Relationship:* The manner in which power is passed to the executive machinery and assessment of the use of that power.
4. *Board Process:* The manner in which the board represents the "ownership" and provides strategic leadership to the organization.

Next Chapter

Having established universal categories in which to conceive and to store the board's policies, let us now investigate policy-making in more depth. In Chapter Three, I invite you to look at the traps in policy-making and the characteristics of effective policy-making. I show how the board can gain greater control with shorter documents. We see how the revered practice of approving budgets, plans, and other administrative material—a process that cripples strategic leadership—becomes unnecessary when boards enact policies that make a difference.

Chapter 3

DESIGNING POLICIES
THAT MAKE A DIFFERENCE

Most governing boards conceive of themselves as policy boards. We have a general understanding that board leadership is largely a policy task. A policy approach prevents the flurry of events from obscuring what is really important.

Yet it is rare to find a board that seriously attends to policy more than to the various details of policy implementation. Fewer than 5 percent of the boards I have encountered over the past decade were able to furnish me with board policies! Either they did not have them or what they had was scattered through years of minutes. Documents purported to be policies were almost always executive compendiums in which the board had played a reactive part.

Even searches of minutes failed to turn up much more than single-event decisions disguised as policies. To be sure, there were "personnel policies" and "administrative policies" or general "policies and procedures manuals." But these were basically staff documents upon which the board had stamped its approval. In none of these was it clear what portions or aspects the *board itself* had contributed or decreed.

The most frequent exceptions to this state of affairs have been school boards. These boards have so many policies that they cannot possibly keep up with them. As would be expected, their policies concern mainly staff practices and are usually prescriptive in detail. Few would qualify as legitimate board policies under the definition developed here.

I divided board policies into four categories in Chapter Two. Before investigating each category separately beginning in Chapter Four, I will explore principles that apply to all categories. This chapter begins by describing what is often wrong with board policy and the general characteristics of effective policy. We next consider how a board can utilize the different "sizes" of policies to govern more efficiently. Then I argue that proactive policy-making can replace approvals as the dominant board style of leadership—and why it should. I conclude by looking at the format of policy and the refinement of policy content over time.

Getting Serious About Policy

Current operational definitions of policy impede governing by policy. Any sort of action by the board is often granted the legitimizing title of policy. The fuzziness of the definition is a loud signal that the whole area of policy has not been taken seriously. Consequently, the claim to be a policy-making board is ordinarily belied by "policy" that is staff material with a large component of implementation specifics, only blessed by the board. In practice, I have found that a board's professing to be a "policy board" offers little clue to what the board actually does.

Board policy can be dead, but unburied. I once supervised the collection of all previous (but still official) board policies of a large public organization in Indiana. The paperwork was inches thick. Many of the policies were long since forgotten, but still on the books. Were these policies really useful in running the organization? They had been painstakingly assembled at considerable cost for they were sprinkled through a wide range of documents. For all the rhetorical glamour afforded the board's policies, they turned out to be an impotent, self-contradictory collection too unimportant to be kept up to date.

Board policy can be alive, but invisible. Although it is hard to find true board policy in written form, it is always possible to find it in unwritten form. Actually, it may not be found so much as suspected. Ironically, unwritten policy is sometimes thought to be so clear that no one feels the need to write it down and, at the same time, so variously interpreted as to border on being capricious. In a sense, there is never a de facto lack of policy; it always exists in the actions taken. *Implicit* policy not only fills in for the missing explicit policy, but is even used to excuse the absence of the latter.

Unfortunately, both unwritten board policy and written board policy left untended are of questionable utility. We have difficulty either in agreeing on what the unwritten policy actually is (what it would say had it been explicit) or in knowing which old written policies are still in effect. Curiously, the criterion used to judge which written statements should be taken seriously and which should be ignored is itself *always* an unwritten policy! Why? Because boards are loath to admit they have policies that do not make a difference. Making a major investment in board policy-making begins by establishing principles and formats to guide policy content. Board policy-making, within the categories set out in Chapter Two, is explicit, current, literal, centrally available, brief, and encompassing.

POLICY-
MAKING
MUST BE...
①

Explicitness. Policies must be in written form. This is the only way all parties (including the policy-makers) can know just what the policy is. It is the best way for members to realize which policies should be questioned or changed. Explicitness is often made more difficult by two forces. First, as "everyone" understands this or that precept, it seems silly to dwell on actual language. It seems silly, that is, until the writing begins and we discover our agreement was not as precise as we thought. Second, being explicit carries a danger similar to that of being proactive. It means laying one's values on the table, exposing differences, and confronting them openly.

②

Currentness. Up-to-date policies are the only ones that work. A board can ensure that policies are kept current more by compulsively operating from its policy manual than by vowing to do annual reviews. When a board lives from its policies, the policies will either work or be changed. The policies will not then collect dust. Policies must never end with a whimper, but a bang; they must not be allowed to fade away into oblivion. Staff can help by acting as if the board sincerely means *every* policy not yet rescinded.

Literalness. Policies must mean what they say. If they do not, then they should be amended or deleted. We have come to accept organizational language that is meaningless. Learning a job is time consuming when you must discern bit by bit which words mean what they say and which do not. Governing is a verbal job; if a board's words have little integrity, governance cannot be excellent.

Central Availability. When board pronouncements are all kept in one place, the task of determining what the organization represents becomes easier. Policies are virtually the only medium through which the board speaks, and thus should not be scattered about, discoverable only by scouring years of minutes and multiple staff documents. Centrally visible board values go far in preventing board intentions from being idiosyncratically interpreted by individual members, officers, or committees. Board policies, to make a difference, must be focused into a single repository that has obvious preeminence over other organizational documents.

Brevity. Brevity may be the unheralded secret of excellence. Peters and Waterman (1982) point out the stultifying effect of reams of procedures. It is certainly possible to tie an organization up in procedures manuals. Similarly, in the creation of board policies, "too long" and "too many" are enemies of good leadership. Organizations seem to be impressed with complexity, however, so brevity in policy-making encounters the opposing need to look sophisticated ("It just *can't* be that simple!"). Boards need to seek the compelling elegance of simplicity.

Encompassment. Design of the board policy framework must support the encompassing wholeness that boards want governance to be. Then the board need not address all value issues, only the larger ones. By sticking to the discipline of resolving larger questions before smaller ones, starting with the broadest in each category, the board ensures that its policies will encompass the entire range of corporate possibilities. The next section, by examining the nature of policy "sizes," explains how policy can be encompassing.

Policies Come in Sizes

Inasmuch as there are fewer policies than decisions based on those policies, the board's task is already easier than if it had tried to address all the single decisions. Dealing with policies moves the dilemma from the impossible to the merely improbable, for there are also more policies than a board has time to consider. As policies are merely our values or perspectives, written or unwritten, they can be revealed in every event that occurs in an organization. We value one pen over another. We have values about length of meetings, coach airfare, group insurance, wax for the floor, and the need for a waste treatment plant. How can the board address such an inherently pervasive, large body of policy material, yet have a manageable task and product? This dilemma of too many policies to deal with has, happily, a simple key: policies come in sizes.

Logical Containment of Policies

Larger values or perspectives logically contain, that is, limit the logical content of, smaller ones. Having decided an encompassing value, a plethora of narrower value issues still remain to be settled. It is this characteristic that leads many board members to see policy as vague or not specific. To escape their discomfort, they are tempted to leap prematurely to the highly specific. A board is just as likely to be too broad as to be too detailed, so the anxiety of board members is not without foundation. The phenomenon of logical containment can help boards debate the question of policy breadth in an organized manner.

No matter how broad a policy is, it is always *more specific* than if it had not been said and *less specific* than it might have been. Therefore, it delimits the universe of specificity yet to be encountered, though it does not resolve those specificities. In other words, the *range* of further possible choices is smaller because the large value has been resolved. Say that you personally place more value on owning a new car than on having $15,000. This value statement both introduces and delimits further value issues, about colors, models, and stereo systems. Similarly, selection of a mission is at the broadest level of values about organizational results. Making that choice leaves many questions of priority unresolved, but it clearly limits the range of choices remaining.

A community may feel that the goal of establishing a "healthier local economy" is sufficient reason to operate an economic development agency. Bringing about a healthier local economy is an appropriate choice of mission. Whether to establish a broader employment base or to be a regional retail center is a subsequent, and slightly smaller, value choice that is confronted *within* the mission. Similarly, a public school mission to produce "competent, employable citizens" still leaves large issues to be decided, though at a level of abstraction lower than that of mission. These issues include the balance among academic, job skill, and life-planning competencies.

A journey in values clarification challenges boards who would govern by policy. Policies within each category, described in Chapter Two, can be arranged by size. Like mixing bowls, they "nest" together, largest to smallest. The board, after addressing the largest of value choices (the biggest bowl), can either proceed to address the next level (second largest bowl) or be content with having clarified the first level. The CEO then inherits the right to make choices within the second and subsequently smaller levels.

By attending to the largest issue(s) in each category, the board can responsibly limit its work. As it attends to the specificity in each decreasing level of policy in turn, it reaches a point where a majority of members are willing to accept *any reasonable interpretation* of the policy language. Until the board considers the full range of reasonable, subsequent possible choices permissible, it has not yet reached the stopping point. When that point is reached, the board can safely stop. The argument of "vagueness" is not relevant, only whether the remaining range is acceptable. How much the board trusts the chief executive is not relevant, only whether the range is acceptable, because if the board "trusts" the CEO to make a certain choice, then the board is harboring an unspoken expectation that should be committed to further policy specificity. When Ends and Executive Limitations policies are created with this integrity, management can be safely empowered with the authority to make all further choices.

Phyllis Field of the Rhode Island Board of Regents refers to this phenomenon as "controlling the inside by staying on the outside." As the board's policy is written, there is no doubt at just what size of "mixing bowl" the board stopped nor what the board has explicitly pronounced. Without such a scheme for creating policy, boards tend to make a policy about this, that, and the other. A patchwork of policies can leave dangerous gaps. Boards are reasonably fearful of having overlooked some important policy feature, so the solution is to become supermanagers, reviewing and approving everything. Powerful delegation is impossible in these circumstances, as is respite for the board to attend unceasingly and vigorously to the big issues. Making use of the principle of logical containment enables a board to have its hands firmly on, though not in, an organization.

Board Policy Versus Staff Policy

Starting with the big questions first is simply good problem-solving technique, even for individuals. But when delegation is involved, the utility of this approach goes beyond merely good problem solving. It enables the board to define the boundary between itself and its executive. The boundary always lies just below the point that the board last addressed. There is *no set boundary* for all boards or even for the same board at different times. As long as the board approaches all policy-making from the largest to the smallest issue, this method will continually redefine the boundary as circumstances and board values shift.

The board's job differs from staff jobs, then, not by topic, but by *levels within topics*. Exceptions to this rule are the unique board job contributions to be discussed in Chapter Seven. This approach recognizes and legitimizes that everybody, not just the board, makes policy. Every clerk and janitor, by her or his actions, is making implicit policy at all times. It is inescapable that everyone does so, though the policies made are of vastly differing sizes. What is important is that all policies that live in the organization be consonant with the broader policies enunciated by the governing leadership. Thus, the board can control without meddling.

In dealing with policy issues of different size, the board creates policies that make a difference if it observes the following principles:

- *The board should resolve the broadest or largest policy issue in each category before dealing with smaller issues in any category.* This requires the discipline to stick with the highly subjective, tough choices to be found in the broader policy issues.
- *The board should, if it wishes to address smaller levels, never skip levels but move to the next smaller levels in sequence.* This requires the discipline not to reach into the organizational decision process for instant fixes, even if specific board members are more expert in a subject than staff.
- *The board should grant the chief executive authority to make all further choices as long as they are "within" the board's Ends and Executive Limitations policies.* This requires the discipline to let go, to delegate.

The provisions of Ends and Executive Limitations policies are binding directives, but within those bounds, the executive is free to choose and move without the stultifying, over-the-shoulder involvement (some might say meddling) of the board. If the board has done its job, such detailed involvement not only is unnecessary, it destroys staff creativity and efficiency. Only boards that have failed to be proactive policy-makers have any need to meander in or retain approval authority over staff activity and plans. Moreover, unless the chief executive has such authority, he or she can never delegate parts of it to subordinates without onerous bureaucratic strings.

Prerogatives that fall within board policies in the Board Process and Board–Executive Relationship categories may be given to the board chairperson. Because these categories deal with the board's own means, they should not be delegated to the chief executive. But within the Ends and Executive Limitations categories, the CEO *must* be the person authorized to make further decisions. In any event, it is in delegation to the CEO where board fidelity to good principles is most critical. Even when the staff is small, by far the preponderance of further decisions lies in the executive's arena. Consequently, almost all my further comments on the concept of residual decision latitude relate to the Ends and Executive Limitations categories.

There need be no prescribed limit to how far a board may delve into smaller issues, as long as it starts with the largest and progresses *in sequence*. The likelihood of a board's going "too far" (even in the judgment of staff!) is small, simply because the further it goes, the more complex becomes the task of balancing all the ramifications of any one choice. Lower-level issues branch out much like a table of organization does, so the number of factors to coordinate increases at increasingly lower levels. Juggling such permutations is one reason a full-time staff stays busy.

It is instructive to envision the "size of issue" phenomenon as a matrix. The board's level of involvement is across the top of all topics. Just beneath the board's level is the chief executive, and just below that the first echelon of staff, and so forth throughout the organization. Everything below the board is the chief executive's domain, though the executive turns over lower levels of issues to staff. Columns cutting across all levels consist of any topic with which the agency might deal.

Each topic includes issues that are very large (at the top) and those that are very small (at the bottom). A budget, for example, embodies a few sweeping values and a great many small ones. The board itself fills in the top cells with policy. The chief executive and his or her subordinates fill in all other choices consistent with the board's statement. Board policies are embodied in a board policy manual consisting of all the board's pronouncements, but not cluttered by the more voluminous ones subsequently made by staff.

In other words, instead of an agency "policy and procedures" manual, there should exist a board policy manual separate from staff-written, staff-owned documents. Instead of a board-approved budget, there should be a board budget policy. Instead of a board personnel manual, there should be a board policy on the treatment of personnel. Instead of a board-approved wage and salary administration plan with compensation schedules, there should be a board policy on compensation. Each policy might be approximately one page in length. The board's document would be a conceptually *horizontal* collection of these three and other board policies.

Contrast this with the conventional approach in which agency documents are arranged *vertically* by topic. Commonly, we would have an agency personnel manual, a budget, and a single compensation package. Each document is a mixture of the trivial and the profound, *mostly trivial* simply because the greatest number of issues are at the lower levels. Moreover, document content is not in explicit values at all. Board-level choices cannot be distinguished from staff choices. The content is overwhelmingly the specifics of implementation, generated largely by staff, from which the controlling, broadest values *may only be inferred.*

Policy Architecture

When a board policy is longer than one sentence, the internal structure of the policy reflects the nested levels of issues it addresses. An outline form serves this need handily. The policy preamble would be the highest level, major headings the next highest level, and so on through the outline format. The board will have debated and resolved higher levels prior to lower levels within what will become a single policy. It will not have dealt with the document as a whole, except perhaps in the final review.

Consequently, the very appearance of board policies reflects the discipline of nested sizes of the board's values and perspectives. Policies can be rigorous and yet succinct. To be a compact document wherein every word counts, a policy must not repeat what can be found elsewhere.

The Approval Syndrome

This kind of unembellished policy-making may appear stark and suspiciously terse to boards accustomed to adopting policies in monolithic rather than articulated format. Finding, much less extracting, the broadest, most encompassing policy issues from such conglomerations can be quite difficult. It is customary not only to adopt various levels of policy as an undifferentiated mass, but to adopt whole documents. Whole documents, like budgets, personnel "policies," and compensation plans comprise multiple levels from the least to the most detailed. To control their top-level considerations, boards are thrown the entire documents complete with a preponderance of trivia. So it is that approval of total management documents is the current norm in governance.

Only respect for tradition prevents our noticing how ritualistic, trivializing, bottlenecking, and reactive this "approval syndrome" is. The inherent flaws in this time-honored method are severely detrimental to the quality of both governance and management:

Reactivity. Document approvals place the board in a reactive position. The board is moving after the fact inasmuch as the document has already been created (using criteria the board did not establish). For practical reasons, often little can be done but to approve the measure. Many times, to avoid feeling like rubber stamps, boards nitpick, particularly in approving budgets. No matter how much intelligence goes into playing this reactive role, it is clearly not leadership.

Sheer Volume of Material. Board members must read and understand sufficiently to critique. That calls for studious attention to many low-level issues. Boards are burdened with material to study. The resultant tomes are necessarily filled with staff-level material and issues on which board members spend conscientious and prodigious time. It is unlikely that any board can be truly complete in this endeavor, and therefore overlooks important items in the flurry of small ones.

Mental Misdirection. A strategic leader must continually struggle against smallness. The larger, important values are vulnerable and easily displaced by concrete, short-term matters. The "approval syndrome" invites boards to deal with primarily low-level issues and detracts their attention from high-level, more subjective issues. One board I worked with spent time going over every nook and cranny of an almost $200 million budget each year. Looking back over several years of such exhausting work, they were hard-pressed to find even one half of 1 percent of budget improvement thus produced. Yet during the same time, they had failed to wrestle with and clarify just what this large organization was to produce!

Letting Staff Off the Hook. When the board gives formal approval, it becomes the owner of the document. Whatever is inconsistent with what *would have been* a board policy (had there been one) can no longer be held against the chief executive. Who is to be held accountable when a board-approved staff plan fails to accomplish the desired results? The board has been co-opted in the process. But staff judgment may have been co-opted as well, inasmuch as staff plans are designed not only to accomplish results but to garner board approval. It is not uncommon for staffs to give disproportionate attention to this political feature. Under these conditions, CEO accountability to the board loses both legitimacy and rigor.

(5)

Short-Term Bias. Low levels of organization generally have a short time horizon. Because the document is created from the bottom up, rather than on the basis of high-level values pronounced by the board, it may have a short-term bias.

(6)

Lack of Clarity in the Board's Contribution. When the document is approved, it is impossible to determine just what the board said! The board either said everything because it now owns the document in its entirety, or said nothing because it merely passed what someone else contributed, or said something between these extremes. But no one can tell. There is no distinct pronouncement expressing the values of the board. Thus, the voice of leadership cannot be heard. Under such obscurant conditions, a board may remain busy reviewing and approving, but *making no substantive contribution at all,* and no one notices.

(7)

Subsequent Staff Agility. Since we cannot tell what the board has said, we cannot tell what others in the hierarchy have said. Consequently, we cannot tell who has the right to restate or change some part of what has been decided. Any request for change must be put to the board regardless how undeserving it may be of their attention. Thus, the board is involved in trivial matters both in the initial approval and in amendments. The management effect is either to flood the board with staff-level issues in order to be agile and flexible with activities and plans or to accept the bottleneck caused when plans and procedures cannot be amended in a natural flow by the persons most intimate with implementation.

(8)

Fragmentation. The board is faced with a sequence of disconnected and unmanageably voluminous vertical slices of the whole instead of a holistic, manageable fabric of horizontally connected policies. We all profess that boards should view the big picture. Yet what most boards confront in meeting after meeting are pieces that are too specific.

The approval process provides boards with a handily available, easy, tradition-condoned *imitation* of leadership.

Instead of separating the board's domain from the staff's domain, the "approval syndrome" confounds both into an undifferentiated mass. The stage is set for the board to do unnecessary work at the staff level or for the staff to wield undue influence at the board level. The former, depending on one's point of view, is perceived as detailed, trivial, burdensome, or involved. The latter is perceived as rubber stamping, staff dominance, or comfortable passivity. Of course, both situations may exist at the same time, the board doing staff work and the staff doing board work. However talent is wasted, neither strategic leadership by the board nor effective management by the staff is well served. When the approval process is taken lightly (rubber stamping), it reduces board action to a charade. When it is taken seriously, it reduces the CEO concept to a charade.

Curiously, there are times when the board goes through the approval process not intending to withhold authority from the CEO, but to confirm it. A board might declare its support of the CEO by cloaking some controversial executive decision in the prestige of the boardroom. Board motivation is usually expressed as "we want the staff (or others) to know the board is really behind the CEO on this." As long as the board and CEO understand that the decision is truly the CEO's, this approval seems not only harmless, but a healthy show of solidarity. The board should, however, consider that such a gesture of board support is called for only if the board has been sending weak signals about the nature of delegation. This kind of support is ordinarily not warranted if the board has made it clear to all that the CEO's decisions within board-stated bounds are *always* supported by the board. Official support of a specific action implies that such support is necessary or, conversely, that the general philosophy of delegation is weak.

Policy Development

Policy-making, then, is proactive concerning the broadest issues rather than reactive on issues of all sizes. Policies of the board, brief though they may be, become parent to all executive action. Because these policies are central, their currency is critical. Brevity will make keeping them up to date far easier. Such brief, current policies developed by a state board in Ohio were said by Dr. Robert Bowers to "reduce the Board's Policy Manual to 34 pages from 422 pages and make it a constantly used reference rather than a collector of dust" (personal communication). Governing by policy means governing *out of* policy in the sense that no board activity takes place without reference to policies. Most resolutions in board meetings will be motions to amend the policy structure in some way. Consequently, policy *development* is not an occasional board chore, but its chief occupation.

From time to time, a board discovers that its values and perspectives have changed, that a previous statement was not fully cognizant of the range of options, or that the risks and opportunities in the external world have shifted. Even large shifts in board values can usually be accommodated more by altering existing language than by adding to it, thus changing the volume of policies very little. It is very important that the collection of board policies not grow so large that it fails to remain a truly living document.

Policies or policy changes can be initiated anywhere. It is not important to restrict the sources from which the board receives its impetus to establish or change its policies. But it is important to fix the *responsibility* for continual, informed weighing of policy issues. That responsibility must rest squarely upon the board itself, not upon the chief executive. In practice, the CEO plays a meaningful role in the board's continuing inquiry. But, to remove from the board the central responsibility for its own job would be a rash flight from responsibility. The board may charge its officers or committees with parts of its task, but let there be no mistake *whose* responsibility is being assigned.

An optimally working board is constantly fueled to develop policy by the nature of the discourse in which it engages. Proper boardroom dialogue spots value inconsistency, seizes upon value issues, and is impelled on an exciting discovery in relative worth. In an environment of value awareness disciplined by principles relating to value size and category, a board can enact policies that make a difference.

Next Chapter

Now that we have better defined the nature of effective policy-making, we will study each policy category in turn. In Chapter Four, we examine those policies that direct the most critical feature of any organization: the Ends. No feature is more central to the policy-making responsibility than the governing of organizational ends.

Chapter 4

FOCUSING ON RESULTS: CLARIFYING AND SUSTAINING THE ORGANIZATION'S MISSION

The most important work of any governing board is to create and re-create the reason for organizational existence. This is not simply the approval of a purpose statement. Nor is this a task once done, then forgotten. It is a perpetual obligation, deserving of the majority of board time and energy. It is far more important than any other board undertaking, including budgets, personnel issues, risk management, and even choice of chief executive.

The only justifiable reason for organizational existence is the production of worthwhile results. Worthwhile results always relate to the satisfaction of human need. Whose needs, which needs, and what constitutes "satisfaction" are the unending, subjective quandaries confronting a board. Resolving the important, even existential value dilemmas inherent in these questions is the very heart of leadership in governance.

In this chapter I begin by arguing for boards to focus more on the world outside the organization than the one inside. I then relate that external focus to the creation of mission and the results-related (Ends) policies built on mission. Next, I look at two powerful distractions that draw boards away from Ends: the confusion of ends with means and premature anxiety about evaluating Ends. I conclude with the board's largely Ends-related role in long-range planning.

Transcending the Organization

Board leadership of an organization is jeopardized more by the organization itself than by any other threat. I am not referring to the reluctance of staff to be governed, but to a more insidious phenomenon: the captivating allure of organizational events and issues. Typically, a high percentage of board time is spent on internal matters. Even when the subject matter is related to services or programs, the focus tends to be on personnel, fiscal, logistical, or other organizational aspects of programming. In other words, the most compelling subject matter deals with structure and method, not results.

Leadership for results begins outside, not inside the organization. Because of the seductive intrigue of organizational activity, board discipline must be designed to overcome entanglement in internal matters. Our understanding of what constitutes board "involvement" must change. The most effective way to help a board rise above organizational myopia is to let the board taste the grand expanse of the larger context.

The Larger Context

Although organizations are worlds in themselves, each is part of something bigger. We must start from this larger context to grasp the underpinnings of an organization. This outside world existed prior to, is larger than, and likely will go on after the organization. It is this larger context that gives meaning to the organization's mission and makes the organization's very existence possible. Further, board members' primary identity lies not within the organization, but in some part of the external context.

To the extent a board fails to consider its results from a context external to the organization, it narrows the vision of which it is capable. Sometimes, leadership differs from nonleadership only in that leadership views the world with a slightly wider lens. That wider lens or, if you will, taller perspective, is achieved in governance by viewing not the organization, but its environment as the setting for analysis and debate.

Transaction with the Environment

The organization lives in this larger context and, hence, affects it. That the organization exists makes a difference to this larger world, and the difference it makes can be characterized in two ways: (1) The world is richer, happier, less in pain because of the care, knowledge, cure, or support produced. (2) The world is poorer, more depleted, more in pain because of the talent, capital, and space consumed. These two impacts on the world, corresponding to benefit and cost, should be the chief interest, even obsession, of the governing board: What good shall we do, for which people or needs, and at what cost? It is important that organizational results be viewed in terms of both cost and benefit.

The concept here is exchange, a transaction between the organization and the world. Something of value consumed is swapped for something of value produced. I use the words *results, ends,* and *outcomes* interchangeably to describe the organization's swap with the world. So these terms, as used here, refer to both 'product (changes for people) and efficiency (amount of change per dollar).

The usual vocabulary of organization contains *goal* and *objective.* But, alas, both goal and objective can be applied to either means or ends. Legitimately and commonly, objectives are established in the drive to attain a desired amount of activity or a desired outcome. Therefore, it is misleading to equate goals or objectives with the concept of ends. Although I use these terms in their common meaning, as some desired achievement, I do not employ them as special management concepts, choosing instead to focus on the ends–means difference.

Similarly, the word *strategy* includes both ends and means components. A planned shifting of outcome priorities over the next five years is an Ends issue. Long-term staff retraining and replacement strategies to make the shifts possible are means issues. As important as strategy is, the concept itself does not determine the best way a board can address it. So as much as this text is a plea for boards to be strategic leaders, good strategy flows from the board's proper treatment of the ends–means distinction.

Confusing Ends and Means

My point is not that means are unimportant, just that means and ends should not be confused. Means will be best decided by the persons who must use them, persons whose choice of means is measured chiefly by whether they achieve the expected ends.

Kirk (1986, p. 40) charged that boards "become so engrossed in doing an infinite variety of discrete things, pursuing an endless number of routines, that they lose sight of the results, if any, that the activities are supposed to accomplish." The distinction between ends and means seems simple. Ends and means appear often in the common language as a way of usefully classifying events around us. But closer inspection reveals difficulty in this apparent simplicity. For a board to take advantage of the ends–means opportunity for governance, it must recognize the ways in which ends and means are confounded.

Means Mistaken for Ends

In the absence of clear dictates about intended effects on the world, a number of means come to be treated as if they were ends themselves. In some nonprofit and public endeavors, these counterfeit result areas have received the blessing of tradition, an unearned legitimacy that—more through default than through deliberation—is accorded to the familiar.

Commendable Activities. The most insidious counterfeits are activities associated with good intentions or with well-accepted reasoning. For example, because making available more handouts for training sessions shows good intent or sense, the number and quality of handouts can come to be judged more important than the effect of the training. The bounds to which such confusion can extend are endless. In response to public clamor in the mid 1980s to compensate teachers on the basis of competence, numerous plans were proposed to establish incentives for those teachers who took more graduate courses!

In social service fields, a revered counterfeit is unit cost. Unit cost is the cost in dollars for providing a time unit of service. Pupil-day expenditure is a comparable public school term. Unit cost comes to be the measure of whether a service organization is doing as much per dollar as it should. But unit cost is not related to the effectiveness of the service, so it does not measure productivity (efficiency in producing benefits per dollar) as social programs pretend it does. For example, the unit cost mentality leads to the assumption that $50 per hour is better than $65 per hour when there is absolutely no reason to believe so. Perhaps the $65 per hour service is 150 percent more effective in attaining the results sought! Unit cost would simply be an innocuous measure, if institutions had not come to rely upon it.

An organization can become so permeated by the belief that well-intended or reasonable actions (rather than results) are the reason for existence that no one realizes something is awry. A striking example is the allegiance given to services and programs as if they were results. Services and programs are often treated as if they have value in themselves; however these are only packages of prescribed activities. Under a results orientation, services and programs are seen only as means to some end. It is that end that should be judged. Otherwise righteous busyness becomes not just as meaningful as results, but *more so*.

The *threat of good activity* is so great that it can hardly be overstated. Without constant vigilance and systems to support it, said Odiorne (1974, pp. 1–7), "People tend to become so engrossed in activity that they lose sight of its purpose. . . . They become so enmeshed in activity they lose sight of why they are doing it, and the activity becomes a false goal, an end in itself. . . . Falling into the activity trap is not the result of stupidity. In fact, the most intelligent, highly educated people tend to be those most likely to become entrapped in interesting and complex activities."

It is not that good intentions or sensible actions by staff are unimportant. It is that they in no way constitute the reason for an organization's existence. Commendable activities are only a means to an end.

Commendable Conditions. Similarly, commendable conditions can also masquerade as results. Staff credentials may be the foremost of these conditions. Credentials and training can easily inspire admiration. It surely seems reasonable to think that a person with impressive training will do a better job than one without such training. Such reasoning has been called "paying persons for where they've been, not for what they are contributing." On this basis, for example, a professor with an impressive publications list is assumed to be a better teacher than a professor without such credentials.

High staff morale is another commendable condition. Some boards show more interest in staff morale than in results: If morale is high, then we must be OK; if turnover is high, something is wrong. One does not have to favor low morale or high turnover to see that although these indices may be symptoms, the organization exists neither for high morale nor for low turnover. The point here is not to ignore the signs of possible problems, only to put them in perspective. Boards that monitor morale but not results have an inverted ends–means perspective.

Conditions within an organization are important, but they are not the reason the organization exists. Commendable conditions are only a means to an end.

Commendable Structure. The arrangement of jobs, reporting lines, and distribution of decision centers through an organization constitute the structure of an organization. A short-hand representation is the table of organization. Structural factors have great influence on how an organization functions. To illustrate, narrow spans of control may reflect undeveloped management potential and extra hierarchical levels. The existence of a majority of staff officers (as opposed to line officers) in close proximity to the CEO suggests fragmented delegation and underutilized, underdeveloped line managers. Very wide span of CEO control may demonstrate unusually high precision in delegation, but could also mean that the CEO is too busy and not sufficiently reflective. A deputy CEO to whom everyone else reports when the CEO is unavailable is almost sure to involve wasted managerial power. More than two executives vertically configured, each with supervision over only one person, almost certainly means someone has a position but no job. Structure does make a difference.

Streamlined, efficient structure is to be admired and much sought. But an organization neither deserves points for it, nor loses points for lack of it. Whether an organization is good or bad is revealed in the results and in its prudence and ethics. If an assessment of performance against the criteria set forth in board policies shows no problems, then the concern was misplaced anyway.

Organizational structure is important. Yet, even the best structure is not the reason an organization exists. Structure is only a means to an end.

Commendable Technology. High-technology electronics has become increasingly important in nonprofit and public organizations, but the technology of operations has long been an issue to managers. Examples range from the hardware technologies of typewriters, filing systems, and telephones to the concept technologies of queue theory, operations research, and decision-making techniques. Management has graduated to word processing, extensive data banks, and other computer applications. But techniques and technologies can be undeservedly promoted from supporting to leading actors.

In the late 1970s the Environmental Protection Agency was set to require use of a certain type of scrubber to rid smokestack discharge of particulates. EPA's intent was that particulate emission be no greater than some critical level. Yet its criterion was the technology used to reach the result. By diverting attention from the desired result, the EPA would have sabotaged its own long-term effectiveness. Government bureaucracies often operate in this manner. Although they sacrifice long-term effectiveness, in the short run they maximize control (even if over the wrong things). In a supervisory situation, this might be viewed as the difference between managing and bossing. Technology-driven operation, very much like commendable activity-driven operation, is susceptible to what has been called the "tool illusion." To a child with a hammer, objects to be pounded become the most important things in the world. An object's "poundability" becomes its most salient characteristic.

Technology within an organization is important, but even the best technology is not the reason an organization exists. Technology is only a means to an end.

Ends Mistaken for Means

In failing to focus on the ends–means distinction, we can also confuse ends for means. In some instances, there is such a singleminded focus on means that results are not recognized when they come along. I observed a public school board spend its usual long, cluttered meeting moving from one executive means issue to another. Most of the means issues were not very large. In the midst of this unnecessary flurry was an agenda item concerning the outcome of extensive tests of reading ability throughout the system. The busy board spent only enough time to notice the item, say something nice, and move quickly back to the flurry of trivia!

The confusion that surfaces most often is between "subends" and means. Parts of the overall result can accurately be viewed as means to the final end. The concept of means in such a case differs materially from the concept of means used here. In everyday language we use the word *means* for both. Assume that the board's overall result (mission) is "normal community living for the developmentally disabled." The board, in dealing with the next lower level of abstraction, determines which "products" make up the mixture that most closely corresponds to its vision of the broad result.

Perhaps the board will decide that the desired mixture comprises independent living skills, occupational skills, and

receptive employers. The megaresult (the mission) will comprise several sub-results, which in turn will comprise sub-
sub-results, regardless of where the board chooses to stop and
allow executives to take over. This procession of ever smaller
sub-results continues to the most specific short-term result
concerning an individual consumer. One *could* look at any
sub-result as a means to the next higher result. Returning to
the example, occupational skills can be viewed as a means to
"normal community living." There is nothing wrong with
this construction, but it is not the kind of construction that
yields a managerially useful differentiation between ends and
means.

The hybrid *sub-result as means* represented by "occupational skill" is quite different from the *pure means* represented by, say, "skills training." Skills training, an activity, is
a means now and forever; it cannot be an outcome. On the
other hand, it is easy to conceive of occupational skill as an
outcome—a reasonable organizational result in itself. Occupational skill can even be pictured as the single product of a
smaller or less ambitious agency, that is, the mission itself.
Occupational skill can be mistaken for a means *only* if there
exist broader results of which it is a part.

In the ends-means differentiation discussed in this
book, the sense in which a sub-result like occupational skill
can be considered a means will never be used. The powerful
utility of the ends-means differentiation in enabling better
governance rests on using one definition rather than the
other. *Activities are always means no matter how complex or
important. External outcomes, results, and impacts are ends
whether or not they are parts of a broader end.*

Mission as Mega-Ends Policy

A written mission can be conceived in different ways. One
popular and creditable manner is to summarize in a short
statement all the major values to which an organization as-
pires, for example, "We will be the most respected regional
provider of Widgets by our customers, our employees, and

our suppliers." This type of mission can be extremely useful, even inspiring. I make no case against such a formulation when I call upon boards to produce another kind of statement. The two (this type and the one I propose) could, in fact, coexist. Because the mission described in this book is a different sort, there is a danger in using so familiar and widely defined a label as mission. It is very important that nonprofit and public boards develop the type of mission I describe. It is very unimportant that they call it mission.

Although Ends can be considered at various levels, it is only the broadest expression that should initially concern a board. Mission, defined as the briefest, broadest Ends statement, does not determine everything about an organization's intended results; but it tells us the range within which all further results will occur. Mission defines the arena and answers the simple questions "What is this organization for? How will the world be different as a result of our being in business?"

MISSION

What Makes a Powerful Mission

Stating a mission can be the most powerful single action a board takes or it can be a waste of time. Not infrequently, boards engage in meticulous mission-writing sessions. This intense exercise takes much more time than most boards intend, particularly in the light of the physical product. More times than not, the completed work finds a quiet resting place in a grant application, annual report, or brochure. It bothers no one until it is time to find it, dust it off, and go through the grueling project once again. Often, the board is driven by one member who is sold on the importance of writing mission statements.

A powerful mission is a broad Ends statement with six critical characteristics:

CHARACTER-ISTICS OF A MISSION STATEMENT

(1)

1. *Results terminology:* Mission should not be couched in terms of the activities necessary to achieve some change. *It is the change itself* that is the mission.

2. *Succinctness:* A long statement usually means that a board has not come to terms with its mission. Long statements clutter and smother the actual mission with explanation, intended methods, and excess verbiage. The real mission is often found buried in the several paragraphs, but boards are hard pressed to identify it, and CEOs are not able to organize around it. Ideally, the mission should be stated in a few words, no more than a sentence.

3. *Authoritative generation:* The mission is too close to the heart of governance for the board to act passively and simply approve another's statement. If the board is not actively involved in determining the mission, why should it be involved in anything else?

4. *Horizontal integration:* The mission is developed from the extraorganizational context by a board accountable to an "ownership." That same ownership may have other boards doing its business. There is disjointedness in public service and weakening of the public fabric when boards do not speak with other boards. There is no more meaningful subject about which community boards can converse than mission.

5. *Ubiquity:* Unless a mission is pervasive, it will lose its compelling power in organizational affairs. It simply cannot be repeated too much (which is another reason for succinctness). The mission should appear on all documents, on the phones, and in the conference rooms. *Live* with the mission.

6. *Vertical integration:* The mission must be the theme and the backbone of the organization. An elegant mission does little good if it is not connected to the goings-on of the organization. The mission connects the board's job with the CEO's job and thence to all others. Every department, every program, every job, and every objective must be tied to the mission. Placing the mission on this pedestal is comparable in a summative sense to a "bottom line" mentality. Because of their peculiar market status, nonprofit and public organizations have been able to develop

disjointed, internal islands of excellence that are not forced to sum to a bottom line.

Examples of statements that fulfill the first two requirements are "a community free from poverty" (a community action agency) and "every child a wanted child" (American Birth Control League, then its successor, the Planned Parenthood Federation of America—though never as a formal mission). To accurately cover the "swap" aspect of Ends, the actual policy document might add "at state of the art efficiency" or other expectation pertinent to the acceptable cost of producing the desired effect. This part could be omitted when the mission is used for slogan purposes.

Expanding on the Mission

The first "vertical integration" takes place in the mission's clear connection to further policies created by the board. The board, not the CEO, is therefore likely to be the first to expand upon mission, and it does this by creating a second level of Ends policies, just one order of abstraction below the mission itself.

I have argued for phrasing mission in a few carefully chosen words, then adding more detailed policy statements that further determine the organization's results. It is common for boards to write paragraph- or page-long missions. Aside from obscuring the focal mission statement, this *conglomerate form* is far harder to debate and to amend. In contrast, mission-related expressions espoused here are in an *articulated form,* that is, characterized by a progression of cautiously segmented parts beginning with the broadest and moving to the discrete parts. The process of deciding on "headings" before "subheadings" (as in an outline) yields greater integrity in establishing intended results than lumping results into an undifferentiated mass. In effect, the articulation of results into separable, descending parts yields a "value map" that both boards and staffs find instructive, with respect not only to what has already been resolved, but what is to be addressed next.

The brief mission statement at the very highest, broadest layer encompasses all further value choices about results. Though unlikely, the board may choose to address no further results after it has adopted a mission. If the board were to agree that any reasonable interpretation of the mission language by the CEO would be acceptable, then it need say no more. That is, if all the possible priorities, choices, and costs are acceptable, there is no reason for the board to narrow the expected results by passing more policies. The board would simply refrain from further pronouncements and allow the CEO to resolve all submission choices among Ends. Most boards are understandably reluctant to leave such broad issues to the CEO, so they do not stop at this point.

The Ohio State Board of Education policy titled "Mission" (Exhibit 1) illustrates a slightly expanded mission statement. The board collected in this statement the megaproduct of the Department and, if you will, the three "product lines" or major outputs. Note that the outputs are what the state agency contributes to the whole of education; there is no pretense that it is contributing what local school systems are producing.

Consumers, Products, and Costs

The board's next step after stating the mission is to discuss which portions of the topic it wishes to define more narrowly,

---

Exhibit 1. Ohio State Board of Education Policy: "Mission."

This mission of the State Board of Education and the Ohio Department of Education is *Literate Ohio Citizens.* Necessary to that mission, consistent with the State Board's unique representation of citizens with respect to education, and statutorily appropriate to the Ohio Department of Education, there are three distinct Department contributions to Ohio.

Statewide Vision: There will be, enriched by diverse viewpoints, a common public vision of what education is to be and to achieve in the future.

Quality Outcomes: There will be statewide definition of quality in education, and the actual achievement of that quality by Ohio school districts.

Informed Decision Makers: There will be ample information about realities and possibilities that enable the governor, general assembly, and individual citizens to make informed judgments about education.

---

thereby reducing the submission latitude available to the CEO. The board may choose to create further policy in one, two, or all aspects of Ends.

Products. Mission statements are broad enough to encompass a wide range of potential products. Products are the benefits to be produced (cure, knowledge, broader employment base, housing, job skills) or the accessibility/availability of the products (within every county, only a 1-800 call away, five days a week).

As a trade association, the Metropolitan Indianapolis Board of Realtors exists, as is clear in their "Purpose of MIBOR" policy (Exhibit 2), so that members can thrive. Like the Ohio State Board of Education, the MIBOR board stated no priorities among the five outcomes. The Executive Director would, therefore, have the right to make that decision, as well as to decide, for example, just which skills will be emphasized in area 2. The board can, of course, create another policy expanding upon any part(s) of this policy it wishes. It is obvious how such expansion would reduce the executive director's latitude.

Beneficiaries. Mission statements are broad enough to encompass a wide range of potential beneficiaries. Beneficiaries might be differentially "targeted" by age, type of disorder or

---

Exhibit 2. Metropolitan Indianapolis Board of Realtors Policy: "Purpose of MIBOR."

The mission of the Metropolitan Indianapolis Board of Realtors is enhanced demand for Realtor services. In pursuit of this mission, MIBOR will bring about results in five areas:

1. A positive public image of Realtors.
2. A highly skilled Realtor membership.
3. A favorable environment for Realtors' commerce in real estate.
4. Accurate and timely information and business tools for the conduct of Realtors' business.
5. Free housing choice and equal professional services to all persons as prescribed by the Voluntary Affirmative Marketing Agreement and the Code of Ethics of the National Association of Realtors.

deficit, severity of need, party membership, location, income, or other consumer characteristics.

"International Food and Development" by Lutheran World Relief (Exhibit 3) describes the third-party (in this case, U.S. government) actions that it seeks to influence. Advocacy is an activity, but the results of that advocacy are legitimate Ends. These changes in government policy are products of the organization just as much as its direct Third World development benefits are. Note that the board chose not to first determine a preamble that would subsume its seven points.

Cost. Although putting a dollar value on changes in the human condition is not an easy task, we do so implicitly all the time. The board may decide how much any given benefit is worth or, at least, the cost not to be exceeded in providing units of that benefit. The apportionment of cost also might be addressed, for example, the subsidy of certain consumers by other consumers, by donors, or by the public.

Exhibit 3. Lutheran World Relief Policy:
"International Food and Development."

LWR will advocate U.S. policies which:

1. Contribute to international development and humanitarian assistance activities at levels commensurate with U.S. resources and with the contributions of other donor nations of the world.
2. Provide sustained support for efforts of developing countries to become more self-reliant.
3. Give high priority to assisting small farmers, landless laborers, and others among the very poor.
4. Make development, humanitarian, and food assistance available on the basis of need without discrimination as to gender, ethnic origin, or religious or political persuasion.
5. Recognize and facilitate the work of American and developing country private and voluntary organizations, at the same time respecting their independence and privateness.
6. Support the work of multilateral organizations which express a shared international cooperative approach in meeting human needs.
7. Address the causes of poverty and suffering through social and economic changes, seeking reconciliation and healing rather than division and strife.

There is interaction among these three areas. Consider, for example, a dental health project in a ghetto. For a given level of expenditures, we can fill the cavities of 500 children *or* we can fill cavities and straighten the teeth of 150 children. Which is the best choice? We must juggle product and worth to resolve the issue. In a public school system, students with behavior problems cost more to educate. The extra costs mean that other children do not get as much as they otherwise would. To what extent should the benefits to some children be sacrificed so that troubled children can be more fully served? Public library products cost more per user in rural areas than in urban areas. What is the right balance between cost per rural user and cost per urban user?

The "Service Priorities" policy of the El Paso Center for Mental Health and Mental Retardation (now the Life Management Center) (Exhibit 4) addresses the board's concern that various disability or need areas receive a fair share of service. Note that the board chose to incorporate latitude for the executive director by using percentages that do not add up to 100 percent.

Obviously these are but a few of literally thousands of value choices regularly facing organizations. Usually they are hidden from direct view, buried in the many pages of program descriptions, budgets, and other staff documents. Board leadership, newly aware of this hidden richness, will at first seem to have uncovered an unmanageable number of value dilemmas. These were always present but previously settled by default—massive value choices about organizational nature and destiny that have been decided by not deciding.

These all-important variations on "what are we here for?" should be the board's consuming business. Reducing the clutter of conventional governance enables boards to approach these choices systematically. The first step is determining mission. The second step is establishing those aspects of products, consumers, and costs about which the board feels strongly enough to make further pronouncements. The third step is subjecting those issues to analysis, debate, and vote.

Exhibit 4. El Paso Center for Mental Health and Mental Retardation Policy: "Service Priorities."

The Center exists in order to bring about higher functioning in persons or families whose functioning is impaired by developmental or mental/emotional disabilities. With respect to the balance of services between concerns of developmental disabilities and concerns of mental health, the numbers of persons or families impaired by developmental disabilities in relation to the numbers of persons or families impaired by mental/emotional problems shall approximate the proportion of these disorders in the community.

With respect to resources expended for developmental disabilities services, approximately equivalent emphasis shall be placed on the relief of (a) deficits in early infant stimulation, (b) deficits in independent living skills, (c) deficits in work skills, and (d) family stress due to the presence or care of developmentally disabled persons. Resources thus expended (on a through d) shall constitute no less than 80 percent of all developmental disabilities resources.

With respect to resources expended for mental health services, areas of substantial emphasis and moderate emphasis shall be observed:

1. Substantial emphasis shall be reflected in resources intended for the relief of the mental health problems listed below. Each type shall be demonstrably served. The resources expended for all shall be no less than 45 percent of all mental health services expenditures.
   • Dysfunction due to alcoholism
   • Dysfunction due to drug abuse
   • Family disorder due to presence or care of disturbed persons
   • Disturbance due to criminal attack or abuse
   • Moderate emotional disturbance of whatever source

2. Moderate emphasis shall be reflected in resources for the relief of mental health problems listed below. Each type shall be demonstrably served. The resources expended for all shall be no less than 30 percent of all mental health services expenditures.
   • Living problems of the seriously, chronically emotionally impaired
   • Acute reactions to life crises
   • Emotional dysfunction associated with criminality
   • Lack of public information about available services

3. The remaining 20 and 25 percent for developmental disabilities and mental health services, respectively, shall be proportioned at the chief executive's prerogative.

With these policies in place, the board has the opportunity to venture still further. The policy-making process is fluid. Policy-making stops at whatever point the majority of the board is willing to allow the CEO to make further decisions. The idea is not to extend policy-making to the smallest possible value choice. It is necessary for the board to go only as far as its values compel it.

Staffs sometimes worry that a board will address the lesser values so extensively that no latitude is left for staff decisions. Such overextension by the board is improbable. As a board addresses increasingly lower-level issues, relatedness among issues grows geometrically. It becomes exceedingly difficult to coordinate all the many value choices, much as traditional personnel and finance committees must take extra time to deal with the interface of their respective work on staff salary increments. The board finds that time requirements get out of hand. Coordination of these many interdependent variables is part of the reason a staff is needed. As long as the policy-making principles presented here (particularly, going one level at a time) are followed, a board's incursion into lower and lower levels of involvement will be self-limiting.

Policy Product

The concrete product of this series of value considerations by the board is a set of Ends policies. Most boards are able to govern well with only a handful of Ends policies, including the mission. Because the number of policy issues and the depth of value levels addressed vary from board to board, the exact number of such policies a board should have cannot be stated. Under usual conditions, it would be surprising for an ordinary community social service agency board to have much more than a half-dozen Ends policies averaging more than a page in length. Reams of staff program descriptions, of course, will be developed on the basis of these brief board directives.

Long-Range Planning

It is important that the board prescribe results from an appro-
priately long-term perspective. *Creating Ends policies with a
long-range perspective is the greatest board contribution to
long-range planning.*

It is mandatory that boards be forward thinking. It is
important that organizations have long-range plans. By extension of these two ideas, it is assumed that boards should be
involved in long-range planning. Boards should, indeed, do
their work with a long-range mentality. But boards can govern with excellence and never be involved in actual construction of the myriad parts of a planning document.

Good governance calls for the board role in long-range
planning to consist chiefly in establishing the *reason* for planning. Planning is done to increase the probability of getting
somewhere from here. Enunciation of that "somewhere" is
the board's highest contribution. In a manner of speaking,
boards participate most effectively in the planning process
by standing just outside it. Boards can make an invaluable
contribution to planning; however, except for planning the
improvement of governance itself, *boards should not do the
actual long-range planning.*

By casting its Ends policies out toward the planning
horizon, a board lays out those values on which the staff
makes plans. Of course, planning can become mere "blue-
skying" if the board has spoken to its Ends policies in too
cavalier a manner. To deliberate responsibly, a board must
interact greatly with staff and outside parties. This interaction
does not relate to the staff's present concerns and job under-
takings. Staff–board interaction here is designed to ensure
inclusion of staff insights, passions, and environmental scan-
ning in board deliberation. It should not be, as is common in
conventional board–staff communication, the case where the
board moves to staff-level issues. To the contrary, this process
richly stretches staff upward to the board's long-term, deeply
value-laden world so that all participants grow a little.

The board's creation of Ends policies requires penetrating deliberation about big questions. There is simply no time to drift into current staff issues. Difficult as this challenge might be, it is easily the most exciting, creative, responsible task in which a board can engage. Board data, dialogue, and decisions include the probable environmental circumstances of the future, shifting public needs, big-picture strategic swaps, and the intentions of other boards working on their own visions, in other words, highly informed dreaming.

Planning is more effective when kept simple, yet the greatest resistance to board leadership as defined here is that, although not easy, it seems so simple. The principle is not "so complicated that it's hard to grasp," as R. James LeFevre of Planned Parenthood of Northern New England, Burlington, Vermont, puts it, "but rather, because it is so maddeningly simple it's easy to have it slip away" (personal communication). There is a fair amount of rigor involved in determining even at a broad level what an organization's contribution to the world should be. But when that has been done, the nuts and bolts of planning become merely the executive tool to bring it about. Waterman counsels to "think and rethink basic direction, but keep the statement of it simple and general (even though) you will frustrate the people who are looking for 'the strategy.' Our idealized image of strategy as a complete game plan is so strong that general statements . . . seem unsatisfying" (1988, p. 71).

In short, the board's job in long-range planning is not long-range *planning* itself, but exploration of vision. The board's job is to maintain and behaviorally demonstrate a long-range *mentality*. And that critical mentality is demonstrated through continuous obsession on the value issues inherent in deciding what good is to be accomplished for which people at what cost. These values about ends lie at the core of organizational existence. They are reduced to a few, succinct Ends policies. So it is that with the same stroke, boards can do their part in long-range planning and govern organizational results as well.

Evaluating Ends

Evaluation of Ends is an integral part of the management process. And it must be integral in governance as well. Evaluation (as discussed in Chapter Six under the larger rubric of monitoring) should ideally be a precise, systematic, nonintrusive, criteria-focused method that constantly answers the question "How are we doing?"

The word *evaluation* has come to be associated with service or program success more than with other areas of performance, such as financial status or compliance with purchasing guidelines. The model presented here does not differentiate, however, among the various instances of performance monitoring. The board is obligated to check performance against those matters that the board found important enough either to prescribe (in the case of results) or to proscribe (in the case of staff means). As with other policy types, then, evaluation of Ends is important to leadership in that it discloses unacceptable deviation from the desired values, it enables the board to relax about the present so it can keep its mind on the future, and it keeps board policies constantly in the spotlight and, therefore, more likely to be amended as they grow out of date.

Well-Placed Concern for Evaluation

Nonprofit and public organizations—generally free of the harsh, inescapable Ends evaluation of the market—often find their results difficult to evaluate. If, through the mechanism of market, consumers could tell nonprofit and public organizations what their products are worth, the topic of evaluation would never have attained its lofty status. Business organizations do market research and product research, but never have to do the type of program evaluation popular in nonprofit and public agencies, at least not for the same reasons.

Public and nonprofit organizations need to evaluate their services precisely because they have no natural, consumer-based, behavioral measure of whether a service is effective enough to be worth the cost of producing it. They claim that evaluation is difficult because they are producing services, not widgets. The argument is specious. Consumers are as able to evaluate services as they are concrete items. There is nothing inherently more difficult in evaluating a service *when consumers do the evaluating.*

Evaluation assesses not simply whether organizational activity is effective, but whether it is sufficiently effective to be worth the cost. If the muted market voice is to be overcome by a board (that is, if evaluation is even possible), the relative worth issue cannot be neglected. The separation of effectiveness from worth is a rampant disease among nonprofit and public organizations. It is a fundamental flaw of public administration. This is why the model presented here assiduously focuses on the simple idea of the organization's swap with the world: what is consumed compared with what is produced.

In the face of this difficulty, it is understandable that professional evaluators and lay persons alike bemoan our inadequacies in rendering good evaluation of nonprofit and public services. The field of "process evaluation" offers to circumvent the problems by intentionally evaluating the means rather than the ends. Texts on the problems of measurement validity and reliability often suggest well-considered strategies around the dilemmas. Evaluation of effectiveness is primitive even without the conceptually burdensome question of whether what is achieved is worth the cost. We truly are not very good at it.

This technical inadequacy in *how* to evaluate is not the largest evaluation problem facing nonprofit and public boards. The biggest problem, far and away, is that we do not know *what* to evaluate! Misplacing our concern for evaluation is part of the cause for this dilemma.

Misplaced Concern for Evaluation

Ironically, premature concern about evaluation of Ends can be a formidable deterrent to leadership. This problem exists in evaluation of the prudence and ethics of staff means and, particularly, in the evaluation of results.

Driven by anxiety about evaluative shortcomings, board discussions of program outcomes are often stopped short: "But we can't evaluate it." "But how would we evaluate that?" Persons are loath to answer such an obvious stopper. An enthusiastic "Oh, yes we can!" surely brands the speaker as naive, which may well be true. It seems that well-read people are armed with impressive proofs that evaluation schemes just do not work well enough to discuss. Given the obvious inadequacies, they make a fine case.

Fearing they might decree something that cannot be evaluated cleanly, boards retreat from decreeing at all. They let a reasonable worry about evaluating program or curriculum block them from saying what the outcomes should be. This process can deteriorate into deciding where to go based on whether evaluators can tell us when we get there. "What do you want to accomplish?" is met for practical purposes with "It depends. Tell us what you can measure."

It is as if we are in a taxi surrounded by fog. Though our view of the surroundings, our progress, and even our arrival would be clouded, we would not refrain from telling the driver where we want to go. Yet that is exactly what many boards do in the face of countless, admittedly tough questions about evaluating program results. The stage is set for slipping into the trap of evaluating means, because means can be seen better and counted with ease. Professional evaluators and boards miss the most relevant matter: Stating the desired results is too important to wait for defensible evaluation.

An authoritative, clear statement of what is to be accomplished has a powerful effect on organizational behavior even if the results are never evaluated. This is not an excuse for omitting evaluation. But there is merit in letting people know what you want, even if you cannot be certain that you got it. The single most intimidating aspect of program evaluation is not the technical difficulty but blockage resulting from premature consideration. We simply place the concern for evaluation too early in the process.

Where to Place the Concern for Evaluation

No Place. First, do not be concerned at all and start at the beginning: State what is to be contributed by this organization to the world, what condition is worth achieving, what you would evaluate if you could. That process is best done in the ends-oriented, stepwise fashion I have described, and must be done without regard for evaluative difficulties.

Wrong Place. Second, avoid evaluating the wrong things. Measuring the wrong things is damaging in two ways: (1) "You get what you inspect, not what you expect," is still a valid principle of behavior. Measuring the wrong things sends a strong message through the organization about what matters. If in understandable frustration, you throw up your hands and yield to measuring busyness, you are sure to get more busyness. (2) The pressure, even the embarrassment, of having no stated outcomes to be evaluated is a powerful motivator toward developing at least a first, faltering approximation of the results to be achieved. Evaluating the wrong things removes much of the healthy pressure, even more so if you do it well. The appropriate counsel here might be "Do it badly if at all!" When we are able to take pride in how well we do the wrong things, there is little incentive to begin a wobbly start on the right things.

Right Place. Only when the board has created Ends policies should it stop to consider evaluation, because only when the board knows what it wants the organization to accomplish can it intelligently discuss evaluation. Evaluation without these targets is ludicrous; fretting over evaluation prior to these targets is dysfunctional. The issue of evaluation is merely this: What is the most convincing evidence we can find (and choose to afford) that will show us we are getting what we sought? Evaluative purity is wonderful, but purity is not mandatory. What is called for in evaluation is *reasonable assurance for the cost*, not academic accuracy.

We forget that evaluation in the form of performance

monitoring is an issue not of research, but of management.
The topic of evaluation is dominated, one might say handicapped, by the academic mentality. We unwittingly apply standards of pristine, laboratory-like evaluation to the real-world
necessity to determine if what we do is worthwhile. Managerial mentality, unlike academic mentality, would counsel us
thusly: With respect to influencing organizational behavior, *a
crude measure of the right thing beats a precise measure of the
wrong thing.*

The best approach a board can take in program evaluation, then, is to stick rigorously to the results, not cop out by
prescribing means. If the evaluation is crude, so be it. If it is
worth doing, it is worth doing poorly if that is the best that
can be done. But never, never forsake specifying the desired
results in favor of a less crude evaluation.

The most important real-world evaluation in almost
all nonprofit and public organizations is extremely crude.
The public judges an organization's worth continuously.
These evaluations may be too global to be managerially useful. They are usually too hard or too soft on management,
because authoritatively pronounced criteria on which to base
fair judgment are rarely available. In other words, implicit
crude evaluation of results is proceeding anyway. The task of
the board is to make that judgment of worth explicit, to direct
it pointedly at preestablished criteria and away from capricious or confounding expectations, and only then to fret,
deliberate, and act toward making the evaluation less crude.

Board leadership in the matter of results evaluation lies
not in being seduced by sophistication, but in persevering in
a compelling, disarmingly simple quest: "What did we want
to accomplish? Are we achieving it?"

My contention, of course, is that what really matters in
the long run is the effect an organization has upon its world.
Boards betray their trusteeship when the attractions of staff
practices prevent an undeviating obsession with attaining
intended ends. To return to our cab ride, as long as we know
we are not being cheated, it is usually best to let the taxi
driver decide the route and the lanes in which to drive.

Next Chapter

Strategic leadership lives in the board's Ends policies more than anywhere else. But the board is also accountable for how its staff achieves these results. In Chapter Five, I invite you to consider how the board can safely keep out of staff business, yet still be accountable for the conduct of business. We will see how a relatively few Executive Limitations policies can provide both the board and its executive the freedom to be innovative, bold, and attentive to their respective jobs.

Chapter 5

SETTING LIMITS: STANDARDS OF ETHICS AND PRUDENCE

The board must have *control over* the complexity and details of staff operations. It is also important for a board to be *free from* the complexity and details of staff operations. The board needs control because it is accountable for all organizational activity, however obscure or far removed. Yet the board needs to be free from operational matters because it is a part-time body with little time to get its own job done.

It is common to sacrifice one need for the other. Some boards relinquish control to be free from details or to grant the CEO freedom from board intrusion; such boards may be guilty of rubber stamping. Others forego freedom in order to control many details; such boards may be guilty of meddling.

The responsible board cannot escape its obligation to prescribe at least the broad sweep of Ends and perhaps a few levels below. In other words, with a broad brush the board determines where the organization is going. In this chapter, however, I am concerned not with where the organization is going, but with what staff does to get it there. I deal with the myriad of "how to" questions facing the CEO and his or her staff. Or, more accurately, I deal with how the board might best relate to the staff's "how to" issues. The board's challenge is to be reasonably certain nothing goes awry and at the same time to grant as much unimpeded latitude as possible to those persons with the skill and talent to get the work done.

To make the case for freedom through limits, I start with the often dizzying array of organizational means, their seductive appeal, and the board's legitimate interest in them. I then look at how a board can maintain control of internal operations by setting limits instead of becoming directly involved. Next, development of the documents capable of exercising proactive control (Executive Limitations policies) is dealt with and is followed by a discussion of typical policy topics in this category.

The Enticing Complexity of Operations

For most boards, the greatest source of complexity is not the Ends, but staff operations. Boards struggle with budgets, personnel procedures and issues, purchasing, staffing patterns, compensation, and staff plans. Self-perpetuating cycles are in effect wherein staff members bring their issues to the board because they think the board wants to hear them. Board members request information and attend to staff-level issues because they believe that the staff will feel abandoned if they do otherwise. Sometimes, staff bring matters to the board to avoid making a choice—"This item is a hot one; we'd better get the board to decide." Often no prior board guidance has been given; consequently, there are no parameters within which the board guarantees to protect staff's right to choose. On the other hand, boards delve into staff matters because a particular board member has either the relevant expertise or merely curiosity about some aspect of operations. It is not uncommon for an entire board to be drawn into an issue only because of the minority concern. The board's job is thus defined, not by a carefully constructed design of the task, but by the laundry list of individual interests.

Boards study, invest meeting and committee time in, and worry and argue about that complex, neverending, intriguing body of staff activities. To the detriment both of carefully deliberated results and of effective board process, boards are entangled in and seduced by the means of their subordinates:

ARES WHERE
A BD IS
SEDULED

Personnel: job design, hiring, firing, promotion, discipline, training, grievance up through the chief executive, deployment, evaluation

Compensation (except that of the chief executive): salary ranges, grades, adjustments, incentives, benefits, pension

Supply: purchasing, bidding, authorization, storage, inventories, distribution, salvage

Accounting: forecasting, budgeting, depositories, controls, investments, retrenchment, growth, cost center designation

Facilities: space allocation and requirements, rentals, purchases, sales, upkeep, refurbishing

Risk management: insurance, exposures, protective maintenance, disclaimers

Consumer record keeping: forms, waivers, consents, service tracking, actions taken or services rendered

Reporting: grant reports, tax reporting, law and regulation compliance

Communications: memoranda, telephone systems, meetings, postings, mail distribution

Management methods: objective setting, staffing patterns, team definitions, feedback loops, planning techniques, control methods, participation level

The foregoing list is not exhaustive. Means issues with which staff contends are endless. There are always far more issues than any board can keep up with, even if the board totally neglects its own job to do so. Keeping up with all these issues—much less providing leadership for them—is utterly impossible. Reviewing and approving everything is illusory. Yet the board must attend to its legitimate interest in these matters, an interest that can be overlooked only with severe damage to the concept of accountability.

The board's challenge is to exercise oversight with respect to staff operations without obscuring role differences and without taking the staff off the hook for making decisions. The appropriate expression of the board's legitimate interest is not to make a staff issue into a board issue, but to curtail or confine the available staff choices to an acceptable range.

The Board's Stake in Staff Practices

The preceding partial list of executive means includes important aspects of organization. Such material in board mailings and meetings may be so impressive that it seems to capture the essence of organization. No matter how important, how technically sophisticated, how impressively carried out, or how long the professional training of experts in the various areas, these items are *means,* not ends. They are not what organization is all about; they *serve* what organization is all about. And, for the most part, it is the degree to which they serve Ends well that they derive their value.

For the most part, but not totally. Boards have more than one interest in staff practices.

Effectiveness. By far, of course, executive means are of importance to a board because of their effectiveness. Do they work? That is the primary test and the only justification for having means. The major measure of means is attained not by looking at means, but by looking at what they were intended to produce. We assess their effectiveness by focusing on Ends. In fact, the greatest impediment to measuring the effectiveness of means is to look at the means themselves.

In this area, nonprofit and public administrative practice is prone to a monumental flaw. There is a great deal of inspection of means in site visits, certifications, and agency evaluations, but very little inspection of results. Rewards are handed out on the basis of purported excellence of the means rather than attainment of results. Organizational means come to have a life and momentum of their own, driven by our overpowering tendency to assess them apart from their ability to produce results. Perhaps this source of managerial perversity should not surprise us. Individuals and particularly disciplines or professions are heavily invested in—and, in large part, formed around—distinctive methods or practices.

So if a board is willing to make judgments about means based primarily on attainment of ends ("effectiveness"), then this largest single concern about executive means can be laid aside. I dealt with it in Chapter Four and the board deals with it by measuring how well the organization performs with respect to the board's Ends policies.

Approvability. Granting that the board's central legitimate interest in executive means is discharged by assessing Ends, we must now deal with the fuzzy concept of approvability. Most boards would be unwilling to rest with mere effectiveness as the only test, but would invoke a requirement that, apart from effectiveness, executive means be carried out in an *approvable manner.*

What is meant by an approvable staff activity or plan? By observation of boards proceeding through a traditional approval process, three phenomena are noted:

First, as a body the board is not quite sure what "approvability" means. Consequently, boards tend to go through the motions. Different board members question different items, usually against idiosyncratic criteria. Sometimes, they question effectiveness, but are likely to fall back into the trap of trying to judge effectiveness by closer inspection of the means. A telling test is for a board to ask itself what it would *disapprove.* If a board does not know what it would disapprove, its approval is a process without direction and, at worst, a sham.

Second, board members may equate "approvability" with the question "would I do it this way?" When an approval is rendered from this point of view, the real chief executive finds that there are a number of would-be executives to contend with. Board members sometimes see it as their prerogative to play part-time chief executive. This phenomenon leads the more political chief executive to manipulate documents so as to please the various board member interests. Such maneuvering is not without cost. Ends suffer a loss of primacy and staff's selection of means is less true to its own best judgment.

DOES THIS ALL APPLY FOR START UP?

Third, board members have an interest that staff means—however effective in reaching prescribed ends—are prudent and ethical. And to the extent that inspection and approval of executive means fulfill this board interest, these are justifiable.

Legitimate Control of Means. To summarize the foregoing points: (1) Effectiveness requires no inspection of means and, in fact, is best measured by intentionally not looking at means. (2) A simple preference that means be arranged or selected in a certain way is an indulgence the board may want to allow itself, but one that reduces the integrity of management. (3) Prudence and ethics cannot be covered through the measurement of attainment of Ends. Unlike mere preference, the board has a moral obligation to ensure the prudence and ethics of operations.

SUM OF POINTS

Consequently, the only legitimate, direct interest a governing board need have in how the staff conducts its business is that all is prudent and ethical. Stated more pointedly, *apart from being prudent and ethical, what goes on at and below the level of chief executive is completely immaterial.* The board need only involve itself in executive means to determine that acceptable standards of prudence and ethics are being met. Much board time, as well as a great deal of executive frustration, can be saved. And it becomes clear what the board, in its best moments, was approving or disapproving about.

Control Through Proactive Constraint

Most means are justified by the ends because producing results is what justifies means. Some means, however, are not justifiable regardless of how effective they are. If this were not so, a board would need *no* test of executive means except their effectiveness. Focusing on which means are *not* approvable, rather than on those that are, simplifies the task and makes it less onerous on management as well.

A board that wishes to ensure that the organization's actions are prudent and ethical must delineate *ahead of time* exactly what is imprudent and unethical. Any staff action that does not violate the board's standards, then, is automatically approvable. Note that the board's standards are negative or limiting rather than positive or prescriptive. The board has neither the time nor the expertise to state everything that should be done. It does have the sense of values necessary to recognize what should not be done. The principle is simple and, perhaps more than any other principle, enables excellence in governing:

Although the board speaks to Ends prescriptively, *with regard to executive means the board should remain silent except to state clearly what it will not put up with.*

A small number of policies can enunciate the board's values with respect to minimum levels of prudence and ethics. The board can govern the vast array of executive means through policy, not through direct involvement in staff activities. The category of policies that limits or constrains executive authority is called Executive Limitations.

The total message the board sends to staff, then, is comprised of what outputs are to be achieved (Ends) and what may not be done in the process of achievement (Executive Limitations). Board thought is proactive and general rather than reactive and specific. Such a policy saves the board from making countless separate decisions in the future.

Despite the breakthrough in board effectiveness that this approach makes possible, some board members find it difficult to place limits on staff means. As persons and as governors, they desire to be positive rather than negative. Such a motivation is commendable, but it overlooks an irony of downward communication in an organization.

The most positive approach a board can take toward the means of its subordinates is verbally negative. Conversely, the most negative approach is prescriptive and positive. Telling a subordinate how to do a task automatically eliminates all other methods. Telling a subordinate how not to do it leaves open all other possible methods. Better supervision leaves as much freedom as possible.

No one can presume to know ahead of time all the

innovative combinations of means. No one can divine all the possible ways to improve tasks, systems, structures, and relationships. Even persons carrying out a task stumble across innovation as often as they bring innovative ideas to the task at the outset. Moreover, running an organization involves not only innovation within single tasks, but continual re-creation of interrelationships among tasks and persons. The ability to make and change decisions and to move quickly, particularly on the part of those people closest to the action, is paramount. In the best of enterprises, leaders "define the boundaries, and their people figure out the best way to do the job within those boundaries" (Waterman, 1988, p. 7).

Board prescription of means is a stultifying and anti-innovative process of control. This would be true even if a board were available full time and were fully versed in all organizational areas of expertise. But boards are available to render decisions only a few hours per year and do not have knowledge of every part of organizational life. The common, albeit incomplete, prescription of means not only produces an untenable amount of work for the board, but unduly hampers staff effectiveness. Such board positiveness is a serious cause of lost staff potential. Given the availability of a more effective alternative, it is completely unnecessary as well. In Fram's fictional exploration of the "Corporate Model," a character boasts, "We have a REAL BOARD . . . a real board tells its executive director exactly what to do." Fram's protagonist politely withholds his thought: "You don't have a real board. What you have is a parent–child relationship" (Fram, 1988, p. 74).

There is a subtler way in which a board does the same damage without directly prescribing executive means: it retains approval authority over staff plans. When staff must bring specific decisions to the board for approval (for example, of annual budgets and compensation changes), the board is implying that only staff actions it approves are legitimate. Although the board-approved actions are generated by staff, the board empowers them. For staff, means that have board approval, regardless of their origin, are frozen in place unless the board has time and sees fit to approve changes. The effect on management is only a little better than if the board had generated the means prescription itself. Consequently, board approvals, even of staff-submitted documents, constitute unnecessary interference with the CEO's staff delegation system and decision flow.

Consider the alternative of being minimal but "negative" in dealing with staff means. *Ignoring* staff means, except to prohibit by explicit policies, frees both board and staff. The board is free of the endless details of staff work and can do its own job. The Rev. G. Taft Lyon, Jr., chairperson of Life Management Center, El Paso, Texas, was happy that he "didn't have to get involved in (the CEO's) business and tell him what he needed to do." Anne Saunier, chairperson of Planned Parenthood Federation of America, speaks of the ability to "safely withdraw, as a national board, from administrative details, with the emphasis on being 'safe.' " The staff is left free to choose, change, and create within clearly stated boundaries. Norman Barth, CEO of Lutheran World Relief, New York, is happy to be "freed . . . not that I can do anything I want to, but rather I know the bounds of my authority . . . the board does not second guess me." Without this explicitly bounded freedom, the CEO of a large zoo wrote that she "continues to feel as though I am walking through traps and land mines. Fortunately, I am guessing where most of them are; I am guessing a lot." J. Gregory Shea, CEO of Tri-county Mental Health Services of Lewiston, Maine, says his board, "clearly feels . . . that it knows . . . how far the CEO can and will go . . . that both my day-to-day functioning and the board's policy setting and oversight are done with much greater freedom . . . and (with) flexibility . . . to sometimes very rapidly changing circumstances. Without those policies, there would be a lot of 'Monday morning quarterbacking' " (all personal communications). As long as the board-stated Ends are accomplished and the board-stated Executive Limitations are not violated, staff action is by definition supported by the board.

Using this approach, the board is proactive. Approval of staff documents, discussed more fully in Chapter Three, is reactive. Further, approval is a practice in which the board is always "one down"; it can never know quite as much about the details of staff action and planning as the staff itself. Moreover, by being proactive, the board can be more confident that it has dealt with the issues of prudence and ethics. As painstaking as many approval processes might be, they ordinarily focus on the acceptability of *specific* actions or documents rather than on the underlying values that form the basis for board decisions on those actions and documents. Consequently, after approval of specific actions or documents, the board *policy* remains unstated. Another payoff, more important than it seems, is reduction of the board's burden of paperwork. The board can then invest the bulk of its leadership in determination of expected results, rather than in helping staff be staff.

Policies to Limit Staff Action

The task, then, with respect to board oversight of staff means is to create a workable set of policies that constrain or limit executive latitude. In this section, I first review the necessity to say what does not need to be said, even at the broadest and most obvious level, in a negative or limiting fashion. Second, I argue that broad policies should grow out of the *board's,* not the staff's, values and perspectives. Last, I consider the board's worry areas as a natural origin of these Executive Limitations policies.

As with all policy control, proper governance lies an uncomfortable arm's length from the action for some board members. "Being relegated to a position of *simply* setting policies," comments the Rev. Lyon, "seems like a less important job to them." There may be discomfort, but not difficulty, because it is not hard to write policies that safely allow board withdrawal from the prescriptive details of staff means. Doing so does require close attention to the few simple rules proposed here for policy development. For example, as discussed in Chapter Three, we must start with the largest, most inclusive level before moving on to lesser levels.

Remember that the intent of the Executive Limitations category of policies is to prohibit staff practices that the board regards as imprudent or unethical. Though this will be further defined, note that preventing imprudent and unethical behavior is the board's *sole* aim in setting these policies. Note further that the wording here is negative. We could as easily say—positively—that the board is trying to ensure that behavior is prudent and ethical. The meaning is the same; however, because boards face the almost irresistible temptation to slip back into prescribing staff means, they are wise to maintain a proscriptive demeanor throughout, even when it seems pedantic to do so. Establishing the limiting approach at this basic level ensures a board's ability to maintain that discipline in more complex issues.

The first and broadest staff means policy position of the board is a simple constraint on executive authority: *"The chief executive may neither cause nor allow any organizational practice that is imprudent or unethical."* This sentiment is so obvious. Why should the board have to dignify it as policy? There are two reasons for beginning at such a simple level. First, this position is the source from which all further constraints spring. It is the beginning. As further policies are built on this foundation, it becomes increasingly important to maintain simplicity or, at least, clear connections with simplicity. In addition, as we must learn again and again, organizational excellence is attained by doing the simple things well.

Second, approaching constraints from the broadest perspective, regardless how simple, ensures that the board can never, through oversight, leave a policy vacuum. Although the "backup" policy may be broader (allowing more room for interpretation) than the board would like, it is impossible for an issue not to be covered by board policy at some level. If the extent of reasonable latitude under a constraint of "imprudence" is greater than the board desires, then further policy needs to be stated. But at no time is there a lack of policy. In organizations where this principle of logical containment is not followed, executives or boards continually find issues that are not covered by board policy. Consequently, forceful staff action can be bottlenecked, or staff may take an unnecessary risk or miss an opportunity while the policy hole is plugged.

Conventional, prescriptive policy development on staff means requires that the board foresee all possible actions and create policies targeted at these actions. Perfect foresight is, of course, impossible, and such an approach leads to patchwork policy-making. It also ensures that the board forever remains a step or two behind staff, as staff is continually generating new specifics.

Optimal policy-making produces neither a long list of disjointed pieces nor a mere restatement of approved staff documents. It produces a *fabric of values* that, no matter how thin, effectively blankets all possibilities. Creating this fabric, with respect to executive means, must begin with the broadest proscription. Without this broad statement there is no all-inclusive point of departure for further, more detailed explicit board constraints.

All CEOs know better than to assume there is no limit on staff behavior. But he or she would have to assume what that limit is . . . and might not come up with what the board would have stated. The CEO would have two choices: first, to ask with each concrete plan or activity and all changes thereto whether the board is displeased (this takes us back to approvals again); second, to be safe and assume more limitations than the board is likely to intend. Unnecessary constraint often reduces performance, a consequence the board may not have wanted. It does so by raising cost or lowering product quantity or quality; nothing is free, including constraints.

The most effective move a CEO can make is to inform the board of the unspoken constraint he or she is assuming and ask for confirmation. *If* the CEO asks about the broadest level instead of a specific application, the board creates policy by answering the question. It is simpler to begin from that point, rather than have the process depend on the CEO's motivation and integrity, not to mention luck.

Making Board Policies the Board's *Policies*

For integrity of governance, board policies must be generated
from board values, not parroted from staff wishes. A side
effect of traditional patchwork policy-making is repeated ven-
tures by staff to the board for approvals. As staff obviously
knows what it needs, boards ordinarily issue approvals after a
cursory review. Even a detailed review would not change the
fact that board policy is being passed without *the board's* need-
ing it. In the governance design presented here, the board
adopts only policies for which its values dictate a need. Board
policies are not passed to please staff, even the CEO. The
CEO is already empowered to adopt policies, as long as they
are consistent with the board's policies. The CEO is unlikely
to request that the board restrict executive latitude further. As
he or she is already empowered to make such choices, it
would be clear that the CEO is merely using the board to
avoid making a decision.

    Despite the churning commotion of implementation, a
board's ethics and prudence standards remain constant. The
board's standards written into policy serve as an anchor for
all staff action. There is room for staff to move around when
tossed about in stormy weather, but there is not so much
room that staff loses its bearings or strays from what the organization holds itself to be. Like an anchor, good policy-making is not complicated; its simplicity is why it works. Staff
must be given a free hand to do what they know how to do,
but should not be abandoned by failure to define boundaries.

    Boards can provide this leadership only if they are not
subjected to the same short-term pressures. If the board is
tossed in the same stormy seas as staff, it will have difficulty
seeing past the next wave, much less to the horizon. The
stability of a relaxed governance arena allows the board to
ride above the fray fairly unperturbed. Board energy is saved
for the more contemplative struggle about underlying values.
A board job that is more hurried than contemplative has probably fallen into staff-level issues and ceased to govern.

    Having prohibited only "unethical and imprudent"

behavior, the board may worry that its brush has been a little too broad. Any staff practice that fits within a reasonable interpretation of this range must be considered acceptable. A "reasonable" range is that determined by the board to be a prudent person's reading of the policy. If the majority of board members feel that practices that pass the reasonable person test are not acceptable, then the constraint on staff activity must be further defined and narrowed. As might be surmised, I have never found a board that did not wish to constrict the acceptable latitude further.

Transforming Worries into Policies

The broadest constraint (no imprudent and unethical behavior) applies without differentiation to all areas of organizational activity. Building policy beyond this general proscription, the board will doubtless apply its caution more to some subjects than to others. That is why moving to the next lower level takes the form of addressing specific aspects of organization. Thus, policy not only drops to a lower level, but begins to differentiate among organizational topics.

Differentiated subjects for further constraint could be seen as specific "worry areas." The most common worry areas in which policy is then written, thereby further defining unethical and imprudent, concern financial condition, personnel, compensation, asset protection, and budgeting. Addressing each of these subjects (1) affords board members the opportunity to come to one mind on what is unacceptable; (2) sends the executive a clear message about what must be avoided, an explicitness that most executives find refreshing albeit less manipulable; (3) enables the board to streamline future monitoring because criteria are established against which performance can be measured; and (4) enables the board to codify its anxieties and, consequently, to relax.

In conceiving these policies, it is best that board thinking not be bound by *current* worries. A board should create Executive Limitations policies that cover the entire range of unpalatable circumstances. What a board would find unpalatable is not a function of recent agency problems, even though heightened sensitivity to one or another condition might be. Reactive policy-making will seem to be the responsive action at the time, but this would mean the board's leadership is driven by circumstances rather than by ideals. When it is free from immediate concerns, the board uncovers values that have not heretofore surfaced, values that will be relevant to events as yet unforeseen. Still, the safety net effect of the logical containment principle saves the board from having to be perfect in its comprehensiveness.

Listening to worries voiced by board members helps to establish Executive Limitations policies specific to an organization. One member of an Arizona board wondered aloud how disruptive it would be if the CEO were to be unexpectedly lost. The others were persuaded that this was a legitimate board worry. Converting that worry into an Executive Limitations policy resulted in immediate relaxation from the problem. The board adopted a policy requiring that the CEO never have fewer than two senior staff substantially familiar with board and executive officer activities. The majority of these board members felt that this policy provided all the emergency preparedness needed. The policy fit their values, precluded further worry, and was stated in two sentences.

It is important that policies represent the values of the board that establishes them. Policies are not chosen from a catalog, issued by an agency of government, enunciated by staff, derived by consultants, or taken from books. Policies are personal to the board.

Typical Executive Limitations Topics

Because Executive Limitations policies spring from a board's sense of prudence and ethics, they are more likely than other categories of policies to be similar to the policies of other boards using this model. Prudence and ethics are relatively common across boards, more so than Ends. Note these few, common Executive Limitations policy titles.

Vendor relations	A "floor" for their fair treatment
Treatment of parents	Minimum standards for interactions with parents of students
Asset protection	Unacceptable risk and treatment of fixed and liquid assets
Indebtedness	Limits on circumstances in which the executive could allow the organization to incur debt
Financial condition	Conditions of fiscal jeopardy to be avoided
Budgeting	Characteristics unacceptable in any budget
Funded depreciation	Limits on amounts and conditions under which the executive can expend funds from the funded depreciation reserve
Growth	Limit on the amount of growth that can occur from one fiscal year to the next, regardless of the availability of funds
Compensation and benefits	Characteristics not tolerated in any wage and salary plan

All Executive Limitations policies are messages from the board to its chief executive officer. They are *not* messages from the board to staff, for the chief executive is the only staff member to whom the board gives directions. Further, the policies do not give the CEO power to do this or that. They take power or latitude away ("You may not . . ."). The CEO has whatever power the board does not withhold: "go 'til we say stop" rather than "stop 'til we say go."

To illustrate three Executive Limitations areas, let us look at board concerns with respect to financial management and personnel administration. The financial concern is traditionally expressed in two ways: monthly reports on the actual financial condition and annual inspection of budget. The personnel concern traditionally manifests as approval of personnel "policies."

Financial Condition Policy

Boards put great stock in monthly or quarterly financial reports. Yet a substantial number of board members do not understand these reports. Even in boards composed of persons competent at analyzing financial statements, it is uncommon for the board to know *as a body* what it finds unacceptable. This renders the approval process of questionable importance and repeatedly invites discussion about financial details. Actually, even if the standards were clear to everyone, "approval" of a financial report is simply an acknowledgment that the data exist, that the preceding month or quarter actually took place.

In converting to control by Executive Limitations policies, boards are usually unwilling to let the standard rest simply on avoiding imprudence. Some practices or conditions might not be imprudent in the general sense, but are outside what a given board is willing to countenance. To adopt a policy that further defines the acceptable boundaries of ongoing financial conditions, the board must discuss and debate those circumstances it finds unacceptable. Financial condition is a wavering phenomenon; most of its squiggles are of no consequence. Some aspects, however, are worrisome or even frightening. Ordinarily, the top level within this policy is that the financial condition never result in fiscal jeopardy or disruption of programmatic integrity. Beneath this broad proscription, foremost among the several considerations is usually that spending never exceed revenues. If the agency has the ability to borrow funds or has reserves, the prohibition might be to limit the amount of indebtedness or withdrawals from reserves. Or it might be to prohibit indebtedness or withdrawal except under specified conditions. Moreover, that an executive has not yet spent more than has been received might be a rather hollow datum if expenses have been put off and revenues rushed into the reporting period. Further, shifts of wealth hidden within the overall numbers may obscure important fiscal jeopardies such as a decreasing ratio of current assets to current liabilities. Fine-tuning the policy language can address these points and, at the same time, add to board appreciation of the issues of fiscal jeopardy.

The board must discuss and understand these and related issues to create a financial condition policy. In the short run, as much value is derived from the new level of understanding as from the policy itself. A board can use expert counsel in producing such a policy, as long as the expert does not create the policy. The expert should help create completeness in understanding. The understanding supplies data on which board members' values about risk, safety, conservatism, brinkmanship, and so forth can operate. The aggregated and debated board values create the policy. For most boards, the list of unacceptable conditions thus derived is more complete and more systematic than the items it would have routinely inspected using the standard approval method. Though more complete, the subsequent monitoring of financial statements requires far less time than is traditionally spent by many boards and finance committees.

Voyageur Outward Bound limited its Executive Director in the policy titled "Financial Condition" (Exhibit 5) on criteria that the board felt to be conditions of jeopardy. The board felt it could accept any reasonable definition of "timely manner" in criterion 7, though another board might have the need to restrict the range by using words like "within the discount period or thirty days, whichever is earliest." Figures in criterion 9 would be periodically amended.

Budget Policy

A financial condition policy establishes the boundaries of acceptable monthly or quarterly financial status. Boards can go further and establish those characteristics of financial *intentions* that would not be acceptable. Financial intentions or financial planning takes the form of a budget and often numerous budget adjustments during a year.

Most nonprofit and public boards consider the budget approval process as sacrosanct. To suggest that board budget approval might not be a necessary element of fiscal steward-

**Exhibit 5. Voyageur Outward Bound School Policy:
"Financial Condition."**

With respect to operating the School in a sound and prudent fiscal manner, the Executive Director may not jeopardize the long-term financial strength of the School. Accordingly, he or she may not:

1. Cause the School to incur indebtedness other than trade payables incurred in the ordinary course of doing business.
2. Use advances from the Cash Reserve Fund or the Building Fund other than for ordinary operating expenses.
3. Allow advances from the Building Fund to remain outstanding for more than 90 days.
4. Allow advances from the Cash Reserve Fund or the Building Fund to remain outstanding on the August 1 next following the advance.
5. Use earnings on the Scholarship Endowment Fund for any purpose other than scholarships.
6. Use restricted contributions for any purpose other than that required by the contribution.
7. Settle payroll and debts in other than a timely manner.
8. Allow expenditures to deviate materially from Board-stated priorities.
9. Allow the Cash Reserve Fund to fall below $90,000 in 1988, 6 percent of operating expenses in 1989, 7 percent in 1990, 8 percent in 1991, and 10 percent in 1992 and beyond.

ship runs against a firmly held belief, a belief so firm that some board members contend that no regularly occurring board act is as important as budget approval. The reason given is that the board must have control over the budget because of the board's fiduciary responsibility. In addition, some say that the budget is the most important "policy document" the board passes.

Both contentions are correct. The board must have control over that for which it is accountable. And the budget does, usually implicitly, represent much of what is important to an organization—its aims, its risks, its conservatism. Neither argument, however, dictates *how* a board should control a budget and the budget's policy implications. The starting questions for any board are "What is it about the budget that we wish to control?" and "If we were never to see a budget, what specific conditions would we worry about?"

A budget concerns events that have not yet occurred. It is a plan. Like all plans, it makes suppositions, conveys intentions, and designs process or flow. It is a rather special plan inasmuch as it is denominated in money. Most budgets, moreover, are line item budgets rather than program budgets or result-package budgets, so they illustrate some of the less salient aspects of creating the future. For example, the expected cost for a certain outcome is of central interest when a board debates its Ends policies. How much the group insurance component of support staff compensation is expected to be has less intrinsic value. What is it that the board wishes to control?

If the board had to list every possible dollar figure and ratio in the budget, it would give up and go home! Only the most compulsive board members want to know the budget for stationery, much less to control it. In fact, there are very few aspects of a budget that even very responsible boards need to control. Boards want and need control over *certain* budgetary characteristics to fulfill their legal and ownership responsibilities. Few boards have any idea what characteristics these are.

To fine-tune its fiduciary responsibility, a board must decide which aspects of the budget must be controlled. If the board has been checking these budgetary characteristics all along, jotting them down will take but a few moments. If the board finds it cannot do this readily, there is reason to question what the detailed budget approvals have been seeking. What, in fact, was approved? Is it possible that the admittedly high principle of fiduciary responsibility has been used to justify a process less effective than we thought? In my years of watching budget approvals, this is exactly what goes on.

Enlightenment is nearly inescapable when a board sets out to codify its worries about financial planning. What would worry us about a budget? What would cause us not to approve a budget? The important features begin to stand out and the less important ones recede. The vast array of figures becomes less intimidating for nonfinancial people. Financial people are afforded the opportunity to connect their technical expertise to their wisdom. It is on the wisdom level that they meet the other board members; they are no longer strangers divided by a language barrier.

On this journey, the board gets serious about the meaning of fiduciary responsibility. It does not mean controlling
the number of phone lines, but it does mean controlling the
ability to pay the bills. It does not mean controlling out-of-
state travel, but it does mean controlling the conservatism
with which revenues are projected. Or are those wrong?
Debate ensues. Values about risk, brinkmanship, judiciousness, proportions of effort, and so forth begin to get more
attention than the mundane factors. And the process throughout is disciplined by progression from big questions to small
ones, as it should be in all policy creation.

As in all other Executive Limitations policies, the message is directed to the CEO and is one of limitation, not
empowerment. The CEO is already empowered by the "go
'til we say stop" system of delegation. What he or she needs
to know are the limits to power, the acceptable latitude in
exercising it. How liberal may I be in counting chickens prior
to their hatching (projecting revenues)? How low may I let
the current ratio slip to save programs? How much may I dip
into reserves when pinched for cash? To what extent may I
meet cash flow necessities by shifting money temporarily
among special-purpose funds? These and other value questions confront financial planning, whether for next month
or next year. Agile, empowered management can address
these choices within board values far more effectively than a
board can.

An additional bonus is the applicability of the policy
to *all* financial planning, that is, the plans for next month
and next year and all the replanning that occurs in the real
world of constant change. An organization rarely has one
budget for a year. As conditions shift and assumptions fail to
pan out, it may have many. Every budget alteration made by
the CEO, no matter how many, must meet the test of the
board's budget policy. CEOs can respect the stability of this
type of board leadership. The only fixed aspects of budgets,
then, are the policies on which they are based and the cer-
tainty that specifics will be endlessly amended.

Most boards that I have helped through this process

have had a hard time coming up with more than half a page
of budgeting constraints. What message does this send? All
those years of painstaking board budget approvals, not to
mention finance committee time, resulted in half a page of
unacceptable conditions. The approval process had always
gone far beyond checking for unacceptable conditions. Having no policy that delineated the unacceptable conditions,
the board foraged about wherever individual interests and
fears directed them. Moreover, this painstaking scrutiny seldom resulted in material change in the submitted budgets
and not infrequently overlooked dangerous conditions until
almost too late.

Boards are accountable for budgets, but not more
accountable than they are for what the organization accom-
plishes in actual results for people per dollar. Budgets are
simply *not* the board's most important job. What good is
done for what people and at what cost is its most important
job. Missing on Ends even by a small percentage costs the
world far more than most budgetary errors. Gwedolyn Calvert
Baker, executive director for the National Board of the YWCA
found that when dealing with financial planning in this way,
"the program drives your budget, your budget doesn't drive
your program" (personal communication).

Except for balance and conservative projection of revenues, the board of the Milwaukee Association for Jewish Education felt comfortable in relying largely on harmony with
Ends priorities as the major budget criterion (Exhibit 6). This
is a small organization; however, even large organizations
have difficulty producing more criteria than those found in
this policy entitled "Budgeting."

Personnel Policy

When boards are asked to show their policies, they invariably
produce their personnel "policies." It is ironic that the one
document in which the word *policy* is almost always misused
is the most frequent example of board policy that comes to
mind. The question for boards, beyond the broader ethics-

Exhibit 6. Milwaukee Association for Jewish Education Policy:
"Budgeting."

With respect to planning fiscal events (budgeting for all or any
remaining part of a fiscal period), the Executive Director may not
jeopardize either programmatic or fiscal integrity of the organization.
Accordingly, he or she may not cause or allow budgeting which:

1. Contains too little detail to enable reasonably accurate projection of
   revenues and expenses, separation of capital and operational items,
   cash flow, and subsequent audit trails.
2. Plans the expenditure in any fiscal year of more funds than are
   conservatively projected to be received in that period.
3. Deviates materially from board-stated priorities in its allocation among
   competing budgetary needs.

---

prudence proscription, is "What is it about dealings with
personnel that we need to control?" The answer is anything
that might be considered by a reasonable person as ethical or
prudent, but which the board does not want to happen. The
board of the Orchard Country Day School decided that secre-
tive decision processes, which it found unacceptable, constituted mistreatment that might slip by as acceptable under the
"don't be unethical" rule. Another board decided the same
about any prejudice toward an employee who had filed a
grievance. Most boards have decided to omit references to sex,
race, and age discrimination insofar as the law now covers
these items. Violation of the law is so patently a case of imprudent behavior that no additional words need be wasted. But a
board that believes that the law does not go far enough could
increase the constraint beyond the law's protection.

The board does have a personnel policy under this
model, but it is unlikely to be more than a page long. The
previous board personnel manual becomes the property of
the chief executive, to change as he or she sees fit, within the
board constraints.

"Employee Protection" is the title chosen by the board
of Social Advocates for Youth to address the personnel issue
(Exhibit 7). Because they were dealing only with the "don't"
list, their only concern about personnel was that they not be

---

Exhibit 7. Social Advocates for Youth Policy: "Employee Protection."

The Executive Director's authority, with respect to the treatment of
paid and volunteer staff, is limited so as to assure that the rights of
employees to fair, equitable, and humane treatment are not impeded.

1. The dignity, safety, and right to ethical job-related dissent of employees
   shall not be impaired; grievances by employees shall receive fair
   internal hearing through procedural safeguards.
2. Employees and candidates for employment may not be judged on other
   than their own job-relevant qualifications and/or job performance.
3. Staff will not be left unprepared for prompt action in case of
   emergency or disaster.

---

mistreated. Note that the board demands "fair internal hearing" but does not go so far as to require "due process."

Range of Executive Limitation Policies

In Executive Limitation policies, different boards differ on
what they have to say, both in volume and in restrictiveness.
One board may find another's policies too restrictive or irresponsibly loose. It is critical only that the chief executive and
board always know precisely what the marching orders are at
any point in time.

Although a number of policy topics such as the three
just discussed will be faced by most boards, the full list of
policies will differ from board to board within the same
type of organization and will certainly differ from one type
of organization to another. An international development
agency will have policies different from those of a family
planning agency. Boards of County Commissioners, library
boards, chambers of commerce, and trade or professional associations will all differ, though they are subject to the same
principles.

The Executive Limitations policies of the Metropolitan
Waste Control Commission (Exhibit 8) and the Southeast
Georgia Area Planning and Development Commission (later
renamed the Southeast Georgia Regional Development Center) (Exhibit 9) illustrate two very different types of constraint

Exhibit 8. Metropolitan Waste Control Commission Policy: "Communication and Counsel to the Commission."

With respect to providing information and counsel to the Commission, the Chief Administrator may not cause or allow the Commission to be uninformed or misinformed. Accordingly, he or she must:

1. Cause the Commission to be aware of relevant trends, public events of the organization, material external and internal changes, particularly changes in the assumptions upon which any Commission policy has previously been established.
2. Submit the required monitoring data (see policy on Monitoring Chief Administrator Performance) in a timely, accurate, and understandable fashion, *directly* addressing provisions of the Commission policies being monitored.
3. Marshal as many staff and external points of view, issues, and options as needed for fully informed Commission choices.
4. Not present information in unnecessarily complex or lengthy form.

Exhibit 9. Southeast Georgia Area Planning and Development Commission Policy: "Protection of Assets."

To prevent disrepair, excessive risks, untraceable transactions, or conflict of interest in the management of SEGAPDC resources, the Executive Director:

1. Will not allow any one individual to have complete authority over a financial transaction.
2. Will not permit any person who is not bonded to handle cash.
3. Will not deposit Commission funds in institutions where they are not fully protected by FSLIC or FDIC. Returns must be maximized and costs minimized.
4. Will not allow abuse or misuse of APDC assets. APDC property will be inventoried and a security system in place to ensure adequate safeguards to prevent loss, damage, or theft of property.
5. Will not insure APDC vehicles for less than what is considered necessary for prudent risk management. Liability coverage will not be below the federal requirements. Employees will not be allowed to drive APDC vehicles if their driving record increases the premium or cancels the vehicle insurance.
6. Will not allow insurance coverage of stock and equipment, furniture, and fixtures to fall below 90 percent of co-insurance level of replacement value.
7. Will not allow Public Officials Liability Insurance to expire without board notification.

a board might impose. The first ensures that the board is sufficiently informed to do its job. The second limits the risk that the board finds palatable. An Executive Limitations policy may be as simple as "Administrative Clarity" by the board of Southwest Counseling Service (Exhibit 10). The board had little interest in the exact content of operational documents, but did have strong feelings that such provisions be clear and available to those who need them. The policy is not necessary to ensure that Ends are achieved, for the board will assess Ends on their own merits. The provision springs from the board's opinion that the prohibited condition was simply not fair to staff and, therefore, should be avoided on that basis.

In practice, most boards get by with fewer than ten Executive Limitations policies. These tend to average less than a page in length. But the vessel is adjustable to as much restriction or freedom that a board feels is right. In the final analysis, however, boards must realize that no matter how narrow a policy is intended to be, there is still room for interpretation. The CEO's job is largely one of making those interpretations as he or she delegates to others. Unless the board itself wishes to do the organization's work, this will *always* be the case. Interpretation is so integral to the nature of management that one could describe managers' jobs as translation from one level of abstraction to another.

Consequently, it is *never* legitimate to complain that board policy with respect to the CEO and staff is fuzzy or open to interpretation or speaks in generalities. It is on that *degree* of fuzziness, interpretive range, and generality that board debate must turn. A board member who feels that certain policy language allows too great a range of interpreta-

---

**Exhibit 10. Southwest Counseling Service Policy:
"Administrative Clarity."**

The Executive Director may not operate without:

1. Procedures to assure operational/administrative continuity.
2. Operational policies and procedures known and available to employees.

---

tion is obligated to argue for language that narrows the range. The member only detracts from his or her good argument to complain, in effect, that policy should not allow any range. It is in studious management of the generalities that a board enhances both its contributions and those of staff.

Board and staff need as much freedom as possible to perform. The board is responsible for creating the future, not minding the shop. Chait and Taylor (1989) bemoaned boards' time being "frittered away on operations" (p. 45), mired in minutiae, and thus unavailable for policy and strategy. "Rather than do more, boards would be better advised to demand more" (p. 52). The staff needs freedom from the board's friendly intrusions to do its work. The board cheats the mission by constraining too much; it risks cheating standards of acceptable conduct by constraining too little. Proactively setting relatively few limits for the CEO increases the freedom of both the board and the CEO.

Next Chapter

We have now looked into the minimal verbiage and high leverage power of Executive Limitations policies established to ensure that staff action is prudent and ethical. Simultaneously achieving delegation that is simple and powerful, however, requires a certain kind of relationship between governance and management. In Chapter Six, I turn my attention to the relationship between the board and its chief executive officer.

Chapter 6

STRONG BOARDS
NEED STRONG EXECUTIVES:
THE BOARD-EXECUTIVE
RELATIONSHIP

No single relationship in the organization is as important as that between the board and its chief executive officer. Probably no single relationship is as easily misconstrued or has such dire potential consequences. That relationship, well conceived, can set the stage for effective governance and management.

It is often said that the most important task of a board is the choice of chief executive. Although choice is surely important, establishment of an effective relationship is even more important. Good executives have been rendered ineffective as a result of poor relationships with their boards. Poor executives have been allowed to remain because of inadequately structured relationships with their boards.

To accomplish an effective relationship, we must attend to the board's job, the executive's job, and the link between them. In this chapter, the focus is on the executive's job and the link between board and executive. Board policies on empowerment of staff and on the nature of staff accountability constitute a category called Board–Executive Relationship. In this chapter, I begin with a definition of chief executive officer and the nature of accountability and empowerment it implies. Then, I deal with the kind of information the board

109

needs for responsible oversight of the CEO and what this has
to do with the executive's performance evaluation. I end by
discussing how to keep the roles of board and CEO separate
and complementary.

Defining a Chief Executive Officer

Except for a few unique functions of the board, almost all
organizational activities are performed by staff. Even in relatively small organizations, the sheer volume of staff activity
would overwhelm a part-time board. Further, the myriad
interrelationships among separate functions in an organization frequently awe even a full-time staff.

Boards ordinarily choose to coordinate these intricate
parts by employing a "chief executive officer" to put all the
pieces in place. More than a mere coordinator, a CEO is
accountable for all the parts coming together in an acceptable
whole. The board is therefore able to govern by dealing conceptually only with the whole and personally only with the
CEO. The CEO becomes the board's bridge to the staff, a role
more distinct than merely lead staff member. A powerfully
designed CEO position is a key to board excellence. It enables
a board to avoid the intricacies and short-term focus of staff
management and to work exclusively on the holistic, long-
term focus of governance.

Nonprofit and public organizations have chronic problems with the CEO function, resulting from its being over-
or underpowered. In either event, its promise can be lost, and
with it much of the board's opportunity for excellence. If a
strong executive causes a board to be weak or if a strong
board causes an executive to be weak, the role has been ill-
designed. Many boards unwittingly invite their chief executives to be either milquetoast or manipulator.

The "Delegation to the Executive Director" policy of
Naperville Park Commissioners (Exhibit 11) expresses the
method in which power is passed. Pay particular attention to
point 2, wherein the Commission as a body has limited its
own rights as individuals to commandeer resources through

Exhibit 11. Naperville Park District Policy:
"Delegation to the Executive Director."

To facilitate optimum effectiveness, the Board of Commissioners of the Naperville Park District recognizes the board's responsibility as being generally confined to establishing topmost policies, leaving implementation and subsidiary policy development to the Executive Director. "Results and Priorities" policies direct the Executive Director to achieve certain results; "Executive Limitations" policies constrain the Executive Director to act within acceptable boundaries of prudence and ethics. All board authority delegated to staff is delegated through the Executive Director, so that all authority and accountability of staff can be phrased—insofar as the board is concerned—as authority and accountability of the Executive Director.

1. The Executive Director is authorized to establish all further policies, make all decisions, take all actions and develop all activities which are true to the board's policies. The board may, by extending its policies, "undelegate" areas of the Executive Director's authority, but will respect the Executive Director's choices so long as the delegation continues. This does not prevent the board from obtaining information about activities in the delegated areas.
2. Only the board, by majority vote, has authority over the Executive Director. Information may be requested by a board member or committee, but if such request, in the Executive Director's judgment, requires a material amount of staff time, it may be refused.
3. The Executive Director may not perform, allow or cause to be performed any act which is unlawful, insufficient to meet commonly accepted business and professional ethics or the "prudent person" test, in violation of funding source requirements or regulatory bodies or contrary to explicit board constraints (see Executive Limitation policies) on executive authority
4. Should the Executive Director deem it necessary to violate a board policy, he or she shall inform the board. Informing is simply to guarantee no violation may be intentionally kept from the board, not to request approval. Board response, either approving or disapproving, does not exempt the Executive Director from subsequent board judgment of the action nor does it curtail any executive decision.

seemingly benign requests for information. This provision is clearly consistent with a strict interpretation of the "one voice" philosophy. The Commission chose to impose the blanket proscriptions of point 3 in this basic delegation policy; these could instead have been written as a single overview policy in Executive Limitations. In point 4, the Commission does not excuse intentional violation of board policy, but, recognizing the rare occasion in which a violation would represent *good* CEO judgment, prohibits its being hidden.

Placing the CEO Role

Understanding an effective CEO function requires us first to look beyond the distraction of titles and, second, to grasp the peculiar organizational phenomenon of cumulative responsibility.

The traditions of various pursuits bring with them preferred CEO titles: Superintendent, Executive Vice President, City Manager, Administrator, Headmaster, County Executive, President, and Executive Director. In recent years there has been a trend among some nonprofit agencies to switch from executive director to president. The reasons given are "to be more businesslike" or "to adopt the 'corporate' model." When this occurs without changing *functions*, only the cosmetics have been affected. The exact title itself has no managerial relevance. The function is what is important. Chief executive officer, sometimes used as a title, is used here to refer to the CEO *function*, regardless of job title.

The CEO function can be vested either in the top staff person or in the board chair, although the latter is rarely recommended. There is a long tradition in business of one person both chairing the board and being chief executive. Historically, in business corporations, however, entrepreneurs have gathered boards around them as their enterprises grew. Even large, publicly held corporations often operate with a "good old boy" circle centering upon the chair/CEO combination. Standard practice or not, some have recognized the conflict of interest this method presents (Geneen, 1984).

Almost all nonprofit and public organizations are best served by vesting the chairing function and the CEO function in separate persons. The CEO holds final authority "outside of the broad powers held by the board. To invest this final authority in the hands of a part-time board member would seem inappropriate" (Fram, 1986). Regardless of the board's choice in placing the CEO function, it is necessary for managerial integrity that a board clearly use one method or the other and not wander back and forth.

Some boards state in their bylaws that the board chairperson is chief executive officer, yet operate as if the paid executive is CEO. On the other hand, some boards clearly state that their paid executive is CEO, but allow the board chairperson to play that role as he or she sees fit. Such caprice in a critical relationship is damaging to an effective board–staff linkage. Still other boards hold the executive responsible multiply to board treasurer, chairperson, and several committees (most notably, the executive committee). Such a situation gravely confounds the relationship. A board–CEO relationship is weakened when it is allowed to become an officers/committees/board–CEO relationship.

For board and executive peace of mind, it is very important to describe the board and CEO functions as simply as possible. The case made here is that the CEO's *only* accountability is to *the board*, not to officers of the board nor to board committees. This seemingly harsh prescription does not prevent a great deal of interaction between the CEO and committees or individuals as long as the CEO is instructed only by the board as a whole. Board process and structure must be in harmony with that wholeness.

The CEO, by definition, is the topmost single person through whom all upwardly accumulating accountability flows. A chief operating officer, one step below the CEO, might be a single funnel, but not the topmost. Regardless of titles, the topmost such position is de facto the CEO. If the top paid executive must get the approval of the board chair or is seen as being supervised by the board chair, then the board chair is really the CEO.

Being held accountable to the full board for agency performance is a distinct characteristic of the CEO function. That accountability derives from the accumulation of responsibilities in the staff. In describing the executive's job, the board's job, and the relationship between board and non-CEO staff, upward accumulation of responsibility is a key phenomenon.

Accountability as Cumulative Responsibility

Each individual is responsible for his or her own behavior. When individuals come together in organizations, they are still fully responsible for their own behavior. Supervisors, too, are responsible for their own personal contributions and compliance, but they are also responsible for the behavior of their subordinates. Supervisors have, then, two kinds of responsibility: direct or personal responsibility, similar to any other individual, and "cumulative" responsibility, which accumulates from the bottom upward.

In designing hierarchical relationships, job design, and performance evaluation, these two types of responsibility must be treated in different ways. I assign the word *accountability* to the responsibility that accumulates. Therefore, each manager is *responsible* for his or her own job contributions and compliance and is also *accountable* for the total contributions and compliance of his or her entire team, however extensive that team might be. The accountability burden increases as one goes up the organizational ladder, though responsibility may not. In other words, the personal job responsibility of the chief executive may not be more difficult than that of the manager of word processing, but it is encumbered with far more accountability.

From the board's point of view, the important lesson is that the *board's relationship with the CEO must be formed around the accountability of the position, not its responsibility.* In other words, it need be none of the board's concern just what job responsibilities fall to the CEO. The board's concern is confined to what it holds the CEO accountable for.

The Commissioner is not separately elected, but reports to the Board of Regents in Rhode Island. The "Commissioner's Responsibilities" policy (Exhibit 12) reflects the simplicity of a CEO's task (in the describing, not in the doing!). Note that the Board of Regents uses "Results and Priorities" as its title for Ends.

**Exhibit 12. Rhode Island Board of Regents Policy:
"Commissioner's Responsibilities."**

The Commissioner is the Board of Regents' single official link to the Department of Education. The Commissioner is accountable for all Department of Education performance and exercises all authority delegated to the Department by the Board and by law. Inasmuch as the Board of Regents governs through explicit and succinct policies which address the topmost level of organizational values, the Board of Regents will evaluate the Commissioner based on the Department's performance in the entirety and in the following areas:

1. Department accomplishment of the provisions of Board policies on "Results and Priorities."
2. Department operation within the boundaries of prudence and ethics established in Board policies on "Executive Limitations."

Consequently, the Commissioner's performance will be considered synonymous with organizational performance as a total and will be annually reviewed.

By the definitions just given, the CEO is accountable for no less than the entire product and behavior of the agency. That means everything except the board and its functions. And the CEO is accountable to the board as a body. This seems straightforward enough, but consider the implications.

The Board Has Only One Employee. For most official purposes the board has only one employee, the CEO. The CEO has all the rest. If something goes wrong in the organization (for example, a failure in producing Ends or a violation of the board's Executive Limitations), there is only one person at whom the board can point its finger. The CEO is no more accountable to the board for his or her direct actions than for the actions of the most distantly removed staff member. Everything is part of the CEO's accountability package. The board has no *official* connection with staff members except at the CEO's behest.

The CEO's Work Is Immaterial. The CEO is accountable for the entire enterprise's working up to expectations. His or her personal work is only a means to that end. The working job description of a CEO (what he or she actually contributes personally) is not for the board to decide and certainly not for the board to use in evaluating CEO performance. The skills sought in a CEO are not those associated with responsibility, but with accountability. For example, grant writing, plant maintenance, and accounting are not the point. Executive job design, leadership, strategic organization, and setting a climate of creative achievement are.

Board Members and CEO Are Colleagues. The relationship between the CEO and any *individual* board member is collegial, not hierarchical. As the CEO is accountable only to the full board and as no board member has authority individually, the CEO and board members are equals. This relationship of supportive peers is true for the CEO and board chairperson as well. They are *not* hierarchically related, because to be so would shift the CEO function to the chairperson.

The job of the CEO is to work whatever magic it takes to ensure an acceptable amount, type, and targeting of benefits in prudent and ethical ways. Although allowing no escape from performance, the board needs a strong CEO. Some boards are reluctant to empower the executive to this extent. Their reasons vary from being unwilling to let go of the strings on decision making to being unwilling to burden executive and staff with such momentous decisions. But by delegating less authority, the board must constantly forsake strategic leadership to make tactical decisions.

Leadership is being cheated in either case. As to burdening staff, in most cases they work no more in making decisions than they already do in *almost* making decisions, such as writing recommendations or providing support to board committees. Granting performers the right to choose is not perceived as a weight, but as an energizing boost.

Boards would do well to discard the traditional distinction of "day to day" management in describing the CEO's purview. Does this imply that the board's job is "month to month"? If so, both are working dangerously close to their noses. The board should be looking years ahead, and the CEO, almost as far most of the time, except perhaps in quite small organizations. "Day to day" is *not* the CEO's task and, even when said symbolically, misleads more than helps.

The CEO role is sufficiently different from that of both board and staff that the common two-part breakdown of board–staff would better serve as a three-part phenomenon: board–CEO–staff. In a formal sense, the staff is insulated from the board and the board from the staff by the CEO. The "insulation" is not one that rigidly prohibits contact between board and staff members. On the contrary, those very human connections are never problematical *if the formal roles are clear.* The rule is merely that the board can never direct or judge staff performance, though it may impose as many requirements on its CEO as it deems fitting.

Because of its summative nature, a list of CEO job contributions (not of job activities) is the simplest in an organization: *The chief executive officer is accountable to the board of directors for (1) achievement of Ends policies and (2) nonviolation of Executive Limitations policies.*

This is the long and the short of the job. The CEO function neither takes over board prerogatives, nor stands meekly aside while the board does staff work. It is a position that is as invested in having a strong board as in having a free hand. It is a function that, being strong, can afford to bid both board and staff to grow.

This highly focused CEO job description is true only *when the board does its job.* The board's desires must be clear to both board members and the CEO. As many CEOs have discovered, if you do not know what the board wants, it may be impossible to please it. The reverse is also true. Boards that lack standards and systematic monitoring are not displeased when they should be.

Monitoring Executive Performance

With the board operating at policy arm's length and delegating so much authority to the executive, how can it know that its directives are being followed? Boards receive much information, only some of which is of monitoring significance. We commonly fail to distinguish among classes of information and, thus, cloud the question of monitoring. It is helpful first to separate information into three types.

Types of Information

Decision Information. Decision information is that information the board receives to make decisions, for example, to create a budget policy from among alternative positions, to decide on an approach to use for the governing process itself, or to establish the qualities it desires in a new CEO. This type of information is used solely to make board decisions. It is not judgmental; any measure of performance implied is only incidental to the purpose. It is prospective in that it looks to the future and is used to value some aspect of the future.

Monitoring Information. Monitoring information is used to gauge whether previous board directions have been satisfied. It is judgmental in that it intentionally measures performance. It is retrospective in that it always looks to the past. Good monitoring information is a systematic survey of performance against criteria. In being aimed at specific criteria, it is more like a rifle shot than a shotgun blast. It does not demand "tell us everything," but "tell us this, this, and that."

Incidental Information. Information that is used neither to make decisions nor to monitor falls into the incidental information category. It often masquerades as monitoring information. Thus, boards hear staff reports, read lengthy documents on activities, or even scrutinize performance, but *without criteria against which to judge the information received.* Such conscientious activity creates the illusion that the board is effectively monitoring agency performance. Even the revered monthly or quarterly financial report stands indicted here. To the extent that the criteria against which the financial report is judged are not obvious, it yields incidental rather than monitoring information. Boards do, indeed, get smarter in a scattered kind of way, but they wallow in information more than monitor with it. I have found that the majority of information received by boards is of this type.

A common board folly is to want to "know everything that is going on." Although this thirst can never be sated, such boards do review and often dabble in much staff activity. Because they spend their time in this impossible attempt to learn all that is going on, they never really know how their organizations are doing. First, boards that are awash in staff material have little time to create the policies that will serve as criteria. Second, even if boards had such policies, the endless stream of data is largely immaterial to a focused, rigorous comparison of performance against criteria. Flailing in irrelevant information can be raised to an art form by committee reports and show-and-tell agendas.

There is nothing wrong, however, with incidental information. Global impressions of it may lead to better policymaking. If a board studiously extracts from such information insights helpful at a true board decision level, then it has been a diversion well spent. Unhappily, it is more common to find a board that is dragged through such information because its members think it is their duty or because a few members subject the entire board to their specific list of operational interests. The gravest trap in incidental information is that the board may delude itself that the need for rigorous monitoring has thus been satisfied.

Criteria for Monitoring

Good monitoring is necessary if a board is to relax about the present and get on with the future. Preestablished criteria are required for good monitoring. Setting criteria ahead of time is so critical to good governance that I will dwell for a mo-

ment on why criteria are necessary and then on how setting
criteria in a two-step process prior to monitoring taps board
wisdom more effectively than simply letting criteria emerge
while reviewing a document.

WHY
CRITERIA?

Preestablished criteria save board time. Each judging
action will take more people and more time if the criteria are
unclear. Boards can rush through the process with little real
inspection, of course, but if rubber stamping is to be avoided,
each judging action will consume material board time repeatedly. Very little more time is needed to establish the range of
acceptability, after which assessing performance or plans is
an easy task of comparison with these preestablished criteria.
The real work is at the front end, but savings accrue there-
after. The board avoids the continuing start-from-scratch approval struggle that exists when criteria are unstated.

Criteria are also necessary because they save staff time.
Time is lost when staff proposals are based on considerations
later found to be unacceptable. In many cases boards so routinely approve staff plans and reports that rejection is not a
realistic worry. Even under such rubber stamp conditions,
staff time is often spent "dressing up" the report or proposal
to ensure that the ritual is smooth. A great deal of ingratiat-
ing manipulation of boards has been known to go on in this
process.

A third reason criteria are necessary is that judgment
is simply not fair without criteria. Many executives have
received unearned harsh judgment from boards whose values
became clear only *after* executive initiative had been taken.
Such boards find it easier and safer to shoot down staff action
than to struggle with and declare their own values at the
outset.

A fourth reason criteria are necessary is that a board
does a far more creditable job of judging staff performance if
it does so in two distinct steps rather than one. A single step
is the common approach. When a board judges without preestablished criteria, individual board members use idiosyncratic
criteria and share their yes/no responses; totaling across all
the yes/no responses yields an official board action. The vote

records the summary of individual judgments against individual criteria. It is tricky to infer from such a process the board's aggregate values. Group judgment on the exact criteria cannot be gleaned from mere recounting of comments and arguments, because the criteria so inferred merely constitute a laundry list of individual expectations.

A two-step process leads to a far better product. Board members debate and decide at the outset those group values that will be codified in Ends and Executive Limitations policies. The only judgment to take place in monitoring is whether reasonable persons believe that actual performance matches the preestablished criteria. Each board judgment is no longer a new ballgame, but a continuation of a clarifying process in which board values are increasingly well represented in policy language. Monitoring is simpler because the value dilemmas have already been resolved in the creation of the policy. Displaying data against the policy can then be made a rather mechanical, routinized process. With monitoring thus systematized, the board can be more certain that monitoring is diligent, even without squeaking wheels or crises to compel its attention. Such systematic assurance that things are not going awry is less likely to falter due to board fatigue or distraction, more fair to all concerned, more likely to engage the board in an appropriate level of thinking and, conversely, far less likely to invite board members into trivia.

Methods of Monitoring

If the board adopts the discipline of monitoring only what it has already addressed in policy, its anxiety will drive it to develop all the policies needed. "If you haven't said how it ought to be, don't ask how it is," describes the principle that forces a board to monitor instead of meander. The board can then monitor each policy at whatever frequency it desires by one or more of three methods.

Executive Report. The CEO makes available a report that directly addresses the policy being monitored. Unlike the common staff report, it is geared to a specific board policy. The monitoring of financial condition, for example, would not manifest as the standard balance sheet and income statement. It would, instead, follow the format of the unacceptable circumstances spelled out in the board's policy on financial condition. The intent of so directly relating the report to policy language is that no additional interpretation is needed. Staff compliance or violation should be evident at a glance. It is the CEO's responsibility to produce data that enable a majority of the board to feel reasonably assured of performance.

External Audit. The board selects an external resource to measure staff compliance with respect to a specific policy. It is important that the external party assess performance against the board's policy. If the external person judges against his or her own standards, the resulting assessment confounds monitoring and decision information. Fiscal auditors are the most common example of this method, but external audits need not be confined to fiscal issues.

Direct Inspection. The board assigns one or more board members to check compliance with a specific policy. Infrequently, the board as a whole might perform this inspection. Direct inspection might require an on-site visit or inspection of a staff document. This monitoring method should not be used unless the board role and discipline are in excellent order, lest it deteriorate into meddling. Board members involved have no authority to direct anyone nor may they make judgments on any basis but the literal policy.

"Monitoring Executive Performance" (Exhibit 13) was produced by the board of the Washington County Developmental Learning Centers to ensure systematic assessment of agency performance. The board had no Ends policies in place when this policy was created, so point 3 in the exhibit shows monitoring scheduled only for Executive Limitations policies. Note that the board chose to monitor three of the policies by two separate methods.

Exhibit 13. Washington County Developmental Learning Center Policy: "Monitoring Executive Performance."

The Board will track executive performance by monitoring in such a way as to have systematic assurance of policy compliance, yet leave the Board free to concentrate most of its time on creating the future rather than checking the past. To those ends, the Board's approach to monitoring will be based on its governance philosophy and carried out in a relatively automatic way. Board meetings are not, in general, to be used for monitoring.

1. The Board will monitor those agency characteristics which it has addressed ahead of time in explicit statements of policy. The purpose of such monitoring is simply to determine, in fact, if board policies are being met. Since the Board speaks to the executive through "ends" policies and "executive limitation" policies, monitoring finds whether ends are being achieved and limitations are being violated.
2. Monitoring will occur in one or a combination of three ways:
   - Internal Reports: Periodic reports from the Executive Director to the Board.
   - External Judges: Auditors, site inspectors, or other external assessors shall be retained to answer certain monitoring questions.
   - Direct Inspection: Directors on a rotating basis designed by the Board Secretary select at random a policy for on-site monitoring. The Executive Director will "walk through" implementation of the policy. Directors involved have only the authority to state whether, in their opinion, the policy is being implemented (not the authority to determine how it should be implemented nor to direct staff to do anything).
3. Each policy of the Board in "ends" and "executive limitations" categories shall be classified by the Board according to the frequency and method of monitoring.

Policy	Method	Frequency
Protection of assets	External judge (audit)	Annual
Financial condition	Internal report	Monthly
	External judge (audit)	Annual
Compensation and benefits	Internal report	August
Employee protection	Third party	Annual
Budget	Direct inspection	August
	Internal report	Quarterly
Indebtedness	Internal report	When applicable
	External judge (audit)	Annual

The CEO's Evaluation

The CEO's only job is to make everything come out right! That translates into achievement of the board's Ends policies and nonviolation of its Executive Limitations policies. This is exactly what governance expects of the organization as a total entity. Organization performance and CEO performance are the same. Evaluation of one is evaluation of the other. Accountability is gravely damaged when the two are viewed differently.

Monitoring organizational or executive performance is a continual process. The board may wish to punctuate this continuity with an annual CEO performance appraisal. That is fine as long as the board understands that the ongoing evaluation is the most important element. Periodic evaluations are no more than summaries of the ongoing evaluation. Addition of other criteria at the annual appraisal is both unfair and managerially sloppy.

There are three common ways in which boards add superfluous evaluative criteria. First, some boards allow unstated expectations to be part of the evaluation. These are criteria that the board might have included in its policies, but did not. If a single board member is doing the evaluation, these unstated expectations might well be those of that board member alone. Second, one of the many generic personnel evaluation forms which can always be found in circulation might be used. Third, CEO performance might be compared against personal objectives originally proposed by the CEO himself or herself. In this case, the board is inappropriately judging its executive against his or her criteria rather than the board's. These three sources of extraneous standards of performance seriously weaken the powerful synonymity between board policies and CEO accountability.

Any forms developed for CEO appraisal must reflect the single source of evaluative data. I have seen school boards create citizen task forces to design a superintendent evaluation, an action irresponsible to the public as well as to the

CEO. If the boards were to do their jobs, such games with evaluation would be unnecessary. The only relevant questions are: What did we charge the CEO to accomplish? What did we prohibit him or her from doing? How did he or she do against only those criteria? If the board needs public help, it is in the creation of policy criteria.

Evaluating the CEO is an important board task. It seeks to ensure that board values are truly in place. The great utility in executive performance appraisal derives from its being integrated with the board's policy fabric and with the concept of cumulative responsibility. Because of this integral dependence on preestablished criteria, *it is impossible for the board to evaluate the CEO when its own job has not been done.*

Keeping the Roles Separate

Without a clear difference in job contributions, the board becomes staff one step removed. It is not unusual for a board to see its job as "stacked" on top of staff jobs. No wonder boards have problems distinguishing their positions from those of their chief executives! The effective board relationship with an executive is one that recognizes that job products of board and executive are truly separate. Effectiveness calls for two strong, totally different responsibilities. Either party trying to do the other's job is interfering with effective operation. It is not the board's task to save the chief executive from the responsibilities of that job nor is it the chief executive's task to save the board from the responsibilities of governing. Further, who works for whom must always remain clear. The board can respect, even revere, the chief executive's skills, commitment, and leadership, yet never slip subtly into acting as if the board works for him or her.

Two commonplace events in the board–CEO relationship deserve a closer look, each representing a clouding of role distinction: (1) executive recommendations to the board and (2) board involvement in executive plans and practices.

(1)

Recommendations by the Executive

Boards often wait for executive recommendations to move. Some even believe that to move otherwise is either foolhardy or a repudiation of the CEO. As long as boards deal predominantly with staff-level material and decisions, their instincts about this matter are correct. It would be improper if the board were to make such decisions on its own. But if we clear all staff issues from the board's agenda and are left with only those that truly belong to the board, the scenario changes significantly. Now the same behavior is revealed to be the ostensible leader's waiting for its CEO to tell it what to do next. What the executive wants the board to do may be of interest and even of some legitimate influence, but it is surely not the driving force of good governance.

CURRENT
PRACTICE

Current practice is a confounding, then, of two errors: First, boards deal so predominantly with low-level issues that the executive's *not* having a controlling influence would be foolish. Second, boards often avoid confronting genuine governance decisions by falling back on executive recommendations. When it comes to the long-term, visionary, strategic import of an agency, asking the executive, "What do you want us to decide?" is not the language of leaders.

To help the board develop more integrity in leading, the executive would do better to bring the board no executive decisions. And for governance decisions, he or she would help develop policy options and their various implications. The executive might also make spokespersons available to the board for the different alternatives. In this manner, the board's choice is truly the board's choice—a substantive involvement with not a hint of rubber stamping. The vitality of the process engages the board at an appropriate level. Board members become more aware of the important currents affecting agency fortunes and futures. Members leave the board meeting knowing they have been doing the board's rather than the staff's work. This more alive and meaningful board work cannot but have a salutary effect on the quality of management.

Intrusions by the Board

Making staff decisions trivializes the board's job, disempowers and interferes with staff investment, and reduces the degree to which the CEO can be held accountable for outcomes.

Boards make staff-level decisions through any number of single incursions: a motion to hire someone, a motion to award the painting contract to a certain contractor, a motion to change a certain personnel rule, a motion to switch $300 from one budget line to another, a motion to purchase a certain computer system, a motion to purchase new tires for the van, and so on to a level far below strategic leadership. Boards are often inexplicably unwilling to allow their CEOs to make decisions that are competently and routinely handled by persons in their daily lives. I have seen boards entrust a multimillion-dollar agency to an executive, then prohibit him or her from making expenditures greater than $5,000!

In addition to the approval process discussed in Chapter Two, boards also intrude into management by trying to help or advise staff in operational areas. Whether given by individuals, committees, or the whole board, advice to staff from the governors becomes confused with direction. In such cases, staff members have had to exercise their diplomatic skills to maintain social graces while safeguarding the integrity of delegation. When offering themselves as volunteers in tasks for which the CEO is accountable, "board members, now wearing volunteer hats . . . are subject to the direct supervision and control of the [CEO] or the responsible staff person" (Swanson, 1986).

The board has a stake in obtaining the most return on what a CEO costs. Though I am using the CEO to make this point, other staff are out there, eager to make decisions and to perform toward the mission. As individuals, they, like the CEO, are not hierarchically related to individual board members. It would be naive to maintain that disparate social or organizational positions can be entirely overlooked, but organizational culture can minimize their effects. When the roles are clear, it is possible for anyone to talk with or elicit wisdom from anyone with no harmful effects on the "chain of command." People operate better when they are not bound by rigid channels of human contact.

"Return on CEO" is greatest when the CEO's decision power is used to the fullest, bounded, of course, by the board's interpretation of its own accountability. The board would be irresponsible if it allowed even dazzling CEO decision making to take the organization in a direction the board did not desire or to foster activity the board considered unethical or imprudent. If a board establishes what it wants (Ends) and what it does not want (Executive Limitations), it optimizes both CEO power and board power simultaneously. The board's confidence increases as its fatigue decreases. The CEO's freedom to make decisions increases as the limitations on that freedom are made explicit. "Return on CEO" becomes "return on personnel," usually the largest single outlay of nonprofit and public resources. *Even a minor improvement in this return benefits mission accomplishment in one year more than most boards have contributed by involvement in details in their entire histories.*

Mutual Expectations

The board and its chief executive constitute a leadership team. Their contributions are formally separable, and once clearly differentiated, the two roles can be supportive and respectful of each other. As in sports, the team functions only so long as the positions are clearly defined at the outset. Teamwork is not the blurring of responsibilities into an undifferentiated mass. The foremost expectation of mutual support is that each function remains true to its peculiar responsibility. The chief executive must be able to rely on the board to confront and resolve issues of governance while respectfully staying out of management. The board must be able to rely on the chief executive to confront and resolve issues of management while respectfully staying out of governance.

Each can reasonably expect the other to exhibit leadership. If the board's job is well designed, board leadership is discharged in simply doing that job. But the quality of the design is paramount. Vision, values, and strategic mentality must be integral to the position. Leadership in the chief executive has two components: the CEO must influence an organizational culture in which agency impacts on the world are at least up to board expectations and, at the same time, must set a high level of ethics, prudence, creativity, and concern for the development of people. Further, the CEO influences the board toward greater integrity and capability for strategic leadership. Pressing, cajoling, and even embarrassing a board toward greater integrity is a far greater gift than pressing, cajoling, and embarrassing it toward specific content recommendations. It is unlikely that a chief executive can do both well; the CEO leader will choose the former.

The board has the right to expect performance, honesty, and straightforwardness in its CEO. Boards can at times be understanding about performance, but should never bend an inch on integrity. The CEO has the right to expect the board to be clear about the rules and then to play by them. He or she has the right to expect the board to speak with one voice despite the massive currents that flow within the board's constituencies. And the CEO has the right to expect the board to get its own job done.

Next Chapter

Getting the board's job done is the theme of this entire book. In Chapter Seven, however, I focus more on ownership accountability, job description, and discipline of an effective board. These constitute the subject matter of the fourth category of board policies, Board Process.

Chapter 7 🔥

THE BOARD'S RESPONSIBILITY
FOR ITSELF

The subject of this book, of course, is the redesign of the board job. How a board decides organizational results, how it controls operations, and how it relates to staff reveal much about its job design. It still remains for the board to deal explicitly with how it governs its own process, including a job description by which the board can discipline its time and action. These perspectives on the governing task itself are codified in the Board Process category of policies. In Chapter Eight, I deal with officers and committees, the subdivisions of board labor; in this chapter, I address the board's accountability as a whole.

I begin by introducing the concept of ownership, the source from which board accountability derives. I then fix the onus of responsibility for good governance on the governors themselves. Next, I recognize the dynamics affecting the individual board members' ability to fulfill their responsibility as a group. Management of board process is then presented as a natural outgrowth of the board's products. Finally, a board job description is set forth, along with a commentary on board work beyond policy-making in support of governance responsibilities.

"Moral Ownership"

Stakeholders for a nonprofit or public organization may be clients, students, patients, staff, taxpayers, donors, neighbors, general citizenry, peer agencies, suppliers, and others. The board could be said to be accountable to all these groups, and certainly these groups all have ownership in the organization. The special class of stakeholders I call owners are those *on whose behalf* the board is accountable to others. This narrower concept of ownership embodies only those stakeholders who are situated as stockholders for an equity corporation.

Ownership as a special concept serves as the origin of board accountability. The concept of ownership saves this legitimizing, special group from being lost in the general array of stakeholders. Surely the members of a trade association have a different order of ownership than, say, vendors or even staff members. For a city council, the municipal population occupies a position different from other stakeholders.

Various stakeholder groups may overlap, and, in some cases, two groups may comprise the same people. The ownership of an antique auto club is made up of club members; the beneficiaries of the club are the same people. The ownership of a community mental health center is the community at large; the beneficiaries constitute a portion of that community. The ownership of a public school system is the population of the school district; the beneficiaries are the students. Moreover, in the two preceding cases, the staffs of these institutions are members of the community at large and, therefore, also owners. Owners may either constitute a group larger or smaller than the beneficiaries. Even when the same people are involved, the organization's differing responsibilities to the several constituencies are kept straight by separating the concepts.

Ownership and trusteeship, as I use them, are only occasionally legal realities. It is the social obligation of trusteeship, whether or not codified in law or contract, that concerns us here. "Moral" rather than legal ownership is to be the basis on which a board determines its accountability. In cases where state law requires a nonprofit organization to have a membership (a legal ownership), the board must determine whether the moral ownership is a larger body, far beyond the bounds of the formal membership.

The composition of this moral ownership can be obvious, as with a city council, or it can be obscure as with a public radio station. Are the owners regular listeners, donors, everyone in the listening area, or all classical music buffs? For organizations that receive government and foundation grants, it is important that the grantor not be seen as owner. Ownership is not merely paying the bills, although this may be a factor. Grantors are usually best seen as high-volume customers with whom the organization makes a deal. It has the choice to not make the deal. No such choice is available to the board concerning its ownership; the rightful owners do not lose their status because the board wishes to ignore it. The test for ownership is not with whom the board makes a deal, but whom the board has no moral right *not* to recognize.

The board is ordinarily a subset of the ownership, acting as trustee on the owners' behalf. The board's trust relationship to owners *supercedes its relationship with staff.* The primacy of this relationship is easy to forget when the stream of board activity and the high visibility of organizational personnel pull the board staffward. Boards learn to speak staff language, use staff acronyms, and become involved in internal organizational issues. This understandable, intense identification with staff detracts from their being trusteeship driven. It occurs at the expense of interaction with the owners and resolution of the owners' complex interests. The mechanisms of board work must be designed to remind the board that its rightful identity is with the owners, not with the staff.

The Eastway Corporation, in "Relationship of Board to Moral Ownership" (Exhibit 14), establishes not only the composition of the ownership but the way in which the board relates to the ownership. Note that the board has planned that communication flow both ways.

The Board's Obligation for Board Performance

Board members, not staff, are morally trustees for the ownership and, consequently, must bear initial responsibility for the integrity of governance. The board is responsible for its

Exhibit 14. The Eastway Corporation Policy:
"Relationship of Board to Moral Ownership."

The "moral ownership" of Eastway Corporation shall be perceived conceptually as all persons residing within geographic concentric circles. The innermost circle shall be defined as all residents of the East Montgomery County Mental Health Service Area while the outermost circle shall be defined as all residents of the United States. Each intervening concentric circle shall represent all residents of an expanded geographic area. It is understood that residents shall be assigned varying priority depending upon which concentric circle they reside in. Residents of the East Montgomery County Mental Health Service Area shall be accorded priority while a progressively lesser priority shall be assigned residents of each expanding geographic circle.

The Board represents the moral ownership. Therefore, it shall educate itself regarding the values held by the persons it represents and shall act always under the influence of those values. The Board's education may be facilitated by (1) reviewing reports in the media, (2) studying responses in citizen questionnaires and comments by key informants, (3) discussions with elected representatives, consumers, and service providers, and (4) monitoring the demand and utilization of services.

The Board shall report periodically to the moral ownership on its stewardship. At least once each year, the Board shall disseminate a statement of its values and give an accounting of its financial resources and the extent to which these funds have been translated into services.

own development, its own job design, its own discipline, and its own performance. Before any discussion of board process to improve governance, this responsibility must be clear to board and staff alike. Primary responsibility for board development does not rest in the chief executive, staff, funding bodies, or government. These other parties doubtless have an interest in better governance. They may even seize the opportunity to affect governance quality. But they are not where responsibility for governance resides.

Only responsible stewardship can justify a board's considerable authority. Board members who do not choose to accept this breadth of responsibility should resign. If they do not, it is the responsibility of other board members to structure a board development system in which such persons are, if not "converted," eliminated from the board. Being warm, being willing to attend meetings, being inclined to donate money, and being interested in the organizational subject matter do not constitute responsible board membership. These characteristics are desirable but far from sufficient.

It is inviting to rely on the chief executive to provide motivation for a board. This scenario frequently extends further than the provision of an occasional motivation "fix." It may extend as far as spoon feeding. No matter how well the executive tells the board what to do and when to do it, governance cannot be excellent under these conditions. Going through the motions, even the "right" motions, is fake leadership that transforms a chief executive into a babysitter. Only a deluded board waits for its CEO to make it a good board.

Under these conditions, public-spirited and ethical chief executives prod the board to do and say what they think a responsible governing body should do and say. With time, observers of such a situation may question the need for the board to be responsible: If everything turns out well, what is the fuss? Getting the board to be truly responsible may be pedantic and perhaps unrealistic. After all, board members frequently are "just" volunteers; how can a part-time, outside group of largely nonprofessionals presume to tell a professional/technical staff what to do? This litany impedes any further inclination to lead leaders to lead.

The preceding unhappy scenario is the *up*side! What if the chief executive is not public spirited and ethical? The improprieties resulting from lackadaisical governance are easy to imagine. I have observed boards whose laissez-faire, rubber stamping came to an abrupt end upon discovery of misconduct. Most nonprofit boards are too private or too small for public embarrassment to be a realistic threat. Yet they must endure their own awareness of having been asleep at the throttle. Their failure may not lie in misjudging a specific issue, but *simply in not realizing that the throttle belonged to them.*

Boards are responsible for their attendance, discipline, governance methods, development, agendas, and capability to envision the future. Others can help. Surely the chief executive should even be required to help. Helpers, however, can only assist a body that has assumed full responsibility for itself; helpers can only marginally compensate when responsible parties are not responsible.

"Governing Manner" by the board of Loudoun Hospital Center (Exhibit 15) sets the standards to be met in the conduct of board affairs. Pay particular attention to the last sentence.

Diversity and Dynamics

As a board sets out to fulfill its trusteeship, its most immediate responsibility is to deal with the implications of being a group. Indeed, this hurdle can easily keep a board from attending to other responsibilities. Boards are fraught with extensive interpersonal dynamics as is any other group of human beings. People differ in their comfort with confrontation, inability to express feelings, and in the personal defenses brought to an interaction. People differ in fears, hopes, opti-

---

Exhibit 15. Loudoun Hospital Center Policy: "Governing Manner."

The board will approach its task in a manner which emphasizes strategic leadership more than administrative detail, clear distinction of board and staff roles, future rather than past or present, and proactivity rather than reactivity. In this spirit, the board will:

1. Keep its major involvement with the intended long-term impact of the organization, not with the administrative or programmatic means of attaining those effects.
2. Direct, control, and inspire the organization through the careful deliberation and establishment of policies. Policies will be statements of values or approaches which address (a) the "products" (what benefits for which needs at what cost), (b) the boundaries of prudence and ethics to be observed by staff, (c) board roles and responsibilities, and (d) the board–staff relationship.
3. Enforce upon itself whatever discipline is needed to govern with excellence. Discipline will apply to attendance, policy-making principles, respect of clarified roles, speaking with one voice, and self-policing of board tendencies to stray from rigorous governance.
4. Be accountable to the general public for competent, conscientious, and effective accomplishment of its obligations as a body. It will allow no officer, individual, or committee of the board to usurp this role or deter this discipline.
5. Be an initiator of policy and responsible for its own performance.

---

mism, and excitement, all of which contribute to the interpersonal aspects of board operation. These aspects exist quite
apart from models, rational structures, and job designs.

This book does not set out to deal directly with the
interpersonal dynamics of governing groups. The abundant
and useful literature on small-group process obviates the need
for such discussion here. I do, however, recognize the powerful influence interpersonal processes have on governance and
point to a few phenomena peculiar to boards. Most of all, I
want to persuade the reader that taking time to design a
sound board process, before the process becomes personalized,
is the greatest safeguard against the debilitating effects of un-
fortunate interpersonal dynamics. The only other preventive
measure that comes close is to ensure that all board members
are intelligent, communicative, assertive, and mentally healthy!
Alas, even emotionally "together," Renaissance people cannot
compensate for an inadequate governance process.

Carefully designing areas of board job performance will
profoundly channel the interpersonal process of a board. For
example, job design influences the types of conflict that will
be experienced and the decision of members to follow a commonly proclaimed discipline or their individual disciplines.
Diversity is directed toward some areas and muted or eliminated in others. Clarifying tasks and off-limits topics helps to
depersonalize subsequent struggles over the appropriateness
of an issue for board discussion.

A sound, codified board process can ameliorate jockey-
ing for power, control of the group through negativism, and
diversion of the board into unrelated topics. Dealing with the
dysfunctional behavior of a board member is far more difficult if the board has not previously determined what constitutes appropriate behavior. Without board-developed
guidelines, the matter will be considered a clash between personalities, and the issue of acceptable board behavior becomes
lost in ill feelings.

Effectively dealing even with appropriate diversity requires discussion of process prior to the specific disagree-
ments. Diversity must somehow be funneled into a single

position. Not all ideas can prevail, and, if members approach disputes personally, there will be winners and losers. Simple compromise is not necessarily a responsible solution; either of two very different approaches may be far better than a compromise between them. The challenge can be sidestepped by delaying decisions or by squelching dissent as being too painful, too impolite, or too impolitic. Indecisiveness and unanimous votes often result from the desire to avoid confrontation.

Like the family dynamics in *Who's Afraid of Virginia Woolf?* (Albee, 1962), boards sometimes deliberate on inconsequential issues to avoid dealing with a difficult, unspoken issue. What appears as a preoccupation with trivia may be fear of confronting the larger issues in a group setting. Small wonder; we are not very good at it, even as individuals. Moreover, board members deprived of trivia might not know how to spend their time. A board member once asked me, in all sincerity, what would be left for the board to do if detailed review and approval of staff plans and procedures became unnecessary: If we do not do staff work, what will we do? This organization had for years avoided a searching exploration of its mission. The board continued to hide behind the manufactured busyness and apparent conscientiousness of its demanding, staff-driven agenda.

Another way to escape confrontation with diversity is to use board committees, heavily "assisted" by staff, to make recommendations. Operating largely from CEO recommendations is a similar dodge. Conflicts among board members are thus avoided as is any questioning that might be interpreted as lack of faith in the executive. Instead of judiciously resolving differences, the board ignores or smoothes over differences. Instead of eliciting and embracing their differences, board members are embarrassed or even frightened by them. It is a pity, particularly for boards that represent the public, for such differences partly define the nature of "public."

When boards choose to recognize and handle differences, they find that they need a mutually agreed upon system to keep the group on task. Without a good system, the dominant characteristic of any confrontation is personality. Our points of departure may be ideas, but interaction can easily deteriorate into issues of feelings and control. As alliances are formed and personal power is experienced, the person who expresses the idea becomes more important than the idea. And, feeling rebuffed or vindicated may become more important than judging the merit of the idea.

Governing can thus be flavored by personalities rather than issues. Overpoliteness and power-based confrontation, seemingly opposite, both spring from valuing personal aspects more than the issues. Once the calm surface is broken, interpersonal dynamics that squelch dissent are transformed into personal confrontation. The opportunity to develop productive confrontation around issues dies, people are hurt, and the governance experience leaves a bad taste. If the system is poor, even good people bore or bite each other to death.

The chairperson bears a peculiar responsibility with respect to board process; however, more cogent to this discussion, the entire board cannot avoid its share of responsibility. In other words, the existence of a chairperson does not relieve other board members from contributing to the integrity of the process. If the board as a whole does not accept responsibility for board process, the best the chairperson can achieve is superficial discipline.

One way in which the board participates in good process is by placing explicit policies concerning the topic into the Board Process category. The chairperson can then maintain the process by referring to board policy, which is easier than invoking disciplinary measures on the basis of his or her individual sense of what should be. Board members expect too much of the chairperson when they ask him or her to save the board from being held hostage by its most controlling member. Each member has the right to want to run things or never to budge. But, as a body, the board does not have the right to allow individual proclivities to destroy the process.

The Cincinnati–Hamilton County Community Action Agency board incorporated its strong resolve to keep board discussions on target into points 4 and 5 of "Board Meetings"

(Exhibit 16). Some topics are simply off-limits during the board meeting.

Process explicitly designed can produce a discipline controlled more by the will of the board than by individual inclinations or exigencies of the immediate dynamics. When board process is derived from the job to be done, it will be aptly shaped by the planned products. There ever lurks the danger that the products of governance will turn out to be the unforeseen aftereffects of an unplanned process.

Board Products: A Job Description

Construction of Board Process policies begins with consideration of the board's overall reason for existence, because the

---

**Exhibit 16. Cincinnati–Hamilton County Community
Action Agency Policy: "Board Meetings."**

Board meetings are for the single task of getting the Board's job done (see Board Job Description).

1. Meetings will be open to the public except when executive session is officially announced by the president. Executive sessions will only be used when the subject matter is related to litigation, personnel, or contemplated real estate transaction.
2. Any member may request an executive session, but:
   • The reason for the session must be stated.
   • The Board may include no one else or anyone else it chooses.
   • Authority to declare the session is vested in the President unless overridden by simple majority vote.
   • Where possible, announcement of executive session should be on the published agenda.
3. Agenda Control: the Board is the sole authority over its own agenda. The President will exercise this control on behalf of the Board, though any board member—with a majority agreeing—can add or delete business from the agenda. Normally, material related to the agenda will be given to Board members with adequate lead time for preparation.
4. Agenda Content: Only those issues which are within the board's chosen areas of responsibility (see Board Job Description) shall consume Board time. That is, the Board will work only on the Board's job, not on the staff's jobs, though the Board may review staff performance against Board Policies at any time it wishes.
5. Board members are obligated to prepare for meetings and to participate productively in discussion, always within the boundaries of discipline established by the Board.

---

ultimate test of process is whether this reason is fulfilled. The board's "megaproduct" (as opposed to the organization's megaproduct—mission) is the bridge that translates between those to whom the board is accountable and those who are accountable to the board.

Developing an effective board process begins with clarification of the specific contributions of this bridge between owners and producers. Before we can intelligently design board process, we must be sure of what the board exists to accomplish; "form follows function." Appropriate practices are determined on the basis of the accomplishments expected. The board job description is thus the central factor in board process.

Conventional job descriptions are detailed lists of job activities. Their emphasis is on job means rather than job products. I use a more powerful, succinct format that omits activities and focuses on why activities take place: the intended outcomes. This method, convincingly argued by Reddin (1971), yields a job description that, in effect, states the "value added" by the position. How is the organization different because this job exists? What does this job contribute? In describing job contributions, I speak of job "products" simply to keep before us at all times the output aspect of work rather than the activity.

Boards can contribute any number of products to an organization. Only three products cannot be delegated, an irreducible trio applicable to all governing boards. The board's role as a bridge between ownership and staff produces three mandatory products.

Core Board Products

The board must contribute whatever legitimate link the organization has with its ownership. The board's first direct product is the organization's *linkage to the ownership*. Furthermore, the board has the obligation to fulfill fiduciary responsibility, guard against undue risk, determine program priorities, and generally direct organizational activity. We have seen that a board can be accountable yet not directly responsible for these obligations by setting policy. The board's second direct product is *explicit governing policies.*

    Finally, the board is obliged to ensure that the staff faithfully serves the board's policies. If the executive continually fails to fulfill these explicit expectations, the board is itself culpable. The board has no choice but to take the steps necessary to remedy the situation. The board's third direct product is *assurance of executive performance.*

    These three undelegable job contributions are the *unique responsibilities* of a governing board—unique because only the governing body can contribute these products. The board may add other products to this list, but it cannot shorten it and still responsibly govern.

Optional Board Products

Although all other contributions to the organization beyond the core three may be delegated to the CEO, it does not necessarily follow that the board should delegate them. The most common additional board products involve fund raising and legislative action.

    Should a board be responsible for fund raising? The answer depends on the kind of organization and its circumstances. From the perspective of governance concepts per se, one can only say that fund raising, at the board's discretion, may be either delegated or retained. If a board assumes this responsibility, it should define the contribution well enough that there is no confusion between staff and board responsibilities. "Fund raising" is an activity, not a result. Using results language forces the board to confront the task it has taken on and its expectations of staff. Does the board merely make philanthropic contacts and leave responsibility for actually bringing in the money to staff? Or is the board responsible for the funding level, that is, everything up to and including the goal amount? Or does its responsibility lie somewhere between? Wasteful conflict between the roles of the board (or its fund-raising committee) and the CEO (or the CEO's director of development) can be reduced, perhaps avoided, by defining the job in terms of the expected result rather than in terms of the means used to attain that result.

With respect to legislative action, the same points apply. Does the board wish to assume responsibility for legislative strategy? For network notification? For "personal presence" at hearings? Remember, too, that board members can offer themselves as volunteers under staff direction without complicating the board job itself. For example, the board might hold the CEO accountable for certain legislative impact, but guarantee to supply board members as informed volunteers to participate in testimony under the CEO's direction. With this approach, there is no need to add legislative results to the board's job, yet board members are still providing a valuable contribution. It must always remain clear who has authority and responsibility for the strategy and mechanics necessary to achieve the legislative results. In this instance, the CEO is in charge even though board members are involved. Board members work for the CEO or the CEO's designee when engaged in activities for which the board holds its CEO accountable.

Whatever the board decides about assuming more than the basic three responsibility areas, the matter must be made explicit and all further board activities made consonant. It is important that the initial three core areas, because they cannot be delegated, be given primacy. No board should add items unless it is sure its allegiance to the first three will not be diluted.

Some might say that fund-raising is the chief responsibility, even the *raison d'etre*, of a board. I disagree. Fund raising by the board may be important, even critical, to a given organization. It is even more important that the organization be *worth funding*. That worth is what the three areas of basic governance are designed to ensure. I do not mean to denigrate board fund raising in cases in which the board has made sure the agency is worth the donors' money. To the contrary, I applaud it and hold both the skills and the dedication involved in great respect. There is no reason a board cannot attend quite well to the basic three products plus fund raising, but this wholeness is ill-served by lopsided attention to fund raising as the chief board responsibility.

The Basic Board Job Description

The irreducible minimum contributions of governance are restated below. Note that these constitute the board's specific job *responsibility*, but if accomplished, ensure the board's overall *accountability* as well. This responsibility/accountability aspect of managerial job design saves the board from acting as if everything is its job. A limited responsibility list is identified, but so constructed that the board's accountability for the total is not circumvented in the name of simplicity. To summarize the job products of the board:

1. *Linkage to the ownership:* The board acts in trusteeship for "ownership" and serves as the legitimizing connection between this base and the organization.
2. *Explicit governing policies:* The values and perspectives of the whole organization are encompassed by the board's enunciation of broad policies, properly categorized, in an explicit manner.
3. *Assurance of executive performance:* Although the board is not responsible for the performance of staff, it must ensure that staff meet the criteria it has set. In this way, its accountability for that performance is fulfilled.

Each of these three products is a job output, not a job activity, though any number of attendant activities are implied. The board job, however, is neither built on activities nor evaluated on the completion of activities. Within each area of responsibility, the board can set objectives to guide its short-term work. Although the board need not set objectives for staff work, it surely must for its own work.

The Ramsey Action Programs board adopted the basic board job products in its "Board Job Contributions" policy (Exhibit 17). Optional outputs were considered and not chosen, so there are only three parts. Executive Limitations

**Exhibit 17. Ramsey Action Programs Policy:
"Board Job Contributions."**

The job of the agency is to achieve the mission in a prudent and ethical way. The job of the board is to make certain contributions to the total which are unique to its public trusteeship role and necessary for proper governance and management of the corporation. Consequently, the "products" of the board itself shall be:

1. Connection between the agency and its "ownership," the community at large.
2. Written governing policies that concern:
   - Ends (what benefits, which needs, what cost)
   - Administrative constraints (prudence and ethical limitations binding upon the staff)
   - Governance process (how the board carries out its task)
   - Executive linkage (passing of power and measurement of its use)
3. The assurance of staff performance (through control and evaluation of the executive director).

---

appears here as "Administrative Constraints," Board Process as "Governance Process" and Board–Executive Relationship as "Executive Linkage."

The Board's Hands-on Work

The three job products are intended to capture the reason the board exists. In those organizations in which the board wishes to add more outputs to its basic three, the additional job products must be reflected in the job description. In any case, subsequent board work is channeled into activities designed to fulfill these intended outcomes. Previous chapters have dealt with principles and actions pertinent to job products 2 and 3. Let us now consider some aspects and activities of job product 1 and briefly note the work involved when the board adds areas.

Direct Work: Linkage with the Ownership

The identity of ownership and perhaps the favored channels for connecting with it are deliberated and then set forth in the Board Process category of board policies. That explication is, like all policy-making, a verbal undertaking. Making the linkage real, however, is likely to require action.

The board should continually struggle to define and link with its ownership. It should do so with the same vigor it would have if owners were organized and looking over the board's shoulder. " 'Community' ownership," Ewell (1986) wrote of hospitals, "is not clearly defined, and the community does not voice its opinions or require reports on hospital performance as rigorously as industry shareholders do." It is only in rare cases that such owners are organized. In the case of nonprofit organizations, it is even likely that most owners have no idea that they are owners. Any ownership voice that becomes audible is doubtless the voice of but one segment of ownership. Although the board owes that segment its ear, it owes the silent segments the recognition that one group does not represent all. Elected boards seem particularly vulnerable to the error of listening to segments as if they were the whole. I have seen city councils, library boards, school boards and utility commissions be unintentionally unjust to those owners who were not vociferous. Allowing lengthy floor time for a few faction spokespersons makes boards feel democratic, but may cheat the broader mandate. Linkage to the ownership requires a more affirmative mentality than holding open meetings and entertaining spokespersons from the floor.

Linkage with the ownership can be viewed as attitudinal, statistical, and personal. The first, simplest level of obligation is attitude: board members behave in the belief that they are moral trustees for the owners. This intention establishes a frame of mind that, if not particularly schooled, at least leads the board to appropriate considerations and loyalties when resolving value issues. At a second level, the board gathers statistical evidence of the owners' concerns, needs, demands, and fears. Techniques include surveys, interviews by third parties, and statistical data. The third level is more personal; it engages board members in direct contact with owners and owners' representatives. Interviews, focus groups, public forums, invited presentations at board meetings, dialogue with other boards or public officials, and other intimate exchanges might be employed.

Maintaining the attitude of linkage may require no overt action. Developing a board informed with respect to the pure data on ownership and its desires may require no more than study. But the third level, personal contact, requires overt action by board members. They must go forth, sit and listen, make conversation, and struggle with communication. The board may choose to take these actions as a whole, in committees, or as individuals.

The board's status as a subset of the ownership is a built-in mechanism of linkage. Board members do not constitute a random subset, however, as they are selected because they can best fulfill the trust of governance. Because nonrandomness is a factor, boards must ensure that the selection process does not impair the most visible connection to ownership: personal similarity. Persons representative of the ownership in color, income level, geographic location, gender, and other characteristics are obviously connected to the ownership. But it is unwise for an even meticulously representative board to consider its ownership linkage thus discharged. Whether a black person can "represent" blacks or a woman can "represent" women is questionable. The superficial characteristics indicate that specific groups have not been excluded, not that they are adequately represented. Tokenism might suffice for the former, but only an adequate, ongoing linkage to ownership will ensure the latter.

The board can delegate to committees or individual members the responsibility for parts of the linkage task. A committee might meet with a focus group or a delegation from the ownership in partial fulfillment of a board objective relating to the quality of linkage. This means that the board's objective on linkage should be clear, as should any limits on the activities involved and the expected time to completion. In other words, the usual elements of delegation apply to a board's assignment of tasks to subgroups. The board has this option of delegating to a committee or to an officer, just as it may delegate to the CEO, but delegation to board members is a more slippery process. Because the board has much better control over tasks delegated to the CEO than to board members, it is propitious to keep the board's self-delegations to a minimum. The more there are, the greater the care that must be taken to ensure that the objectives are actually achieved and that there is no overlap with tasks for which the CEO is accountable.

One way for boards to link with the ownership is to connect with organs of ownership. In communities, many boards allegedly speak on behalf of the general public. Yet, boards in the same community have virtually no dialogue with each other. Their staffs may interact, but at the governance level there is virtually no systematic interaction. Were they more attentive to their linkage with ownership, boards would realize that they have much to discuss with one another inasmuch as they have overlapping if not identical ownerships. For community boards that truly see themselves as wedded to the larger context, over 25 percent of board effort spent dealing with other boards would not be out of line. The cross section of community leadership thus linked holds the promise of making a real difference in the fabric of the community.

Direct Work: Optional Responsibilities

If philanthropic funding, public image, legislative impact, or other delegable performance areas are made board responsibilities, the board must organize to perform. The board has the option of operating as a whole, in committees, or through individual assignments. In any event, it becomes the responsibility of the board, not staff, to develop and use whatever means are necessary. If the board wants the staff to carry out and be responsible for the outcome of a specific task, then that task should not be part of the board's job. Policy control by the board will suffice. To the extent a board adds direct responsibility areas to its job, the situation increasingly approaches that of the workgroup board mentioned in Chapter

One. The risk of diluting attention to the core governance responsibilities also grows accordingly, as does the risk of confusing board and CEO roles.

The optional areas of responsibility listed in the preceding paragraph enjoy a rich literature concerning ways to organize for optimal performance. I do not presume to add to that body of knowledge here, except to point out how important it is that the board clarify the tasks it has assumed. Taking on an *activity* is not rigorous enough. The board's responsibility in any of these areas is not activity—however busy and impressive—but results. It is both more powerful and more incisive to define the responsibility in results terminology at the outset.

Next Chapter

In the organization of board work, officers and committees emerge as official subdivisions of the board whole. Strategic leadership is best served when this division of labor does not jeopardize the wholeness of the board. In Chapter Eight, I discuss roles and rules for the board's officers and committees.

Chapter 8

OFFICERS AND COMMITTEES

Once the board role is clear, we can make sense of the parts into which a board divides its labor. Officers and committees are the mechanisms by which a board partitions its job. The establishment of officers and committees is a delicate undertaking because subdivisions endanger board wholeness. Preservation of "one-voice" governance and integrity of board-to-CEO delegation are both threatened.

I consider the problems and principles involved in establishing, first, officers and, then, committees. In each case, I examine the topic with respect to three factors: minimalism, preservation of the CEO role, and board holism. Finally, I comment on typical committees in light of the governance principles espoused here.

Officers

I assume that the board has decided to name as CEO its top paid executive, not the unpaid board chairperson. Further, to simplify this discussion, I do not consider the CEO to be a board officer. Commonly, boards establish the chairperson, vice chair, secretary, and treasurer, though it is not rare to find more than one vice chair and often a chair-elect.

Minimalism

Structure is best kept to the minimum necessary to accomplish the task. Establishment of more officers than needed increases complexity with no compensating gain. Consequently, a board should start with the minimum number of officers required by law and add more only as they are needed. In many states, nonprofit boards can get by with two officers, chairperson and secretary.

From the minimalist standpoint it is often hard to justify more officers. The office of vice chair usually exists only so that someone is readily available to fill in for an absent chairperson; however, a board can simply rotate temporary chairing duties in the absence of the chairperson. The treasurer is an unnecessary office in organizations with over 20 or so staff, and in many that are smaller. The CEO can, in many jurisdictions, double as secretary. The point I wish to make here, however, is not which officers are justified, but that establishment of the fewest officers called for by the task will result in clearer rules and process.

Preservation of the CEO Role

Accountability is best when delegation is traceable, unitary, and balanced with respect to responsibility and authority. For delegation to be traceable, each link from superior to subordinate must be clear to all parties. To be unitary, assignment of responsibility to and subsequent evaluation of any person must occur through a single channel rather than multiple channels. If the boss is a board, the principle of unity requires that several persons speak as one, to preserve the single channel.

If the CEO must answer to one voice only, no individual board officer can have any authority over the CEO or other staff. Conversely, the CEO must answer to the board as a whole, not to individuals on the board. Most violations of this principle involve the chair or treasurer, each of whom has been known to assume authority over staff functions. The board–CEO connection is interrupted as much by an officer who assumes individual authority over the CEO, as by any other board member who does so. The executive either works for the board as a whole or does not.

If the board chair has no authority over the CEO, who

tells the CEO what the board expects? The board does. When the board speaks with one voice in explicit statements, what can the board chair legitimately add? If the chair presumes to represent the board to management, he or she either is acting unnecessarily (if nothing is added) or abusing authority (if something is added). Moreover, an executive who is obliged to acquiesce to what the chair adds is now (1) working for the chair alone and can no longer be called CEO or (2) working for both board and chair, which is untenable because it is not unitary.

A similar flaw in delegation is commonly found in the treasurer's role. A board holds its CEO accountable for fiscal integrity. The CEO is given commensurate authority to do whatever is necessary (establishing fiscal methods, record keeping, budget adjustments) to maintain whatever level of fiscal safety the board finds acceptable. Yet, more than half of the bylaws I have encountered state that the treasurer of the board is charged with the books of account, disbursement, and a host of other fiscal management activities.

re: TREASURER

If the treasurer is responsible, then an integral ingredient of management accountability has been taken from the CEO. The case can be made that the CEO role, thus dismembered, no longer exists. Does the treasurer have the authority to carry out this role? If not, then responsibility and authority are not matched. If so, does that mean the treasurer has authority over fiscal staff, perhaps over the CEO? Does the CEO then work for the treasurer as well as for the board? On the other hand, if the CEO is the one accountable to the board for fiscal purity, how can the bylaws assign the job to the treasurer?

The office of treasurer in such an organization is like a vestigial organ. It may have been needed when the agency was so small that the board treasurer truly did fulfill the fiscal function. Or, perhaps that never was the case, but legal counsel inserted a boilerplate provision in the bylaws despite its meaninglessness. In any event, boards, executives, and staff fiscal officers across the land wade through wasteful nonsense every month pretending that the treasurer role makes sense. I often encounter the following process: The fiscal officer and CEO confer with the treasurer prior to a board meeting. At the meeting the freshly briefed treasurer recapitulates what he or she has been told. The treasurer looks informed and the board feels secure because the ritual continues. Substituting finance committee for treasurer in this scenario, by the way, does not make the pretense any more reasonable.

Some boards slightly alter the treasurer issue by creating assistant treasurers who are staff members involved in finance. In this version, bylaws give the treasurer the usual overstated responsibilities, but allow the treasurer to delegate any number of them to assistants. Now there is delegation from a board officer not only to the ostensible CEO, but to the CEO's subordinates. Just who is responsible for what and to whom in these convoluted circumstances?

The truth is, in the presence of a CEO, there is *no role* for a board treasurer that is both necessary and legitimate. If an unnecessary role is manufactured, great care must be taken to see that it is legitimate. One reasonable, albeit still manufactured, role would be to monitor financial performance; however, this role is illegitimate if the treasurer monitors fiscal performance against criteria other than those embodied by the board's policies. When the board's criteria are clear and when monitoring information precisely answers to these criteria, an expert interpreter is rarely needed.

Board Holism

A holistic board is a single organizational position and must officially behave as one. Consequently, board officers exist to help the board do its job, not as powers unto themselves. For the minimum two officer positions, I suggest the following job descriptions, stated in the job product style:

CHAIRPERSON: Responsible for *the integrity of board process*
SECRETARY: Responsible for *the integrity of board documents*

These job responsibilities serve the wholeness of governance. They do not interfere with unitary delegation to the

CEO. The chair is not responsible for the functioning of organization, nor for the quality of the CEO. The chair is responsible for the functioning of the board, which ordinarily proves to be job enough! Using the board job description from Chapter Seven, the chair can trust that if the board works well, CEO performance will follow.

If the chair's job product is integrity of board process, selection of a chair should be based on ability to achieve that output. The chair's job requires skilled handling of group process, an ability to fairly but firmly lead a group to confront and even to welcome its diversity and to adhere to agreed-upon rules for board conduct. Boards should take great care in choosing chairpersons who can develop the leadership that often lies dormant in the group. Rather than foisting a heavy-handed discipline, the good chair incites the board to generate all the rules it needs out of its own wisdom. The chair merely calls forth the board's own statements of discipline when needed, as if he or she has no choice but to deal with the group the way the group itself has decreed. The David M greeting card sentiment penned by Monica Sicile to describe friends aptly describes good chairpersons as well: "Friends sing your song when you forget the words." The good chairperson demonstrates the optimum combination of discipline and group responsibility when, with as much affection as firmness, he or she confronts the board with its own song.

The quality of governance often depends on the skill of the chairing party. The better the board, the more judiciously it chooses a chair; but, ironically, the more responsible the board is as a group, the less the chair makes a difference in the near term. Boards only denigrate their mission when they choose chairs on the basis of length of service or availability. It is better to obtain a good leader who can invest three hours a month than a marginal leader who has thirty hours to give. Many a CEO has seethed under a chair who had time to spare.

The chair's responsibility to board holism extends to his or her ex officio role with public and press. When interviewed, the board chair does not have the authority to venture beyond what the board has actually said. "Representing the board" means stating only what the board has stated unless the board has specifically granted further authority. One workable way to carry out this function is to apply the same delegation principle applied to the CEO, except within the Board Process and Board–Executive Relationship policy categories. This approach allows the chairperson to make decisions about board process and mechanics as well as specifics of the delegation and monitoring process so long as she or he is within the board's broader pronouncements on these topics. The chair cannot, however, interpret Ends and Executive Limitations. To do so would be to instruct staff and, thereby, to be in conflict with the authority the board has given to the CEO.

SECRETARY

While the chair is guardian of what the board *is doing*, the secretary is guardian of what the board *has done*. If the secretary's job product is "integrity of board documents," selection of a secretary should be based on ability to make that contribution. Responsible for no one else's behavior but his or her own, the secretary need only be compulsive about correctness, accuracy, and appearance. The secretary's job may have little to do with taking minutes, but will have much to do with the official record of process and actions. He or she certifies the evidence of board action, including board policies and minutes.

The "Officer Responsibilities" policy of the Planned Parenthood of Metropolitan Washington board (Exhibit 18) carefully focuses the jobs of officers. Note that the Treasurer role is retained, but defined so as to be consistent with the board's relationship to its Executive Director. Note, too, that the Vice President has been made responsible for maintenance of the monitoring system. Board members thought that this role would be excellent training for the person who might next assume leadership of the board.

MINUTES

Minutes constitute the most basic record of board action. Even the all-important board policies are created and altered only when the authority of the minutes so instructs. What any board "says" includes only those statements passed

Exhibit 18. Planned Parenthood of Metropolitan Washington Policy: "Officer Responsibilities."

Officers of the Board are in the service of the Board. As such they are bound by Board wishes and by limits of Board authority. The officers may meet as a group with the Executive Director for purposes of preparing agenda and other pre-Board work (as defined by its policy on Committee Process), but they may not act in place of the Board, except as it specifically delegates.

1. *President:* The President is to assure the integrity of Board process including effectiveness of meetings and the Board's adherence to its own rules. The presidential succession, in cases of temporary absence of the President is the Vice President, the Treasurer, and the Secretary. In the absence of the President, the term "President" shall be construed to apply in due turn to this succession of officers.
2. *Vice President:* The Vice President will act in the absence of the President. The Vice President also will monitor the consistent operation of the monitoring system.
3. *Treasurer:* The Treasurer is to perform duties in connection with finances of the agency as may be required by the Board. Duties of the Treasurer will neither lessen nor add to the Executive Director's accountability to (and only to) Board policies on fiscal conditions and budgeting.
4. *Secretary:* The Secretary, by affixing his/her signature, shall attest formally to the legitimacy of Board documents. The Secretary also is responsible to the Board for reporting on and noting any inconsistencies of Board actions.

in an official process. Detailed, narrative minutes (more than what the board has *officially* said) are unnecessary and detract from the board's "one voice," as well as load the record with material of negligible official significance. In long minutes it is almost impossible for the writer to render an unbiased record of the board conversation. If the minutes are wrong, someone has been misrepresented; if they are right, it does not matter anyway. A record of official motions and members' statements suffices for minutes in almost any board situation.

Committees

Board committees are *to help get the board's job done, not to help with the staff's job.* Like officers, committees should be established consonant with due care for minimalism, preservation of the CEO role, and holism: Have no more committees than absolutely needed; do not compromise the clear accountability linkage between the board and its CEO; disturb board wholeness as little as possible.

Minimalism

Traditionally, we speak of boards and committees in the same breath. Boards are supposed to have committees, aren't they? Boards have told me they determined their size on the basis of how many members were needed for committees! And these were governing boards with nothing to do but govern; they did not need or use committees to make up for lack of staff. Committees can serve a useful function, but the propitious path is to start with *no* committees and add them only when clearly needed.

Even then, the choice to establish committees, no matter how intelligently made, is not simply a decision about ideal structure. There are no "right" committees to have, no list of correct subdivisions for getting a job done. Subdividing the board to get a job done is the personal preference of board members at the time. A particular mixture of persons may work better or worse in subgroups, depending on their personal characteristics. None of the common committees is indispensable; there is no one committee a board must have.

Preservation of the CEO Role

Board committees are established to aid the process of governance, not management. This simple rule safeguards the board–CEO accountability relationship. When board committees are assigned tasks that essentially oversee, become involved in, or advise on management functions, who is in charge of these activities becomes less clear. Personnel, executive, and finance committees are habitual offenders. The CEO role deteriorates as a result of their well-intended, official interference. The board's ability to hold the CEO accountable deteriorates apace.

Unfortunately, many board committees are actually designed to be involved in staff-level issues. This is bound to occur when the boards themselves are involved below their level. The problem seems even greater in committees than in full boards because of the belief that committees should be involved in details and because of the traditional committee assignments.

Level of Work. It is widely accepted that committees should delve into more detail than the board as a whole. To boards that insist on acting on staff-level issues, formation of a sub-group to work through the details may well make sense. To the extent to which boards extricate themselves from staff work to do board work, this need evaporates. If the committee is to help the board do its work, working at the lower level is neither appropriate nor helpful.

Committees should work at the board level. With respect to policy-making, the best contribution a committee can make is to prepare truly board-level policy issues for board deliberation. With respect to the non-policy-making aspects of a board's job (for example, linkage to ownership or fund raising), committees may deal with details, but not in areas that have been delegated to staff.

Topics. As in policy-making, there is no reason for boards to subgroup in categories that are appropriate to administration. When boards create committees with titles that duplicate staff functions, those committees can be expected to drift into staff work. Personnel committees automatically work at the staff personnel officer level. Finance committees usually slip into the same trap. A service committee dealing with a specific program will likely find itself dealing with staff-level management issues concerning that program.

When a committee works at the staff level, the crisp board–CEO–staff chain of accountability disintegrates. Look at the relationship between the committee and affected staff. For whom does the staff work, the committee or the CEO? If the staff works for the CEO, then it cannot take direction from the committee (otherwise, the CEO can hardly be held accountable for the outcome); yet such direction, more or less subtle, does take place. If the staff works for the committee, then there is no true CEO because the board has chosen to delegate to staff through more than one channel.

Some boards have protested that such committees exist only to advise staff, thereby making good use of the special skills of board members. But advice to staff by committees— or even by the full board—is suspect. Although the offering of advice may be an honest intention, the staff are seldom so sure. In most of the cases I have observed, the first time this matter was explicitly considered was when I raised it. That is, the board had not seen fit to define committee–staff relationships. Boards may easily overlook the lack of clarity; staffs rarely escape its consequences. Staff are loath to treat committee input as they would real advice.

What does one do with advice from the boss? If it is truly advice, there is no obligation to pay attention. If it is truly advice, advisees are within their rights to dispense with one set of advisors and select another or no one. If it is truly advice, the staff may, by not attending meetings or reading reports, effectively disband the committee. If it is truly advice, the board will not think ill of its staff for these rebuffs. If the board has made Ends and Executive Limitations clear, evaluation, even informally, of staff on the basis of acceptance of advice is not only superfluous, but pernicious.

Advice should be totally within the control of advisees. Staff members who want advice should obtain it however they deem best and from anyone they choose. Staff may ask board members for advice, but the advice mechanism should not then be confounded with board authority. Board members may then advise freely as long as that counsel is not misconstrued as subtle orders because they are still wearing board hats. Establishment of formal, official board committees to advise staff is not only unnecessary, but damaging.

Joint board–staff committees can be legitimate when they prepare options for the board to consider. This activity should be undertaken only where the respective roles are crystal clear. The joint committee must think at the board's level, not the staff's. By no means should the committee make either board or staff decisions. Board committees need never relate directly with staff except to gather intelligence for use in subsequent board deliberations.

Board Holism

No common practice so threatens board wholeness as the traditional approach to committee work. Let us consider how the work of committees can be useful to a board at minimal cost to its unity.

Traditionally boards with a great many decisions to make have found it only natural to divide their labor. Several committees working simultaneously can digest and form solutions for several times as many problems as can the board working as a whole. Each committee works as a board in microcosm, studying, debating, formulating, and, finally, arriving at a course of action for the board. Committee work yields recommendations for adoption by the board.

What does a board do with recommendations originating from its several committees? It can review the committee's entire process so that all board members understand and participate in the problem-solving experience; however, to do so would unnecessarily duplicate committee work and, in fact, obviate the need for committee work. So, by and large, committee recommendations are accepted. To avoid feeling like rubber stamps, board members may ask a few questions and put the committee "on the spot" before they give approval. Most board members accept that they do not know as much about issues handled by committees of which they are not part. Unless there is reason to believe the committee is incompetent or biased, they accept the recommendations.

In reality, then, the board does not aggregate its values across a wide range of governance topics. It aggregates the values within committees on one topic at a time: the values of Elizabeth, Brian, Tanya, and Kevin about personnel; the values of Angela, Sara, Ivan, and Krista about finance; the values of Lisa, Terry, Hannah, and Jennifer about . . . , and on and on. On the surface the board is fulfilling its obligation to speak with one voice, but, except for a relatively perfunctory approval vote, there is no board. There is only a group of congenial miniboards, inappropriately importing into governance a method that is quite rational in a workgroup.

The governing responsibility is to create a holistic, integrated set of connecting values that, taken together, "cradle" or encompass the nature of organization. Proper governance is not a piecemeal endeavor. Whole-board decision making tends to illuminate those "dark corners" where staff or board members can exercise undue power by pushing an idiosyncratic agenda. *The only way a board can create unified policies is to do so as a whole.* Fortunately, when a board attends to the larger policy issues and refrains from prescribing executive methods, its job becomes manageable and the board can make decisions as a whole. The quality of the policies thus created reflects the value coloration of the entire governing body across all topics.

Consequently, board committees, when they are needed to assist the board in decision making, should do *preboard work, not subboard work.* They may work on matters before the board does, but at the board level. They should not work below the board level, or at staff level. But if bringing a recommendation to the board is not supportive of board holism, what then is effective "preboard" work? In boards that govern by policy, most committee work relates to board decisions on policy. A minor part of board work is "doing" rather than "saying," and in these "doing" instances, committees can be used to accomplish an objective as long as their work does not overlap that of the CEO. For this discussion, I consider only what committees can do to help boards create policy.

If a board is to deliberate and adopt a policy position, it will do a better job if several options are available. Existence of only one option is a flaw inherent in the recommendation practice. The availability of several alternatives, however, is insufficient for making an intelligent choice unless the board is aware of the implications of each option. In other words, the board needs to know the choices and the consequences of these choices. Only then can it ponder, debate, and vote intelligently.

A useful "preboard" job product of a committee is just such a recounting of policy alternatives and their implications. To produce an alternatives–implications product for the board, the committee must proceed through several careful steps. Assume that some problem, opportunity, or situation has arisen. The matter may have been assigned to the committee by the board or the committee may have come across it in the course of related work.

The committee's first task is to clarify just what the board-level issue is. Determining the appropriate question makes it possible to search for optional answers. First, the committee must be certain it is addressing the correct issue, for it is not uncommon to spend prodigious time probing the wrong issues. Issues are incorrect when they belong to someone else or when they have been inadequately formulated. The former situation occurs when an issue is in the CEO's domain; the latter because the issue is at an inappropriate breadth. Second, the committee searches out the alternative value positions or perspectives available to the board in answer to the issue. What are the optional policies to be considered? Third, the committee investigates the cost, public relations, productivity, and other implications of each policy option.

Relevant implications will form the basis on which the final policy is formulated, so they must be approached thoughtfully. Staff may be called to assist, not in selecting a course of action but in ensuring that available options and important implications have not been omitted. External help may prove useful as well; the board's auditing firm, for example, may have helpful input regarding implications for specific fiscal constraints under consideration. The committee's product, then, consists of policy options and their implications.

With this product in hand, board members discuss and persuade and vote. There is no committee choice to rubber stamp; neither does the board redo what the committee has already done. No recommendation is necessary. The committee may communicate its preferred option to the board, but it would be of little utility. In this process, the committee job and the board job are sequential and separate. It is greatly significant with respect to board holism that a member not on the authoring committee is just as capable of casting an informed vote as anyone on that committee. The board on the basis of clearly presented survey of options and implications, makes a choice *as a board.*

Remember that boards that govern by policy need not deal with the flurry of neverending details and low-level issues. They have the time to make fewer, though broader, decisions reflectively. Though they deal with massive value conflicts, these are not boards that react to every staff crisis or that feel nothing should go on that they do not know about. Boards that govern by policy can afford adequate preparation and wide-ranging board consideration of strategic interests.

The Executive Director's relationship with the board is protected by the Bissell Centre board policy entitled "Committee Principles" (Exhibit 19). Note that the policy attempts to prevent committees from becoming overidentified with any single area of organization.

This approach to the policy role of board committees places a high value on the wholeness of board action. It values board-integrated oversight of large issues more than participation of segments of the board in narrow slices of organization. With this approach, the bromide "real work takes place in committees" no longer holds true. The board meeting is the place of action. It is not the place for ritual voting or for carrying out the unnecessary business that clutters most board agendas. It is where leaders come together to make leadership decisions.

Legitimate Committees

If board committees should not be tied conceptually or physically to the specific divisions of staff labor and topics, to

**Exhibit 19. Bissell Centre Policy:
"Committee Principles."**

The board may, from time to time, establish committees to help carry out its responsibilities. To preserve board holism, committees will be used sparingly, only when other methods have been deemed inadequate. Committees will be used so as to minimally interfere with the wholeness of the board's job.

1. Board committees may not speak or act for the board except when formally given such authority for specific and time-limited purposes. Such authority will be carefully stated in order not to conflict with authority delegated to the Executive Director.
2. Board committees are to help the board do its job, not to help the staff do its job. Committees will assist the board chiefly by preparing policy alternatives and implications for board deliberation. Board committees are not to be created by the board to advise staff.
3. If a board committee is used to monitor organizational performance in a given area, the same committee will not have helped the board create policy in that area. This is to prevent committee identification with organizational parts rather than the whole.
4. Board committees cannot exercise authority over staff, and in keeping with the board's focus on the future, board committees will ordinarily have no direct dealings with current staff operations. Further, the board will not impede its direct delegation to the Executive Director by requiring approval of a board committee before an executive action.

what should they be related? Which committees might a board use? Recall that the policy-making job is divided into four discrete categories. One option might be to structure committees around these categories. One committee does preparatory work for board choices about Ends, a second prepares for choices about Executive Limitations, a third prepares for policies about Board Process, and a final one prepares for policies on Board–Executive Relationship. As the categories are exhaustive, the committee topics are exhaustive. If ad hoc rather than standing committees are desired, committees can be established whenever a special need arises and then disbanded. In either case, the nature of preboard work would be the same. When proper principles for committee work are maintained, the actual structuring is of less import. The structure may change as the board's need for subgrouping evolves.

Comments on Traditional Committees

INTERESTING SECTION

The approach to board committees presented here differs substantially from conventional wisdom. To underscore this model's departure from governance as usual, let us look at several frequently encountered committees in light of the new concepts.

Personnel Committees. There is no justification for the existence of personnel committees. After assisting the board on one or two policies, personnel committees have no place to go but into staff work. A board with a CEO *never* has a managerially legitimate reason to establish a personnel committee. But what about hiring a new chief executive and handling grievances? If these tasks are so great as to require a standing committee, the board has a problem that will not be addressed by the establishment of a committee.

Executive Committees. An executive committee tends to become the real board within the board, with debilitating effects on holism. An insider/outsider division among board members is not an uncommon result, as the executive committee "becomes the 'in' group of the board, with a corresponding loss of interest and attention of other trustees" (Haskins, 1972, p. 12). If the board is reduced to governable size, an executive committee as usually defined is not needed; however, circumstances peculiar to a given board may unavoidably impose a large board size, and an executive committee may become necessary to get business done. When not established because of board size, an executive committee ordinarily arises because of a lack of clarity in the board's delegation of authority to the CEO. Therefore, executive committees (1) make or approve executive decisions that could otherwise be left to the CEO, (2) assume board prerogatives that should be left to the board, or (3) do both. In other words, executive committees authorized to act must take power either from the board or from the CEO. Establishment of an executive committee to make board decisions between monthly meetings is specious. Board decisions will not arise that often if the board is proactive and delegating properly.

Program Committees. If the program committee is involved in staff implementation decisions, it can be dropped with no loss. If, however, it is preparing truly board-level issues for discussion, then it is in order. Program committees can be legitimate, as described earlier, doing preboard work with respect to Ends. Most program committees I have encountered, however, are involved in program means rather than program results and relate their work directly to current and near-term staff operations.

Finance Committees. There is scant justification for the existence of finance committees. These are much like personnel committees. They could assist the board in developing a very few Executive Limitations policies on financial matters. After that, they have no place to go but into staff work. Sometimes, legitimate board work in fund raising is assigned to a finance committee, though the two functions are vastly different. In such cases, it would be better to rename the committee (for example, "Development") so as not to invite it into inappropriate activity. With adequate financial Executive Limitations policies and the kind of pointed systematic monitoring described in Chapter Six, boards with CEOs have no need for finance committees.

If, however, the board has retained the function of safeguarding endowment or reserve funds to itself, then a "doing" committee might well be used to carry out that task. In this case, the board job description would include a fourth item like "safety and return of reserve funds."

Nomination Committees. The nominating committee does not exist to help the board create policy, but to replenish itself or its officers. This committee is part of the system that empowers individuals to serve as governors or as officers. It is a proper governance committee. It is the only board committee that may need to be described and empowered in the bylaws, particularly if it acts as a membership committee, selecting nominees for the board.

Traditionally, committees and officers are often used to monitor staff performance. The discussion in Chapter Six argued for monitoring only against the criteria formulated by board policies. If the criteria exist and monitoring takes place as described, the need for committees or officers to monitor is all but eliminated. A group is needed only when the criteria have not been set forth or have been set forth unclearly. If monitoring reports are *precisely aimed* at the provisions of policies being monitored, boards can end the wasteful practice of using board time in meetings to determine whether criteria were met. Officers and committees can then cease their unnecessary work and attend wholeheartedly to helping the board put its strategic leadership in order.

Next Chapter

After designing a technical framework to meet the governance challenge, a board must then confront the hard part: making it work with real human beings in real situations. Too often, board dreams are shaped, constrained, and thwarted by meandering, crowded, and pressing agendas. Board dreams, unhappily, are too often regulated if not determined by their agendas. Let us consider in Chapter Nine how governing board members can ensure that their agendas and discussions serve their dreams.

☙ Chapter 9 ☙

MAKING MEETINGS WORK

In striving for excellence and struggling to conserve time, boards are compelled toward more precise use of their energy and talent. The central resource in governance is the wisdom with which board members enter the boardroom. Eliciting this wisdom on the right issues, at the right time, and in the right form is not easy. Crowded agendas, scattered focuses of discussion, and all the familiar weaknesses of group discipline conspire against the efficient use of board energy.

Like the parent of the two-year-old, the governing board knows it has the power, but never quite feels truly in charge. Because of inadequate information, the changing rules of external authorities, a staff more knowledgeable about organizational activities and time constraints, the board appears to be the seat of organizational power in theory more than in fact. The traditional mechanisms intended to make board members feel they are more on top of things and more involved can themselves drive boards even further afield.

In this chapter, I look at what it is like to restrict a large job, built almost entirely on the use of words, to a small amount of time. I then discuss the care a board must exercise in selecting subject matter, and include instances in which outside expectations dictate ill use of board time. Next, I explore the formal, planned use of board time as manifested in agendas. Having dealt with economy in the use of time, I turn to the central goal of this discussion: transforming diverse voices into a single voice. I end the chapter with a brief consideration of board meetings conducted according to the new model.

167

Managing a Talking Job

Governing boards have precious little time in which to do their jobs. Even a liberal average of six hours per month yields less than two regular work weeks in an entire year. There is little room for inappropriate or wasteful activity when a year's governing must take place in such scant time. Even in small organizations, the number of possible items for learning, discussion, and decision is far greater than the available time will allow. Because a topic is important is not reason enough to deal with it; there are too many important topics.

To further complicate the use of time, each board member has favorite interests to explore or points to make. In large boards the process can slow to a crawl so that all members have their say. It is not uncommon for boards to adopt unstated strategies that deny members this right, not because anyone seeks to throttle them, but because not to do so consumes too much time. As conventional board agendas are wide open to topics of staff means, board actions can easily become a laundry list of individual members' operational interests.

Boards fall prey to the same "clean-the-desk" syndrome that afflicts individuals. In the face of overwhelming choices among competing and profound values, it is attractive to back off and do menial work. For an individual, that may entail nothing more harmful than the diversion of cleaning the desk; for a board it is likely to mean dabbling in details. Damaged delegation aside, the distraction robs even more precious board time, the moreso because boards are able to convince themselves that such diversions constitute being "involved."

There are always staff eager to use board time for show-and-tell. Diversion is particularly inviting because the topic seems legitimate. Staffs are proud of their work and want to talk about it. Attracting praise or even notice from the board can be very rewarding. Tradition fails to warn boards that faithfully listening to staff reports may not be governance at all.

External authorities demand board time. They do so sometimes for legitimate reasons, but often because of a dysfunctional construction of governance. An example is the raft of inappropriate actions demanded of local school boards by state legislatures and demanded of many private social service agencies by their certifying bodies. For public and nonprofit boards receiving public money, the lawfully required wastes of time not only plunder the resource of board talent, but jeopardize the tenuous psychology of strategic thinking.

The expression of visionary leadership by a board in the few hours still remaining is—let us be frank about the probabilities—*thoroughly unlikely*. Tradition, time, and available diversions are stacked against real leadership. This budget needs to be approved. This grant must be signed and sent right away. Financial reports are to be reviewed. A roof needs to be repaired. An aspect of the group insurance needs to be changed. Staff cost-of-living increments and merit raises must be sanctioned. Time's up. Perhaps we can get around to strategic leadership next year. A surfeit of insistent demands makes a mockery of boards' yearning for the long view.

Choosing the Issues

The board's job is a verbal task. The school board coaches no basketball teams. The County Commission constructs no bridges. The hospital board cures no patients. The symphony board conducts no music. The board's job is not to coach, construct, cure, or conduct. The board talks. Debating, clarifying, and enunciating values is a talking task.

Words are the board's tools. When the job is one of words, there must be discipline in the talking. That discipline involves *what* is talked about, *how* the talking occurs, and *when* it is done. It is not acceptable to talk about any issue that might come up. It is not acceptable to talk about an issue in whatever way desired. It is not acceptable to talk about an issue at an inappropriate time. Boards, as trustees for the interests of others, have no more right to converse randomly than employed lathe operators have to cut whatever piece of metal strikes their fancy. When boards wander aimlessly, they are as negligent as the professional shortstop who decides that right field is a nicer place to be today. Boards cannot simply address any topics in any way they wish at the moment and hope to excel.

Screening Form Before Content

Screening issues prior to board discussion brings process criteria to bear on board meetings. Boards can resolve the question "What will we allow ourselves to talk about?" before specific issues arise and their enthusiastic sponsors obscure the discipline that could have been exercised. The board needs to address the matter in a Board Process policy. Institution of such a policy enables a board to judge the appropriateness of an issue against criteria before including it on the board agenda. It is important that no one start speaking to the content of the issue before dealing with its form. The first screening question is "What category issue is this?" Is it an issue of intended effects in the world? An executive means issue? An issue of the governance job itself? Or an issue of board–executive linkage? Answering this screening question concretely labels the issue as, respectively, one of Ends, Executive Limitations, Board Process, or Board–Executive Relationship.

The second screening question is "Whose issue is it?" If the issue belongs to this organization at all, it should be clearly "owned" by either the board or the CEO. If the issue belongs to a staff member other than the CEO, as far as the board is concerned it belongs to the CEO. So the question before the board is, simply, "Is this issue yours or mine?" Finding that an issue is "yours *and* mine" bespeaks unclear criteria or an issue yet to be disentangled. Beware of "shared" responsibility; shared is likely shirked and almost certainly sloppy. In a good system, there are no orphan issues. They all belong somewhere.

The third screening question is "What has the board already said in this category and how is the issue at hand

related? This question looks not only at the content of existing board policy, but at the breadth or level of that policy.
Content is inspected to determine (1) whether the board has
already dealt with the issue and, if so, in what way and (2)
whether the issue at hand is several levels of abstraction below
current board policy or simply the next level lower. If the
board has already addressed the matter, then the only relevant
question is whether the board wishes to change what has
already been said. If the issue at hand is several levels below
board level, the task is to reframe the issue so that it is conceptually adjacent to previous policy.

One way to do this is to ask "What is the broadest way
to address this issue so that it is still 'under' the board policy
we already have? And, having answered that question, "Will
that suffice to deal with our concern?" If *no*, the process is
then repeated. As an example, let us say the board has a
policy that prohibits the CEO from paying staff compensation that is "materially greater than market." This policy
would itself fall just under or "conceptually adjacent" to
the broadest policy of the Executive Limitations category:
"Allow no practice or circumstance that is unethical or
imprudent."

Let us assume that a board member expresses concern
that "market" can mean local or national or a special segment, such as professional. Perhaps there is a worry that,
with respect to clerical salaries, political problems will arise
if the organization is out of line with local governmental
scales. Although not wanting to limit the CEO to the local
market in seeking persons nationally, the board member is
convinced that "market" is unacceptably broad in the light of
this political worry. A majority of the board may feel comfortable enough with the broader level of proscription already
set forth. If a vote reveals the majority is satisfied, then there
is no issue. If a majority agrees with our concerned member,
the compensation policy might be amended to read: "No
compensation may materially exceed the applicable market.
Local units of government will constitute the market for job
classifications that local governments employ." The board

would have, in effect, come in at a lower level, though the policy is still only two sentences long.

These screening checks take surprisingly little time if the board uses the configuration of categories and levels described in previous chapters. The total registry of board policies creates a "value map," which is used to navigate through the otherwise confusing array of established and potential policy issues. Determining the placement of any organizational issue with respect to other issues and with respect to board and CEO "territories" is relatively easy.

It is out of order for board members to talk about content before the form is settled. And if the board has decided that options and implications are needed for informed deliberation, it is out of order to begin problem solving before these adequate data have been developed.

Being Ready for Discussion

Obtaining adequate data before creating policy can be a reasonable cause of delay. There is a danger, however. Boards, like individuals, have a tendency to put off doing something acceptable and wait forever to do it perfectly. Total information is rarely available, so boards, like all managers, must learn to take action on incomplete data. The peculiar situation in this case, however, is that the option to put off policy is often an illusion. A board cannot wait until later to create policy, for even as it waits, the existing *implicit* policy is covertly in effect. A board can delay changing a policy, but cannot delay having one.

Executive action continues whether or not the values and perspectives on which it is based are stated. If those actions are consonant with a previously stated board policy, they remain unchanged until the board changes the policy. If the board does not mind that, then a delay causes no harm. If, however, the board is not happy with certain actions even though they are consonant with the old policy, a delay merely prolongs the period in which such actions must be deemed acceptable. In such cases, the board may adopt a tentative policy that approximates a "final" board position. This policy, although expected to be changed soon, is official.

I have many times led boards through a rapid policy development exercise. Policies can be produced at a rate much faster than thought possible. These policies need no more subsequent revision than policies that have taken much longer to develop. In fact, policies formulated after months of work are, in some ways, worse. Boards are reluctant to alter policies that take so long to develop! So the more quickly developed policies are just as good and, as it turns out, more flexible. Once board members grasp the idea of policies as values and perspectives, they are able to turn their worries and intentions into governing documents with little difficulty.

Rubber Stamping Responsibly

It is hard to find champions for rubber stamping. It enjoys de facto popularity while enduring rhetorical derision. Rubber stamping is the relatively automatic approval of another's plan or performance. Exactly what that means, however, is not as clear as at first it might appear.

For example, if a board believes that whom department directors hire as their secretaries is staff business, it follows that the board should not be involved in the hiring. Most persons would not consider such delegation as rubber stamping. If for some external reason—let us say the law requires it—employment of secretaries must be sanctioned by the board, then it follows that the board will be asked to approve a hiring decision. What if the board feels as it did before? Would the board now be rubber stamping if it approved the new hires without debate and, in fact, without even reading the names? Most persons would call this rubber stamping. But the same degree of governance responsibility was exercised in each scenario.

Even good delegation appears to be rubber stamping when a delegated action passes across the agenda. School board agendas would shrink if the boards were to delegate sensibly. Antiquated, ill-devised laws and tradition *require* that unnecessary items be on the agenda. Because those items are on the agenda, school boards feel compelled to probe, study, and publicly comment on a great deal of trivia, even though doing so makes no managerial sense. Not to do so would subject them to charges of rubber stamping.

When board members have an uncomfortable rubber stamp feeling, they dig in and study the offending issue, ask questions, and stimulate discussion. Such behavior is conscientious and is often the wise response. But not always. Sometimes, the more effective, system-improving response would be to question why the issue is on the board agenda. Certain items on the agenda *should be rubber stamped* because the right to make the decision in question ought to be the CEO's. The telling question is how a CEO decision gets on the agenda in the first place.

Tradition and law. Tradition brings personnel procedures, budgets, plans, and program designs to the board for approval in most organizations. For some organizations, the list extends to hiring, job descriptions, organizational design, and even more mundane matters. These practices are often demanded by accrediting bodies because these bodies are merely following tradition themselves. Some states require that boards of agencies funded by state money approve all payment vouchers. Local governmental boards, such as city councils, county supervisors, and school boards, must conduct extensive reviews of staff operations. Both tradition and law embody a "meat axe" approach to accountability: to ensure order, virtually all staff activity must be passed before the board to be badgered and blessed, even when the activity has already occurred! This myopic version of accountability justifies disproportionate attention to fiscal and legal jeopardies over program outputs. It serves accountants and attorneys who would avoid jeopardy far more than it serves dreamers, creators, and leaders who would add value to the world. This kind of accountability sways boards into spending more time looking over their shoulders than over the horizon.

Mindless rubber stamping of true board prerogatives is a dereliction of duty. Rubber stamping of matters that should have been management prerogatives is not. What are management prerogatives? They are *whatever* means the CEO chooses to accomplish board-dictated Ends that are *within board-dictated Executive Limitations*. If the CEO is within these boundaries, then what reason would the board have for not approving? Disapproval would mean that the board had not seriously constructed its boundaries in the first place. On the other hand, if disapproval is *not* seriously considered, why is board time needed for approval?

When board approval is imposed externally, the board is justified in *intentional* rubber stamping. That is, it can go ahead and approve as it is required to do ("rubber stamp") and move on. *If the board has truly done its homework* and is fully convinced that its responsibility has been faithfully discharged, it need not take the approval seriously, only as a matter of empty form. For empty form is exactly what it is.

This tactic is similar to the "consent agenda" used by many public boards to speed routine items. It differs in two ways: in its origin and in the mechanics and meaning of removing items. Conventional consent agendas are intended to isolate routine, noncontroversial actions so that less board time is consumed. The consent agenda suggested here has nothing to do with noncontroversiality or with routineness. It concerns prior delegation and might more accurately be termed an *automatic approval agenda.* Issues placed on the automatic approval agenda are among the many decisions that the board has already determined are in the domain of the CEO. They may not be routine and they may be controversial, but *they are not board decisions*. Unlike conventional consent agenda items, these items may not be moved from the special agenda to the regular agenda by a single board member's request. These items are on the automatic approval list not to save time, but because a conscious decision has been made that these items not come to the board at all. They show up as board business only because some authority to whom the board is beholden said they must. Therefore, no single board member can have the right to *un*delegate the matter, that is, to have the item moved from the special to the regular agenda. The board as a whole, of course, does have that right.

Finally, a word about rubber stamping done to coddle executive indecisiveness. There are CEOs who do not want the responsibility of decision making. To such CEOs, a tradition that transfers their responsibility to the board is quite comforting. They enjoy hiding behind "the board's decision." Boards collude with these CEOs, thinking that it is kindhearted to let them off the hook on "hot" decisions. It is sloppy management design to differentiate board and CEO decisions on the basis of the CEO's preference. This practice contributes to diffusion of roles rather than to clarity. If the CEO does not or cannot make decisions, the board has good reason to question whether it has the right CEO. As a rule, the board need never make a decision solely because the CEO does not want to make it. When the CEO is not both enabled and *expected* to make CEO decisions, the board is wasting a powerful tool and much of its own valuable time.

Planning the Agenda

Boards must continually struggle with agenda content: "What do we *have to do* this month?" There is an element of passivity in this statement, a hint that we will put on the agenda whatever the exigencies of our world put there for us. The spokesperson for those pressing circumstances is most often the CEO. And, as some hapless boards have discovered too late, he or she who can be oracle for the gods assumes a commanding position even without malevolent intentions.

It is common for boards to defer to their CEOs on agenda sequence and content. To the extent a board is needlessly entangled in staff practices, it is compelled to get its signals from persons intimately familiar with staff issues and timetables. Boards become so dependent on their staffs to fill agendas that many would find themselves adrift without such guidance. "Of course," they say, "our CEO provides most of our agenda content, because she or he is the one *who knows what is going on around here.*" The problem is circular:

Boards are trapped in staff-level issues and, therefore, need staff input as to what those issues are. Staff is called upon to generate board agendas and, therefore, board agendas are composed chiefly of staff-level material. The board job is thereby defined through these actions as a reviewer of staff material, not a creator of board material. In fact "board material" traditionally comes to consist largely of staff material to be re-reviewed. In these circumstances, board and staff lose sight of just what a board issue looks like.

Tying Agendas to the Long Term

Boards are often subject to a zig-zag phenomenon in agenda content. Without staff guidance the problem is usually worse. More than we would like to admit, agendas are developed around routinized rituals, reaction to immediate stressors, and last-minute approvals for external consumption. Suppose a board has carefully eliminated business it does not need to do. It will have disposed of meaningless actions and will have sufficiently empowered the CEO to save it from staff decisions. Yet it is still faced with the concrete, real-time problem of this month's agenda. The board cannot then fall back and have the staff supply enough items to keep it busy. The leaders cannot ask the followers to tell them what their job is.

Board work need not come to a screeching halt. When confronted with an ambiguous or bewildering task, we need only retire to the next higher level of thought to get our bearings. If we lose our way on wooded paths, we can re-establish confidence by hovering over the forest for a few moments. What we cannot do physically, we can do mentally. The board needs to hover awhile, to shift its attention from the immediate agenda to the year's agenda and, if that is insufficient, to the perpetual agenda. This is what wise chairpersons do when, in the midst of confusion, they suggest looking at "the big picture."

The perpetual agenda comprises the basic board job contributions and any optional ones the board has added. These outputs belong to the board; they are not merely a summation of staff work. This perpetual agenda was discussed in Chapter Seven as a board job description. So, to gain control over its own agenda (so that the outcome will truly be *the board's* agenda), the board must begin with the nature of governance itself. What does this board exist to contribute?

Remember that the unique and continuing contributions of the board—its perpetual agenda—include (1) linkage with ownership, (2) explicit governing policies, and (3) assurance of executive performance. A board looking for a starting place would do well to begin with contribution #2: create all four policy categories. Linkage with the ownership occurs only after the board has established—in a Board Process policy—who the ownership is and how the connection will be made, which are *expressed* in a Board Process policy. Executive performance cannot be ensured before Ends, Board–Executive Relationship, and Executive Limitations policies are established, as these policies contain the delegation, monitoring, and performance criteria.

In short, the board should get its policies in order before undertaking any other task. With a perpetual agenda, the board has a starting place from which it can plan major board work into the immediate future. Hence, the perpetual agenda leads to a more specific, time-framed agenda that is neither long term nor near term. The most useful time segment for planning board meeting agendas is the midterm, about one year.

The board establishes objectives for the ensuing year within each of its responsibility areas. The board might determine to forge a dialogue with other boards or to enhance communication with its ownership through public or private media. Policy integrity might be improved through more systematic inclusion of financial experts or dissenting programmatic viewpoints. Assuring executive performance can be upgraded by making the monitoring system more rigorous or less costly. If the board has adopted other contribution areas, such as securing philanthropic funds, objectives for these responsibilities can be set.

Establishing board objectives for the midterm, then,

yields a sequence of single meeting agendas and between-meeting work. Weekly, monthly, or quarterly meetings are thus integrally derived from the larger process. Officer or committee expectations are drawn from the same schedule. Note that annual establishment of the agenda by the board, although open to staff input, *is not staff-dependent.* The quality of the board responsibility is enabled to move two steps forward: Not only is the board producing "answers" without executive ventriloquism, it is generating the questions as well and, hence, exhibiting a significantly greater level of leadership.

This approach to agenda setting makes three major contributions to rational board process: First, it avoids the zig-zag agendas set meeting by meeting. Second, the board is in greater control of its own agenda and less dependent on its CEO to tell it what to do each time. Third, the rightfully dominant board concern with Ends is less likely to be lost in a sea of lesser issues.

Using Ends to Justify the Meetings

I have found that policies in all categories except Ends are rather stable. Mission—the broadest, most inclusive Ends policy—may hold relatively still, but further explication of beneficiaries and benefits seems to change enough to require continual attention. This should not be surprising. In a business for profit, constant awareness of customers and products is the key to success. The late 1980 explosion of concern over quality relates chiefly to a continual, systematic obsession with *customers'* requirements, a parallel to the nonprofit and public duty concerning Ends.

For the public or nonprofit board, one eye should be on customer-equivalents and one on ownership. In other words, one outcome of a good governance system is that the governors are free to concentrate on the mission and on those in whose behalf the mission is pursued. Relative value stability in other policy areas and the strategic importance of Ends lead the board to work on two compelling concerns each year: (1) How can we connect with even more integrity with those on whose behalf we serve? (2) Given new information, new wisdom, or new possibilities, what good for which people at what cost should we strive to do in the years ahead? In other words, the majority of board energy is expended on the first element of its job (linkage with ownership) and the first part of the second element (explicit governing policies concerning Ends).

Although improvement in ownership linkage need not be constrained by specific time periods, long-term vision ties more closely to pursuant staff action like writing budgets and planning programs. It is therefore subject to more "punctuations" in the flow of time. As the board's Ends work is strongly tied to these administrative time lines, for most boards *the annual agenda is best constructed around a yearly cycle of exploring and restating Ends policies.*

The board selects an external event to which the organization directs itself. For some, this is the budget submission date of the major funder. For others, it may merely be the annual meeting of the membership, the start of a fiscal year, or the completion of an election cycle. In any event, the date selected is that at which the executive part of planning must either go into effect or be publicly announced.

To give the CEO ample time to prepare for that deadline, the board's annual update of all Ends policies is set two or three months earlier. To update, the board restudies its mission and all subsidiary Ends policies in the light of new information and possibly new dreams. Then, working backward from the due date, the board calculates a year of agendas to lead it to that point. The same technique is used to establish completion dates for committee tasks. Other board needs can and are considered, but the central organizing factor is the neverending focus on mission and other Ends policies.

The board plans its dialogue with other representatives of the ownership (other boards, councils, and commissions), examines its assumptions about environmental factors, and structures discussion of the implications with the CEO and other staff. The board may entertain speakers on competing viewpoints or on the division of social labor among the various agencies in the area. Board-to-board dialogue and other work designed to enlighten vision may take more time than the board has. Or, too much leadership influence may be needed to bring other boards along. At any rate, the work is sufficient that in the first year a board would not accomplish all these steps. Several annual cycles are required before the board comes near its potential in visionary leadership.

The process, particularly early on, does not occur without stumbling. But it is ever so much more defensible to stumble over mountains than over curbs. The leadership involved in persuading boards to converse seriously about the effects they are seeking for their beneficiaries would be a breakthrough itself. Even small successes would be a giant leap from poring over budget lines or probing into sick leave procedures.

After the annual changes or reconfirmation of the Ends policies, the CEO goes forth to plan. The CEO embodies the first year's portion of the board's longer–range vision in a programmatic plan and budget. In doing so the CEO must adhere to all other applicable board policies as well. The board is not responsible for this balancing act; the CEO is. Except for its normal monitoring, the board's annual work is completed when it reconfirms the Ends policies.

In summary, the board begins to gain control over its agenda when it accepts total responsibility for the agenda. Individual meeting agendas are derived from the larger picture of the board's goals for the midterm. These midterm goals are derived from the board's perpetual agenda. The board avoids governing from its hip pocket and the floundering that invites a rescue by its CEO. The board moves further away from a short-term mentality by tying everything to the long-term challenge. Board time is to be spent largely on creating the future, even beyond the two-thirds proportion argued by Mueller (1974). The regular agenda is designed to develop strategic vision, not by inserting an orphan agenda item (or even a retreat) on strategic planning, but by being formed around and infused by a long-range mentality.

Getting Started

The first year's agenda involves a great deal of startup activity. For example, no matter how long an organization has been in existence, its board may well find that few true policies exist. Most "policies" are either staff documents improperly elevated to governance status or actual policies generated out of staff, not board, values. Moreover, the board will likely have conceived of its job as a collection of traditional activities rather than outputs. It is important to recognize the magnitude of change in concepts and behaviors before embarking on the path to policy governance.

Gaining Commitment

The first step is to gain the commitment of board members to strive toward the new model. This involves discussion of the model itself and of the changes that it portends. It is important to include the CEO in the process and, as far as possible, to optimize all variables that will affect the board's subsequent success (Carver, 1984a). When the decision to pursue policy governance is made, it should be captured in Board Process policies, similar to, perhaps, the "Governing Manner" and "Board Job Contributions" policies shown in Chapter Seven (Exhibits 15 and 17, respectively).

As pivotal an act as this massive alteration of roles and rules will be, as much consensus as possible is in order. The board will be leading in a new order, inviting all the hurdles and detractors Machiavelli warned of. This decision, like all policy decisions, should not delay until full agreement is reached. The past need not cast the deciding vote. Moreover, board discussion should lead not only to a choice as firm as if it had been unanimous, but to a clear understanding that *all* members are obligated to help make the resultant choice successful.

Establishing a Sequence

In most cases, the board should write policy before either linking with ownership connections or ensuring CEO performance. These latter tasks are better defined when the policies are established.

A board may wish to review all its old policies to see what can be translated into the new format, but this course of action is greatly discouraged. Except in very rare cases, the resulting material takes more time to organize and results in a poorer product than starting from scratch. It is at this stage that boards come to realize how inadequate traditional policy-making is, even when done well. The confounding of means prescriptions, activities, results, high- and low-level values, single-event (nonpolicy) decisions, and violations of good delegation principles in previous documents constitutes ordinarily a Gordian knot.

In building policies from scratch, proceed according to the principles given in Chapter Three: start "thin" in all categories and then carefully expand. In expanding into narrower policies, many boards find that the best sequence is Executive Limitations, Board Process, Board-Executive Relationship, then Ends. Policies are to be developed by the whole board, not by a committee. If the latter method is necessary, the committee must have the board's mandate and keep the board informed with respect to the process.

Implementing the Plan

What are the broadest statements for the four categories? These constitute the board's "starter set" on which all remaining policy is expanded. Note the following examples:

Ends	The purpose is stable employment in our community.
Executive Limitations	The Executive Director may allow no practices or circumstances that violate commonly accepted business and professional ethics or common business prudence.
Board–Executive Relationship	The board will relate officially to staff only through the Executive Director.

	The Executive Director is accountable for the entire organization's attainment of Ends and compliance with Executive Limitations.
Board Process	On behalf of the total community, the board will govern with one voice through written policies with an emphasis on long-term Ends.

As simple as these statements seem, some struggle is required in their formulation. To decide "stable employment base," for example, the board would have had to discard "broad base of employers," "high personal income," and other alternatives. They may even have gone a round or two over "community" versus "town" or "county" or "region." They should have compared their optional missions with others in the community. How does this mission relate to the mission of the Chamber of Commerce or the goals of the city planning department?

Expanding the Policies

Following the sequence recommended earlier, the board returns to Executive Limitations and generates "worry areas." Each worry area evolves into a policy topic, as discussed in Chapter Five. These negative policies are dealt with first, to eliminate the board's anxieties. If its worries about budgets, financial condition, risk, and personnel can be relieved, the board can relax and attend to building the future.

Next, the board works more on its own process. Remember that self-examination is where this process began, culminating in one or two policies. Now the board checks back to make this category complete. The reason for isolating part of Board Process earlier was simply to get the sequence started. Now the board can deliberate the remaining topics that deal with its methods of governing. Then it is prepared to establish the ground rules of delegation and CEO functions by creating the Board-Executive Relationship policies.

Last in this startup sequence, the board comes to Ends policies. It might seem that the board should deal with Ends first, and, in a new organization, that would be best. But in going concerns, Ends may be dealt with last for four reasons: First, Ends are the most important policies, and the board will now have considerable experience, having "practiced" on the others. Second, the other policies not only prescribe the board's role with respect to Ends, but go far to remove impediments that block the board's attention to Ends issues. Third, the *implicit* ends remain in place until the board confirms or changes them with written Ends; the organization is already aimed somewhere. Fourth, when the board arrives at the Ends challenge, it stays there forever. Ends work constitutes the bulk of the board's perpetual engagement.

Managing the Transition

The process just described takes from several months to a year or longer, depending on the board's commitment, agility, fear, and reluctance to make the necessary changes. If professionally guided, all the foregoing policies, except Ends, can be developed in one or two meetings. National organizations with far-flung board members, when they choose to use a special task force for initial policy writing, ordinarily take longer. On the other extreme, a community organization with a relatively agile board can finish in six hours. Adjustment of previous board and CEO patterns of behavior takes longer. When this initiation process is complete, the establishment of the annual planning cycle already discussed in this chapter takes over.

During the transition, it is important to balance the need to maintain momentum with the need for the involvement and understanding of the entire board. The longer the transition takes, the more likely the changeover will not be completed, for the old ways pull hard. Staff can play an important role while the board retrains itself. The CEO should take care not to bring the board material inappropriate to its new role. Further, the CEO must actually assume the power the board delegates. With the new policies in place, monitoring under the new regimen should start immediately, to quell board worries as well as to convince board and CEO that the board stands behind its new rules.

At this point, boards usually have to struggle to remain focused on criteria rather than reports. It is easier to think about familiar reports (balance sheets, overdue accounts list) than the criteria for which disclosure data are to be received. During the transition, boards often experience withdrawal from giving up their old traditional role. Accustomed more or less to flying by the seat of their pants, boards must learn in this early period to be comfortable with more sophisticated systems. A jumbo jet cannot be flown using the cockpit technology of a crop duster.

E Pluribus Unum

Whatever the agenda content, the central interpersonal challenge to the board is to convert divergent views into a single official view. It is as important for the board to have multiple minds as it is for it to have a single voice. To weaken the multiplicity of viewpoints would be to rob the board of its richness of wisdom. To weaken the unity of voice would be to rob the board of its opportunity for effectiveness. On any issue, the board must elicit as much divergence as possible and resolve it into a single position.

Pursuing Pluribus

Divergence occurs without prompting in many boards. In others, members must be given explicit permission, perhaps overt stimulation, to diverge. Whether an immediate need exists or not, all boards should discuss and adopt a policy that fosters and manages diversity. The discussion and the resultant policy help ensure that social rewards operate in support of diversity. Are dissenters looked upon askance? Is it socially safe to disagree? The chair should assertively pursue differing viewpoints. The behavioral message is that disagreement not only is tolerated, but is necessary to the health of the process. Further, a board can reach outside to seek opposing viewpoints. The board should be so eager to widen its lens that it imports adversaries to invigorate the process!

The board thus is perceived as a forum of churning debate and exposure, an exciting place. This debate and exposure, of course, must concern the big questions rather than the small ones, the results rather than the methods. This is definitely not staff work, though staff members will undoubtedly have ideas to contribute. In fact, involving both board and staff here causes no problem. As long as roles are clearly defined, the board can invite staff to join in the fun. The board is not being pulled downward to staff-level concerns; rather, the staff is stretched upward to board-level concerns, though as guests in the process, not its masters. As thinking, caring human beings, staff members have much to contribute to the dialogue, and everyone profits by their being invited to do so.

Pursuing diversity has implications for the practice of CEO recommendations. As already discussed, most nonprofit and many public boards unquestioningly use CEO recommendations as a point of departure for board action. In fact, boards often do not depart very far from this point of "departure." In the approach presented here, the CEO is a participant and may well include staff in the process. But he or she brings staff in to provide a variety of viewpoints, not to support some prepackaged CEO recommendation. Staff input to the governance process does not need to be homogenized by the CEO when the input is about appropriate board issues. When the board does its job and allows and requires the CEO to do his or her job, exciting opportunities for "bigness" open up.

Ultimately Reaching Unum

Where do we go with all this richness? It is used chiefly to increase awareness, to decrease smallness (choosing furniture just does not have the same allure anymore), to reveal new ways of looking at the world, and to sharpen the issues. It helps boards to pose new, more penetrating questions. It guarantees that boards will henceforth operate a step ahead of staff rather than a dependent step behind. Boards stop trying to be the *final authority* and become instead the *initial authority*.

This healthy, provocative divergence still must be reduced to a single official position. Disagreement is best resolved from the conceptual top down. In other words, the board should elicit agreement first on the broadest position. To make the point, I will go beyond organizational boundaries to a larger debate. It would be much easier to get a majority to support "human beings deserve a high quality of life" than "business should be allowed to fail in that more efficient economies increase overall quality of life." The larger the question, the more likely that differences can be resolved. This is one reason the policy-making process suggested here starts with the broadest application. It is not that the broadest level is without controversy, but that (1) it must be resolved, in any event, before dealing with subsidiary issues, and (2) it probably will be associated with fewer wide swings in value. Note that this approach requires the articulation of policy parts discussed in Chapter Three. That is, the board should not debate a page of monolithically constructed mission and priorities. It should debate the very brief mission first, then the next level of issues, then the next. Running them all together makes wise translation from diversity almost impossible. Even in single policy statements there can exist at least a couple of levels, the first represented in the preamble and the other(s) in the body of the policy. Should the amount of diversity require it, the board can resolve the preamble level first, and then work on the parts one at a time. This process is only slightly slower and it is a far more accurate way of turning board values and perspectives into hard copy. Furthermore, policies produced in this highly articulated (almost outline) form are easier to modify later through amendments. Remember that the implications of the various policy alternatives will have been sought, so the board is not simply flying by the seat of its passionately held opinions.

Making the policy decision, in the final analysis, means taking a vote and declaring a position. Consensus, if honestly achieved, is certainly workable, but requiring a consensus to move is a prescription for either mediocrity or dishonesty. Koontz (1967) felt the tradition of unanimity poses a major danger to board effectiveness wherein vociferous members can "tyrannize the majority" (p. 54). When the vote is taken, the official pronouncement is as firm as if there had been no disagreement at all. Healthy governance requires that board members agree up front that any position resulting from a fair process is, *and of right, should be,* the position of the board. This agreement on process is embodied as a policy in the Board Process category. Individual freedom of opinion, however, need not be sacrificed. There is no reason the members of a board should pretend they agree on content after the vote when they did not before. But they should agree on and support procedural integrity. Supporting the process only when you win the vote is not supporting the process.

In fact, recurring unanimous votes are suspect. All persons on a board may, on a given issue, agree. But if the voting record of a board is regularly or predominantly one of unanimous votes, we must question whether dissent is being squelched or if the issues are simply not important enough to disagree about. Either possibility calls for examination of board process. Brian O'Connell, executive director of Independent Sector, contends that boards try too hard for harmony and compromise. He welcomes occasional split votes, finding it better to have split votes, even charged debate, than to water everything down so it is mush that nobody takes offense at, but nobody gets very excited about either (personal communication).

Collecting Board Wisdom

Nonprofit and public boards are not good specimens of institutional memory. Some board members have a long memory of the organization's traditions and evolution. Some long-term staff carry similar memories. But the board, as a body may have a hard time remembering deliberations of only a few years ago. Staffs often wonder if such an entity as a "board" exists, except in the most ephemeral way.

Turnover has much to do with this, but there is more to it. I have seen boards behave as if they did not have responsibility for previous board positions. The board as an organizational position goes on, regardless of individual turnover. An individual person becomes, upon induction, a part of a body that has existed for some time. The body's obligations and commitments do not change because the new person joined. The new member mounts a moving train, not one that leaves the station just as the last passenger gets on board.

Turnover and short memory are good reasons to use an explicit, brief policy-making approach. The values and perspectives of the board are assembled in accessible, succinct form. New members can catch up more quickly. They know what their board stands for and with which of its positions they disagree. They "get on board" more quickly because they are not befuddled for two years before they understand what is going on. Institutional memory may still be foggy, but the accumulated value positions are not. Board values and perspectives at their current state of evolution may be found in a few pages. The vessel for better institutional memory is in place.

When explicit policies have been produced over a long period, an organizational "value history" is retrievable from the sequence of amendments. As opposed to sequences of events and personalities (the "story" history), value histories trace shifts in the organization's values and perspectives over time. This type of documentation provides a sense of history and tradition without perforce binding anyone to the traditional.

Consider the collection of values and perspectives in microcosm. In the conduct of board meetings, a great deal is said but not seized. I see little to recommend the standard narrative minutes with all their detail, but I do commend the practice of capturing apparent consensus, majority feelings, or unresolved conflicts as they emerge randomly in discussion. Much wisdom is expressed and has no place to go. Unless the comments are directly related to a policy under consideration at that moment, spontaneous board sentiments are lost.

I once consulted with an elected public board that "developed" most of a policy on the disposal of surplus real estate while they bantered during a break. They did not realize they had set forth the elements of a useful policy until I showed them my notes on the informal discussion. Such gems can be collected by a simple mechanism that does not detract from the topic at hand. The board secretary might persuade certain members to stay alert for such commentary. It can simply be noted for later review, for further focusing, and perhaps for consideration as policy or change in existing policy.

If several board members are frightened by a news report of another agency's bad fortune and express their fear at a board meeting, what should be done? The board goes to the policy manual. Does policy address the worry? If not, how can it be made to? If policy does address the worry, is the monitoring system working? If it is working, does it assess performance closely enough or frequently enough to allow the board to relax? This step-by-step sequence not only diminishes board anxiety but results in a stronger policy position. Jacqueline Jackson, of Palo Alto, California, calls this the "heartburn strategy: I determine what's bothering me, see if the policy covers it, put it in writing" (personal communication). In resolving the problem, the board must remain *focused on the policies.*

With a well-designed system, the board that takes care of its policies finds that the policies take care of it. Truly, *making* the policy system work is the way to make it work. If worries are not dealt with forthrightly and in the self-correcting manner just narrated, they destroy the system, bottleneck board and staff, and crowd out time already critically short for mission development. Handled well, worries provide an opportunity to reconfirm that the system works and that expressing fears is a healthy part of the process.

The Character of Meetings

Let us consider how this process looks and feels. Perhaps the most obvious characteristic of this process is a short agenda. Instead of facing a plethora of issues, the board encounters a much shorter, though deeper, list. The board comes to see a lengthy agenda as a sign that something is wrong. Board time is treated as a nonrenewable resource; it must be used with care and made to count.

Attendance is high. Board meetings are not considered optional. Members attend because the meetings are interesting and they feel that they can *accomplish something*. There is an atmosphere of bigness and acceptance of diversity; the board is a forum to embrace diversity more than to homogenize it. Yet there also exists a businesslike awareness that the board is a deciding body, not a debating society. Meetings are worth board members' time. They may have less exposure to interesting staff operations, but this loss is more than replaced by the active stream of contacts and issues generated from the ownership. At the forefront of the board's mentality is whether the dream is big enough, focused enough, visionary enough. There is a refreshing conception of the board as part of a family of boards that form an inspiring stratum of leaders. Agendas and discussions increasingly reflect that the organization and its mission are integral to the larger context. In short, the board *lives* strategic leadership.

Next Chapter

The essentials of policy governance have now been covered. The final chapter issues both challenge and counsel for attaining and maintaining successful strategic leadership in the governing board. Six strategies are presented; the first five are old friends to us all, but are couched in principles of the new governance. So finally, let us consider strategies for board leadership.

Chapter 10

REDEFINING EXCELLENCE IN GOVERNANCE: STRATEGIES FOR BOARD LEADERSHIP

In this final chapter, I synthesize more than summarize. The following six strategies cut across various aspects of the policy governance model and challenge board members to move from paradigm to performance.

I. Be *Obsessed* with Effects for People

ENDS

It seems obvious that the board's primary concern should be the benefits for people. But in the usual routine, programs, projects, activities, and methods demand so much attention that boards virtually neglect the benefits for people that justify the organization's existence in the first place! The neverending struggle with organizational Ends, according to Richard J. Peckham, formerly of the Kansas State Board of Education, "ought to consume us" (personal communication).

A. Don't Ponder Ends, Attack Them

A

"Passion, commitment and fire for what we are doing must start at this table," pleads Donna Chavez, commissioner for the Naperville, Illinois, park district (personal communication). Being obsessed with Ends demands that the board tackle the difficult questions by mobilizing board time, mechanics, and concern around what good is to be done for which people at what cost. The board cannot forget these questions, even for one meeting.

All other policy categories are easy compared to this one; they are more quickly resolved and stable for longer periods. Adequate development of Ends requires a long-term commitment. The board will forever be involved with Ends issues; the struggle is never completed.

The rigorous focus of this process opens up new insights into what the proper Ends should be. To make Ends policies about poverty in a Community Action Agency, the board is forced to develop a new understanding of the nature and perpetuation of poverty. To make Ends policies for a public school system, the board must become more sophisticated about the skills needed for personal and social success in the world to come. To make Ends policies for a Third World development agency, the board must learn about the nuances of development and underdevelopment. A board that recognizes that such learning is going to occur will not behave as if only the answers evolve. The protocols of debate must enable deliberation of the questions as well as the answers. New questions will emerge over time and transform the degree and substance of the wisdom itself.

Moving mountains an inch often appears less active than moving mole hills a mile. Boards who would be strategic leaders must move at a more deliberate pace than their staffs, but with issues far more momentous.

B. Keep the Mission Out Front

As powerful as a good mission statement is, its predominance is a fragile commodity. It is easily transformed from a compelling authority into mere words and, ultimately, becomes hard to locate and impossible to remember. Purely mechanical practices, such as printing the mission on all correspondence, on the reverse of members' name plates, and on the front of the policy manual, can help.

Brian O'Connell (1985) called for keeping the dream alive in board meetings. The leadership must keep the dream out in front so members always see the relationship of mundane things like budgets and audits in the context of the "glorious outcomes" that they have come together to achieve.

Testing everything against mission becomes the standard check of organizational direction. This mentality is best achieved when every board meeting has some mission-relevant conversation. No board meeting should go by without a debate or presentation on some facet of the Ends development process. The central reason for meeting at all is mission and mission-derived Ends policies.

C. Invigorate the Ends Debate

There is no more exciting topic than Ends. An Ends dialogue that is boring should be considered a symptom of poorly designed Ends work. Atrophy is easily avoided. A quick solution is no further away than the staff. Even a small staff will harbor divergent, enthusiastically held ideas about the priority of outcomes. Encourage staff to develop arguments for competing viewpoints. Invite them to be passionate rather than coldly analytical.

Beyond the staff are even more sources of divergence. Some constituents do not believe your organization should exist at all. Listen to them. If your organization is in the public eye, there will doubtless be factions that think your priorities are all wrong. These factions do not agree with each other. Much can be gained from their debate. Rather than avoiding dispute, elicit it. The board should be the forum for public debate in its chosen area. It is, as the Rhode Island Board of Regents agreed to be, the "boiling cauldron" of whatever controversy is afoot.

Of course, none of these invigorating avenues is available if the board neglects to foster acceptance of diversity within its own membership. The board must value, even crave disagreement within its ranks if it expects to be comfortable with the lively dissent outside. A board that believes it must vote as a block in order for its pronouncements to carry weight fails to signal that its one voice *always* grows from and in spite of diversity. Strategic leadership is big enough to embrace diversity and wise enough to be enriched by it.

Divergence is not the only source of richness in the Ends dialogue. Much of the vigor is derived by allowing leaders to dream. In the short term, there is scant place for dreaming, for one must choose between being taken seriously and being visionary. In the long term, however, leadership cannot afford to overlook the wisdom of dreams, even the wisdom of dreamful playing. Vision that bounds higher than the barriers that confine us often springs from earnest playfulness.

D. Drive an Ownership Ends Dialogue

The board derives its identity and legitimacy from its ownership. Some ownerships are broad enough (such as the general public) to have trusteeship vested in multiple boards. Board service to the ownership need not be confined to the specific organization being governed. The board may well reach out to other organs of ownership, that is, other boards. In this extended arena, strategic leadership can be of momentous effect. Bringing the Ends dialogue to the community of boards not only provides leadership to the whole, but infuses the organization as well. It is more exciting and farsighted to be part of an exciting and farsighted whole.

It is important that interboard dialogue focus on the results each pursues in the interests of the shared ownership. Organizations commonly meet on more operational issues, an undertaking appropriate for staff. Boards could profit from discourse on their respective missions and the community-relevant issues they have uncovered in framing missions. Do all their missions in total accomplish the aggregate outcome that this cross section of leaders would have it be? Leaders in such an interaction experience a closeness with the abstract ownership that often eludes them in their separate board meetings. Their minds are stretched beyond the familiar home boardroom.

E. Don't Be Seduced by Cost Control

The quality of organizational results is best served by devoting unswerving attention to greater quality, not to ever more stringent cost control. "An obsession with cost reduction produces narrowness of vision . . . it actually hurts as much as helps," argues Skinner (1986). Crosby (1979, 1984) and Deming (1986) forcefully maintain that costs will decrease when quality increases, although focusing on the reduction of costs does not increase quality. The concept of quality used by these authors concerns the fulfillment of customer requirements with minimal waste, rather unlike the means-oriented professional use of the word typical in many nonprofit and public agencies.

II. Dare to Be Bigger than Yourself

Demand daring. Bring the bigness of this invigorated debate into the boardroom. It need never be small again, for there will be neither time nor toleration for smallness. Conscious strategy is necessary because it is so easy to be more aware of the immediate and near at hand than the unbounded, distant horizons.

A. Keep Trusteeship Up Front

Trusteeship carries compelling obligations, which are obvious to public boards that operate in the limelight. But not-so-public boards, which operate *as if* in trusteeship for the public, are not always known by that public. As a busy public, we do not run around to oversee those who operate in our name, though many a beleaguered school board or city council may think otherwise. Social service and hospital boards operating as nonprofit, private corporations still see themselves as owned by the public, a public who often forgets it is owner. For such boards, the public pressure is less, though the moral challenge is greater. How does a board act as agent for principals who are unaware of the relationship? The board that would respond to its leadership opportunity cannot avoid confronting the problem. If it is to be more than an academic consideration, the nature of trusteeship must be a frequent board topic.

B. Lead Leaders

With respect to the staff, it is pivotal that the board not only lead, but lead leaders. Bigness must be passed on. Leading leaders calls for a mentality that allows others to make decisions. The board should never give the message, by trying to intervene in every potential mistake, that to err is unacceptable. Emphasizing the avoidance of errors rather than the creation of breakthroughs propagates not leaders, but followers. It encourages not decision makers, but bureaucrats. Leading leaders requires tolerance of risk, for leaders do not remain in the safe old ruts. They try and sometimes fail.

One approach is to view governance as *empowerment.* The board passes power to others and expects them to use it as assertively and creatively as they dare. The board will have both the circumspection and the mechanism to empower *toward* something definitive (the impelling criteria of Ends) and to empower *within* something definitive (the boundary criteria of Executive Limitations). The *amount* of risk is thereby controllable. Empowerment is not carte blanche, for delegation need not dissipate into abdication.

Further, the board's ability to keep its own eye on the horizon is prodded by mental bigness in the executive staff. Having leaders work for us is a gift, indeed, for they ally themselves with that which is big in us, save us from distracting side issues, and urge us on toward still greater leadership.

III. Respect Your Words

If saying what we mean and meaning what we say is difficult for us as individuals, as a group the task becomes formidable. Boards have a tendency to author words that quickly become disjointed from their authors, as if the speakers and the spoken are unrelated. Some new board members are delayed in getting "up to speed" because it takes time to learn where all the relevant words are to be found and, after locating them, to learn which words mean something and which do not.

One solution is to use fewer words. When a board's verbal product is voluminous, there is no way board members can fully embrace it. It is common for public school board policies to be several centimeters thick. When a board has that many policies, for practical purposes of governing it has no policies at all. It is far better that a board generate few words after much thought than many words after little thought. Part of the problem arises, of course, when the board acts as if it must approve or adopt all staff documents. Most nonprofit boards should get nervous when their total official paper increases beyond fifty pages. There is nothing magic in this number and it may not apply to all boards, but the minimalist sentiment is the same in all cases.

The second greatest source of volume is duplication. Stating the same board value or perspective in different places increases the volume. There is less of a need to read carefully because the material will probably be repeated. The words at hand, therefore, lose some importance. Board utterances cast in the format of traditional administrative topics restate or imply the same values repetitively, for relatively few values run across all topics. Perversely, if the values are only implied rather than expressed explicitly, in repetition they may be weakened rather than reinforced. Voluminous words, reliance on inference, inconsistency, or any factor that weakens the clarity of board values in their written form impairs the ability to speak with one voice. A greater volume of board words makes board values less clear.

When the board's policies are explicit, concise, and nonrepetitive, there remains the necessity to observe them scrupulously. The integrity of board documents, hence the integrity of the board's word, requires that the board never violate its policies nor create conflicting policies. This mandate would seem too obvious to state, but it is regularly ignored. It occurs when the board creates policy and then lays it aside as if once done it may be forgotten.

Because existing board values can always be found in the single repository of board policies, a board would never consider a new action without relating it to the existing policies. Living closely with the policies enables any interpolicy conflict to be cleared up in the normal course of business. The policies thereby evolve as a consistent expression of board values and perspectives. Not only are they consistent, but they increase in quality. For the monitoring process reveals finer points or new information with which the board can hone its language still further.

Hence, every contemplated board action is pressed against the record of what the board has already said. The compendium of policies will be short and explicit enough to do so easily, so the board need not be a collection of librarians and lawyers. To ensure the continuing fidelity and usefulness of these policies over time, the board must constantly use them or it will surely lose them.

Finally, a board's respect for its policy language may be heightened by cosmetics. Board policies, in this model, constitute a document as condensed as it is consequential. Presenting these few policies in a way that reflects their critical importance helps the board keep their importance in perspective; therefore, the essential governance declarations should not be typed on plain paper or photocopied. Use special printed forms with color if possible and the organization's logo. Make them look like the momentous, center-stage statements they are.

IV. Invest in Selection and Training

Performers—human or machine—can perform only up to their capability. That capability can be diminished or improved, so it is a variable that deserves care. The concept of investment is crucial, for the board can choose to see training as a troublesome cost or as an opportunity to reap a return.

A. *Recruit Those Who Will and Can Govern*

Raw material makes a difference. If the board is able to select its own new members, it should start with a well-deliberated set of qualifications. If the members are selected by others, the board should enroll appointing authorities in using the board's desired qualifications whenever possible. Aggressive recruiting involves not only selling prospective members on board membership, but excluding those who do not fulfill the requirements.

Trusting recruitment to a nominating committee can be useful, but integrity is maintained only if the board as a body has decided what types of people it desires. Nominating committees are too often left completely to their own judgment. They cannot help but develop implicit criteria, but rarely develop explicit criteria prior to becoming entangled in the personality-loaded interactions of recruiting. Even if they were to use a distinctly two-step process (a good idea if the board defaults), the board itself will not have been party to this matter that is critical to future board performance.

If the nominating committee has board-stated qualifications in hand (recorded as a Board Process policy), it can render better service. The board should phrase its committee charge (also in the Board Process category) so that finding the right people is given greater priority than filling vacancies. "We don't do a very good job of assessing prospective board members," said Edward Able, executive director of the American Association of Museums, "We tend to do it in the whole nonprofit sector in a very superficial way" (Blumenthal, 1988). Arthur Frantzreb, consultant in McLean, Virginia, claims the biggest failure is "inappropriate construction of membership—many boards have the wrong people on them" (Blumenthal, 1988). Indeed, boards would do well to tolerate a few more empty seats instead of rush to fill them. Recruiting will be more diligent if it is made known that membership in this board is an honor. After all, the board is selecting those who will bear the privilege and burden of trusteeship.

What qualifications are important? These vary, of
course, but with governance construed as I have designed in
this text, a few universal characteristics logically follow. To
be sure, members "must be knowledgeable, sophisticated, and
politically mature" (McGowan, 1987). To be more specific,
we must start with the job to be done, so we begin by consulting the Board Process policies on the board job description
and style of governing. Members need to have the understanding, the skills, and the willingness to contribute to the governance task the board has so carefully set forth. For the degree
of strategic leadership championed in these pages, five qualifications, among others, are necessary:

QUALIFICA-
TIONS

1. *Commitment to the ownership and to the specific mission
    area:* As agents of the organization's ownership, commit-
    ment to that trust is a prerequisite to board service. Com-
    mitment to the mission is important, though less so, for
    the mission is largely if not wholly a continuing creation
    of the board itself. Therefore, fidelity to those in whose
    name mission is created is dominant over fidelity to the
    current mission.

2. *Propensity to think in terms of systems and context:* Some
    people focus quickly on parts. Whatever the relationship
    of whole to part might be, these persons more readily
    focus on the part itself for inspection, discussion, and
    decision. Such persons, with all good intentions, place
    distractions, if not massive roadblocks, in the way of stra-
    tegic leadership. Prospective members more comfortable
    with parts have a valuable gift, but one that can more
    usefully be shared as a volunteer advisor to staff, not as a
    board member. The board needs members who are cyber-
    netically aware, drawn naturally to the harmony of the
    whole.

3. *Ability and eagerness to deal with values, vision, and the
    long term:* Those members who make the best contribu-
    tions are those who have a natural propensity to look not
    only beyond the stream of single events, but beyond sys-
    tems to the values upon which they are based. It is only a

small step from divining today's values as they are to planning tomorrow's values as they should be.

4. *Ability to participate assertively in deliberation:* Productive board deliberation depends on bringing the foregoing characteristics to the governance struggle. Boards are overly tolerant of members who fail to share their capacities in a way that enhances the deliberative process. It is not enough to have the potential to be a good board member; the potential must be manifested through participation.

5. *Willingness to delegate, to allow others to make decisions:* Board members, with respect to each other, must be able to share power in the group process and, with respect to staff, must be able to delegate. Board members who are loath to delegate will impair the board's leadership by constantly bringing small issues up for consideration. They will impair staff by denying them the opportunity to grow.

The pithiest counsel for choosing board members may be that of O'Connell (1985, p. 25), who was "pained to see others preoccupied with the buzz word 'expertise.' " If he had to rely on one characteristic, he "would single out the ability to start and end every analysis and evaluation with the standard of what is right." What stronger argument can be made that a board member's greatest gift to enterprise is educing, weighing, challenging, and, frequently, fighting over values?

Some prospective members are required to attend board meetings prior to assuming membership. Others are chosen from a pool of persons already familiar with board operations. These are useful tactics. At the least, a board should determine that a prospective member understands the board's governance model, bylaws, policies, current condition, and impending issues. Frankly, a prospective member who fails to ask about such things is probably not a good candidate. Selection of the most qualified members deserves careful thought and design. "Qualified," as is clear from the foregoing list, need not refer to academic credentials or high position. It

need not relate to gender, color, or income. It is more likely
to relate to grasp, mentality, connectedness, and commitment.
As an assessment of *past* selection, consider this test: If fewer
than half the board's members would make good chairpersons, the selection needs improvement.

B. Prepare New Members

Orientation of new members can help institutionalize the
board's governance process as well as prepare new members
for immediate participation. Excellence can be lost simply
through the influx of new members who have not agonized
through the process of improvement. Bringing their expectations about governance from other settings, they may cause a
regression to the norm. Institutionalizing the hard-won process calls for bringing new members to the understanding of
governance already reached by their colleagues. This done,
says Nash Williams, Executive Director of Southeast Georgia
Regional Development Center, Waycross, "new board members can start making meaningful contributions almost
immediately." Orientation is important enough to be a mandatory step rather than an optional exercise. The bylaws can
require that a new member complete orientation prior to a
vote. That members who are ignorant of the organization are
regularly given a voice in board decisions is an absurdity that
only familiarity can explain.

Part of the problem lies in the word *orientation,* which
may smack of learning where the lavatory, the coffee pot,
and the desk supplies are located. Adequate preparation to
shoulder the burden of strategic leadership requires something a bit more substantial. What is called for is job training,
though the term may be offensive to new members who are
accomplished in their occupations or in other board service.
In any event, proper preparation of new board members
requires that they become thoroughly familiar with the process and current values and perspectives of the board they are
joining. Present board members are the best persons to impart
this training. Staff can certainly acquaint new members with

operational matters. "Acquaint" is the distinguishing word inasmuch as new members' primary need is not for operational information. Such information may help members to form impressions of the whole and even to ask good, board-relevant questions, but it is the domain of management, not of governance. No matter how well this information is presented and learned, the new member is still not fitted with the tools he or she needs to participate constructively in the board process. New member training must be built primarily around preparation for strategic leadership.

C. Consider Knowledge as an Investment

All jobs require continual updating of skills and refurbishing of understanding. Turnover would perpetuate this need, even if it were capable of being met for all time for a given group of persons. Greater skills and understanding may often be bought without the expenditure of dollars. If dollars are necessary, the outlay is best approached from the standpoint of investment rather than cost. Instead of depicting training as an irritating cost, see it as an investment made for its expected return.

Consequently, return-on-investment criteria are applied. Although the return in terms of more effective governance will always be subjective, because quantification is difficult, the idea is the same. Boards would learn that education per se is not the issue; it is education about the *right things*. Moreover, decisions about board skill building would give appropriate consideration not only to the cost of training but, as Ronald P. Myers, New York management consultant, points out, to the cost of ignorance as well (personal communication).

V. Surmount the Conventional Wisdom

Until the prevailing understanding of governance changes, leaders must be aware of the deleterious influence of conventional wisdom. Current norms act as a drag on boards that aspire to a higher standard. A board must continually overcome regressive pressures from the general expectations people have of boards, the requirements foisted by funders and authorities, and even the well-intended advice of experts.

Influence of Those Who Expect. When observers see a board behaving atypically, they are surprised, maybe bewildered. Discomfort with deviation has little to do with whether the departure from the norm is productive. When members of a national association watch their board or members of the public scrutinize an elected board, they may be confused, suspicious, and even angered.

In the public sector, the ownership's commitment to a better system is largely rhetorical. We do not petition our public boards to create more effective systems; we assail them for some small instance of implementation that offends us. So the board that would create a better system will find few committed supporters among the onlookers. A survey of what lobbyists lobby for would indicate what aspects of a system truly command our attention. We pursue "fixes" of the element that concerns us, not more integrity in the process itself.

Rituals and symbols of responsible board behavior have grown over the years. Observers (not to mention board members themselves) have come to expect a responsible board to *look* a certain way: It approves budgets, monthly financial statements, and personnel "policies." It might adopt long-range plans, but these are expected to originate from staff recommendations for board reaction and revision. Observers have come to believe that boards that skip these steps are mere rubber stamps for staff wishes. They have seen occasional excesses and even disasters. So there is every reason to believe that boards who follow the prescribed route are responsible and those who do not are not. A board that forges new symbols does so at its peril. The unmasking of empty symbols rarely receives as much attention as their absence.

Boldness and inclusion are keys to success in overcoming these impediments. Boldness is needed to do anything new against the pressure to conform. Inclusion of all relevant parties in the adventure helps to defuse opposition. In other words, the board can seek to include observers throughout its discussion of governance principles and into the adoption of a new model. Those included might be journalists, advocacy groups, unions, lawmakers, and any other relevant stakeholders.

Influence of Those Who Demand. Those who have power over the board constitute a special class of observers. Funding bodies, regulatory agencies, and lawmakers incorporate the conventional wisdom into their demands. After all, in the development of federal or state regulations, statutory language, association certification, and standards of accreditation, there is little but traditional concepts of governance to guide the authors. Consequently, even vastly improved governance can run afoul of accreditation or law because of the improvements themselves. Mediocrity can pass tests that excellence fails.

It is not uncommon for standard-setting bodies to be very prescriptive about what constitutes "good" governance. National associations might dictate that a local board have a certain set of committees, particular officers, or monthly meetings. Federal legislation and regulations might dictate that grantees meet similar requirements. Hospital accreditation may require the board to go through certain approval procedures. State law requires school boards to take action on a host of personnel and expenditure matters. Houle (1989, p. 93) muses that "many a school board member has wondered whether it is possible to get through a single meeting without becoming an outlaw."

Often, little can be done beyond the consent agenda ploy suggested in Chapter Nine. If possible, a board would be well advised to interact with funders, regulators, and accreditors in a manner that takes the threat to their authority into account as compassionately as possible. Sometimes, it is possible to maintain a good governance model, yet give the controllers what they are looking for, that is, evidence that they are in control and will not be viewed as lax by those who evaluate them. Enrolling them in the board's adventure in governance innovation may be one approach. Another may be to proceed through the ritual behaviors expected, but not take them seriously. The consent agenda can be a handy device.

Influence of Those Who Help. Vast experience and expertise are available in the literature and from educators and consultants. Competent help can be obtained on strategic planning, financial oversight, fund raising, endowment building, administrative controls, audits, bylaws, corporate restructuring, and on and on. As part of their ongoing education as well as for specific issues that arise, boards should avail themselves of this body of knowledge.

Because the available expertise and helpful formats have been developed within the conventional governance framework, the board must be a wise consumer. Texts, academic courses, and advice from consultants are likely to be topic specific. The assistance needed concerns the board's *peculiar conceptual segment* of budget, personnel, or planning, not all budget, personnel, or planning activities. The board role can as easily be confused as helped by the board getting smarter about administrative or programmatic topics in their entirety, because the board can expend itself learning how to do the wrong things better.

The challenge to boards is to take advantage of accumulated knowledge, yet reframe that wisdom so that it contributes to better governance within a conceptually useful model, not simply to more information within an impaired model. Some helpers can adapt to this challenge quite well, but boards should not expect adaptation to be either automatic or volunteered. Conceptual struggle might be involved, not to mention a little ego. Staff, for example, may find that their training advice is not as useful to a board fulfilling an appropriate role. Although staff members may have expertise in many areas, governance is not typically one of these areas. To adapt their expertise to what the board needs to learn, staff must have an understanding of advanced governance. That understanding is not so widespread that boards can expect to find it, even in skilled educators and consultants.

Help helpers to be helpful by querying them about competing value issues in the area under discussion. Rather than seeking their recommendation as to what a selected value might be, draw them out on the range of value alternatives available and what they see as implications for options within that range. Implications are not only the predictable consequences, but the "industry averages" with regard to others' experience in making certain choices.

Particularly with regard to development of Executive Limitations policies, helpers can bring a great deal to a board's struggle in setting the ranges within which staff are allowed to act. They can assist the board in discovering, debating, and deciding what the conditions of jeopardy might be in, say, financial condition or personnel management. On these two topics, accountants and labor lawyers can be extremely enlightening if their counsel is taken in a way that relates to the board's proper role in such matters. Do not expect accountants or attorneys to know the proper board role, for they, too, will be operating from the conventional view. Following the "raw material" advice of your accountant or attorney can, indeed, result in poor governance. The use of consultants has always been an important skill; good consultees are made, not born.

VI. Perpetually Redefine Quality

Just as the board's work on Ends policies is a perpetual task, so is its pursuit of excellence in the governing process itself. The definition of quality never stands still. What constitutes quality governance grows as we do, yet always remains a little beyond our grasp. The constancy of change can be unsettling. Ferguson (1980) said that it is not change itself so much as "that place in between we fear. It's like being between trapezes. It is Linus when his blanket is in the dryer. There is nothing to hold onto."

One solution is to give up the chase and settle for the status quo. A second is to continue the pursuit at the expense of feeling not good enough all along the way. The first trap

is always present in human events. The temptation to settle
for the norm is strong in public and nonprofit organizations
because they are not forced to show results per dollar. The
second trap is well known to people who learn fast and continuously. They have only to look back a little to see the last
thing they did which, in light of the new learning, now looks
unwise. Their standards of wisdom and quality are moving
forward. Advancing standards can be an unspoken indictment
of the past. Hence, in addition to the direct cost of working
toward higher ideals, there is a psychic discomfort that
accompanies continual improvement.

A. View the Past as Inspiration, Not Impediment

Continuous improvement may be viewed as harsh treatment
of tradition. Organizations with long histories can cherish
their past without being beaten into inactivity by it. Organizational history, particularly a values history rather than a
narrative history, can serve the purposes of renewal and recom-
mitment by reminding members of what the organization
represents. Traditions can even ignite a secular revival if
treated as a gift, not a chain from the past. Traditions are not
to be discarded, but built upon. Glendora Putnam, Boston,
chairperson of the National Board of the YWCA, spoke of
her board as "moving ahead against long and revered traditions" (personal communication). When tradition boxes us
in and mindlessly determines who we are, it is no longer to
be revered but escaped. The board is, after all, creating tomorrow's traditions with the actions it takes today. Leadership
compels us to be true to tomorrow more than to yesterday.

B. Pursue Excellence More than Solve Problems

Commitment to excellence produces change that is more creative than reactive. Institute change to grow closer to an ever-
receding standard of quality. Such change is not characteris-
tically driven by problems. It is not problem solving as much
as it is ideal creating. It aims to fill the gap between what is

and what can be, more than it seeks to escape what has been. It is a "solution" of the future rather than the past.

"If it ain't broke, don't fix it" loses its charm as a guiding principle because it delays improvement until there is a necessity to move. Imai (1986) points out that if we do not fix the "unbroken," someone else will with predictable market advantage. Peters (1988, p. 3) has altered the old bromide to "If it ain't broke, you just haven't looked hard enough." For "broke" is not a property of the thing itself, but of its sufficiency in our ever-changing world. What was not broken becomes broken simply by virtue of new expectations and new possibilities.

C. Realize that Good Begets Better

The easiest and best time to improve is when things are already going well. Incorporation of better systems is facilitated when it is not perceived as discipline or initiation of a power struggle. When problems are rampant, almost any correction will be personalized. Thus, systematic monitoring of executive performance is best installed when the board and its CEO have a trusting, respectful relationship.

D. Remember that Excellence Begins in the Boardroom

Boards can be successful strategic leaders if they nurture their group responsibility. That responsibility must be accepted by every board member, not just officers. All members must participate in the discipline and productivity of the group. All members must be willing to challenge and urge each other on to big dreams, lucid values, and fidelity to their trusteeship. All members must cherish diversity as well as an unambiguous, single board position derived from diversity. All members must strive for accountability in the board's job, confident that if quality dwells in the boardroom, the rest of the organization will take care of itself. For in the long run, as surely as excellence ends with clients, patients, students, or other customers, it begins with governance.

"To rule is easy," counseled Goethe, "to govern difficult." The greatest difficulty may lie in shifting from old to
new paradigms. Successful strategic leadership demands
powerful engagement with trusteeship, obsessive concern over
results, enthusiastic empowerment of people, bigness in embracing the farsighted view, and the commitment to take a
stand for dreams of tomorrow's human condition. Re-creating
governance can generate a zestful new genre of strategic leadership in the boardroom.

🔥 Resource A 🔥

VARIETIES OF APPLICATIONS

The model of governance set forth in this book was developed to be generic, applicable wherever boards govern and whatever they govern. It is meant to encompass most organizational variations comfortably within a general theory of governance. Adaptation of the model to profit-based corporations, which has not been the subject of this book, requires only slight modification. Public and nonprofit boards face special circumstances that make adaptation appear—and in rare cases be—difficult.

Each organization likes to feel it is different, as each has its own history and personality. Even so, boards would do well to resist focusing prematurely on their peculiarities, and look first to generic principles of strategic leadership in governance. These principles, rather than detracting from the uniqueness of an organization, make its distinctiveness possible.

So it is that a board must deal with its peculiar conditions by first ignoring them. The peculiarities should be viewed through a framework of general principles. Amazingly, boards often find that they are not so different after all. The real payoff lies in being able to apply powerful, generic principles even when lured away by an illusory atypicality.

"Governance is governance is governance" may not be the whole truth, but it is not a bad place to start. Special circumstances do matter, but to deal with them effectively, a board must have a sound footing in the basics. Here are a few examples of application of the generic model to special situations.

City Councils. Four peculiar conditions apply to city councils: (1) Council members are elected individually. (2) Councils have police power or coercive authority over a geographic territory. (3) Councils are tightly regulated as to powers and methods by state law. (4) When an independently elected mayor serves statutorily as chief executive, the board–CEO structure does not pertain. In these cases, the relationship is more like that of the Congress and President, with separate powers.

When each member represents a separate constituency, working together for the whole can be difficult. Further, electorates tend to expect officials to attend to the smallest of concerns rather than the sweeping, momentous ones. A citizen is more likely to complain about a garbage-collection incident or stop sign placement than about the city's long-term maintenance of infrastructure. Police power gives the council authority over third parties, and thus creates a unique area of governance statements beyond the four policy categories of the model, *ordinances.* State-prescribed structure and procedures sharply cramp the latitude available in a council's governance and delegation. Moreover, councils resort to hands-on control so frequently that their time is always over-committed, which results in severe strain on council members. But the greater political consequence, as stated by Ron V. Houser of the City of Grande Prairie, Alberta, is that "society is often unable to attract the best candidates with the necessary vision and talents to lead . . . due to [the job having been defined as requiring such exhausting] time and financial sacrifices" (personal communication).

These conditions make application of good governance principles difficult, not impossible. Condition 4 (independent chief executive) introduces a major difficulty in full application of the model. Even then, however, a council can use some of the same policy-making principles. In the pure council–manager form, this problem does not arise.

School Boards. Local boards of public education have one of the most difficult tasks among public and nonprofit bodies.

They face three peculiar conditions: (1) Individual board members may be elected. (2) School boards are tightly regulated by state authorities. (3) School boards preside in the public spotlight over an emotional topic. Condition 1 is similar to the situation confronting city councils. Condition 2 is so oppressive that school boards misuse *most* of their time in trivial pursuits. Condition 3 intensifies Condition 1 inasmuch as the emotional electorate can be unyielding and irrational. Applicability of the generic governance model, however, is virtually total.

Boards in State Government. Peculiarities range broadly because of the wide variety of statutes establishing and charging such boards. Boards of state government departments, depending on the state, have greater or lesser control by the governor and greater or lesser independence from other organs of state government. They also have various degrees of authority over their respective chief executives and departments. Across these boards, the generic model ranges from largely to totally applicable. What these boards do have in common is their intimate relationship to legislatures and legislation. Legislators, when describing such boards' jobs, have a tendency to write enabling statutes that confound powers, prescribed activities, and outputs. As the conceptual framework used by state boards does not disentangle these managerially distinct concepts, there is much waste of leadership potential. There often appears to be a subtle legislative intent that the board not truly govern, but just as often the problem is simply an instance of naive design. Legislative traditions predate the development of twentieth-century management, so it is no surprise that legislative action often transpires as if principles of modern management never developed.

Foundation Boards. The only peculiarity is that foundation boards (excluding "operating" foundations) give away money rather than run their own programs. Thus, they are like relief agencies, the United Way, the Community Chest, and government funding agencies. The generic model is entirely applicable.

Church Boards. Where the church board is actually the church governing body, the model is totally applicable. When this is not the case, the variety of arrangements makes a single comment difficult. Some local church boards, for example, are merely advisory to a larger hierarchy, some advisory to the clergy, and some in charge, but only of nontheological aspects of the church. In these latter cases, the generic model is partially applicable.

Hospital Boards. Hospital boards have one peculiarity, the "third power" relationship with physicians. Doctors granted privilege to practice in the hospital constitute an organized body called the medical staff. Unlike employed personnel, medical staff do not work for the board, though there may also be salaried physicians who do. The administrative and clinical structure operating under the CEO does work for the board and often finds itself caught in the middle, between board and medical staff. Occasionally, the medical staff is directly represented on the board. Even so, the generic model is totally applicable, usually by treating the medical staff either as a powerful consumer block or as a body advisory to the board on medical quality.

Multicorporate systems in which hospitals are often involved may have an additional peculiarity. It is common to find parent-subsidiary structure and roles that are artifacts of government payment schemes, not designs based on optimal health care delivery. Prolific restructuring is more recently waning, however, as cost reimbursement fades into history.

Boards of Associations of Organizations. In this configuration, otherwise separate organizations have formed another tier of organization, a separate nonprofit corporation to which the constituent entities yield certain of their powers for a common purpose. The peculiarity lies in the nature of the ownership, ordinarily a convention or membership composed of individual organizations. This group would typically elect the board. Improved governance by the association board must be accompanied by greater understanding of governance and some degree of "buy in" by the broader group, because better governance calls on the membership to exercise control more responsibly. As such groups often use the association to set standards binding on themselves, individual organizations in the membership frequently try to end-run the ownership's mandates, placing the association staff in the middle. Power struggles and the ownership's reluctance to being governable even by its own rules ensue and can deteriorate into bizarre entanglements. Association staffs often see member organizations as more provincial and less concerned with the esoteric issues. Constituent agencies see the association staff as running out of control and perhaps even hoodwinking the association board. All manner of patchwork, politically motivated structure and process can grow up around these problems, none of which resolves the fundamental governance flaws that spawned them. Even so, the generic model is totally applicable.

Holding Company and Subsidiary Boards. The parent–subsidiary arrangement of boards is an upside-down version of the association of organization's board. In this case, the single, central board owns the multiple boards. The holding company structure has long existed in the profit sector, but is a relative newcomer to nonprofit organizations. Four peculiar conditions exist: (1) The ownership of subsidiaries usually comprises a single voting member, the parent corporation. (2) There is often a direct, supervisory link between the staff of the parent and the staff of the subsidiary, bypassing the subsidiary board. (3) The chain of successive staffs and boards up through the hierarchy can become a channel of repetitive approvals, taking the power away from subsidiary boards. (4) In some cases, the parent never intends that the subsidiary board govern, only that it provide legal window dressing. None of these conditions causes a problem in application and, in fact, Conditions 2 and 3 are considerably improved by the application of better principles. The generic model is applicable except when Condition 4 exists, in which case the model must be adapted.

Civic Club Boards. The peculiarity is the absence of staff. The board and any club members who can be rounded up are the only "staff" in sight. If the board remembers to wear its governance and workgroup hats separately, the only operational peculiarity lies in the nature of delegation. The board essentially delegates to subgroups of itself or to officers. For the purely governance portion of the board's job, the model is fully applicable though not nearly as necessary as in larger organizations.

Advisory Boards. Advisory boards or committees can most influentially advise about Ends issues. To influence Ends responsibly, a body must do virtually the same things it would do if it were to govern Ends. So, in that sense, advisory groups can use precepts of the model to give counsel within the latitude available to the advisee. In many cases, advisory boards are merely collections of advisors, which means that many voices, not "one voice," are heard. In this role, neither group decisions nor formal meetings are necessary. The role(s) an advisory body assumes depends solely on the person or group seeking advice. The model is partially applicable to stretching the visionary breadth of the advisory body and of little use with the collection of individual advisors.

Business Boards. Business boards, for the most part, are free of the market-surrogate obligation faced by organizations operating in the muted market. They still, however, must determine Ends, delegate some degree of latitude to the CEO, and decide how they will best represent investors. To the extent corporate boards actually represent owners and hold CEOs accountable (remember the skepticism of Geneen, 1984), their need for better governance is almost as great as that in nonprofit and public boards. Drucker (1989) has observed that business boards have much to learn from their nonprofit cousins on this score. The model presented in these pages, with only slight alteration, is completely applicable to the governance of business corporations.

Legislatures and Congress. There are vast differences, of course, between the bulk of nonprofit and public boards and the political "boards" of our state governments (legislatures) and federal government (Congress). Probably the most important structural difference is that the CEO (state governor or the president), as in some cities, is not a subordinate power. In the absence of a hierarchal relationship out of which separate roles and authority can be generated, we have separated legislative and chief executive powers in our chartering documents.

Still, an examination of legislative behavior using principles of corporate governance is a tempting exercise. Controversy over micromanagement receives frequent attention as do legislative excursions into executive investigative areas perceived to have political appeal. Budgeting on an annual basis for gargantuan agencies of government strains credulity, the more so when compounded by the perennial lateness of the budget process. The long-term mentality of government is severely hampered by such budget policy.

The inability of legislative groups to deal well with their own members' individual impingements on the executive process (intervening in grants, influencing procurement) bespeaks an irresponsibility of momentous proportions. "Coaxing, flattering and occasionally threatening federal agencies to meet constituent needs" at the rate of more than three million cases each year (Kiernan, 1989), members of Congress "try to solve the nation's problems one at a time" (Nader, 1989) rather than forcing self-correction in the systems that produce these anomalies. In politically self-serving displays of power, individual legislators damage (or, at best, fail to improve) effectiveness in the very systems their legislation created. Members of Congress were offended when a former Housing and Urban Development administrator suggested that members use oversight power, instead, to ensure proper administrative operation (Felton, 1989).

Former Senator Howard Baker (1989), speaking of the Congress as "a kind of national board of directors," said that body should represent the people on major policy decisions. Its calling is "not to manage the federal establishment to the last detail. We have an executive branch . . . to do that. Congress could do its job better if it did less of it." Nevertheless, the most august of assemblies, shrouding actions in pomp, can do very silly things.

In the words of H. G. Weisman of the Georgia Department of Labor, we "cloak irrelevance in prestige" (personal communication). We have coasted a long time on the design of our founders; arguably, no conceptual breakthrough in republican governance has been created for American government in 200 years. Perhaps it is time that government gained a new understanding of governance. The policy governance model is partially applicable.

☙ Resource B ☙

BYLAWS

This book speaks more to the process and focus with which leaders can better lead than to the initial, enabling mechanism. Yet, mechanics cannot be entirely ignored even when dealing predominantly with principles and concepts. For all nonprofit and many public boards, bylaws create the kind of organ that the board itself is to be. Bylaws, therefore, may help or hinder governance as conceived in these pages.

Bylaws are located in the middle of the hierarchy of documents. The first level is the establishment document, which, for nonprofit organizations, is the articles of incorporation, and, for public agencies, is a statute or other governmental order or charter. The third level comprises pronouncements of the governing body; in the model presented here these would consist almost entirely of policies. Bylaws, the middle document, connect this artificial creature of the state to real human beings. These real beings, acting as a board, for practical purposes *become* the artificial person called a corporation or a distinct agency of the public.

I offer the following guidelines concerning characteristics of the bylaws:

Length. Bylaws are best kept lean. Include only those items that establish the basic structure and empowerment of the board and its members. Whatever can legitimately be put into policy should be omitted in the bylaws.

Membership. Not-for-profit statutes call for a "corporate membership" to which the board is accountable. Membership is

221

the nonprofit equivalent of stockholders. For many groups, such as chambers of commerce and service clubs, membership is a pragmatically useful concept. For others, such as community health clinics, membership is a confusing entity. It is not comprehensive enough to be the moral ownership referred to in the text. Yet it is usually larger than the board and, thus, constitutes a separate body to be dealt with. Some organizations make use of membership in a ceremonial way, conducting annual meetings and board elections as a ritual. For most, however, it is best to nullify the membership in practice by simply constituting the board as the only membership, thus satisfying law and simplicity simultaneously.

Board Size. With respect to board size, the simple rule is to justify any number over seven. There is nothing magic about the number seven; however, as boards grow progressively beyond this size, they pay an increasingly higher price in awkwardness, discipline, and unfocused energy. Large boards have more than their share of flaws. Large boards are easier to manipulate. Members of large groups tend to assume less responsibility as individuals. Large boards have more difficulty setting meeting dates, deliberating issues, and staying on task. Nason (1989), speaking of foundation boards, found that the feeling of unity, common purpose, involvement, participation, and responsibility for the organization is greater in smaller boards. But he also felt the range of viewpoints and judiciousness of final consensus are enhanced by larger boards. Taking these opposing factors into account, I would promote as the guiding principle that a board should be no larger than the task of ownership linkage requires.

Quorum. Set the quorum no lower than 51 percent. A surprising number of nonprofit boards establish the quorum at one-third or, on rare occasions, even lower. They usually do so because of attendance problems and bitter experiences in not making the quorum. But a quorum set low is open admission that attendance does not matter. A board would do well to struggle with expected board member behavior than to hide the issue in a low quorum.

Attendance. One way to deal with the quorum is to require attendance. Public boards have far fewer problems with attendance than nonprofit boards. In the latter it is not uncommon to find an attendance requirement, but written with two fatal flaws. The first error is acknowledging a difference between excused and unexcused absences. In practice, there is no difference, for it is the rare board that can determine if an excuse is good enough. So "excused" comes to be defined as notification that one will not be present. This fulfills the requirement for courtesy, not for attendance.

The second flaw is that termination of membership is not automatic, but dependent on a vote. A motion must be made that George or Loretta be kicked off the board. No one wants to do that, so the attendance provision is not enforced. A workable, though slightly softened provision can be written: "Any member absent from three meetings in succession or four meetings in any twelve-month period is automatically terminated. If such member requests reinstatement within two months, the board may reinstate the seat, though this provision may not be used for any member more than once per term."

Officers. Keep the number of officers minimal and describe their jobs in terms of output areas and authority. Unless the board chooses to name its chairperson as CEO, do not describe the chair's job in terms of a CEO role, for example, that the chair has "general supervision" over the organization. If the organization is large enough to have a staff CEO, avoid having a treasurer unless demanded by law or standard setters. If a treasurer is a must, let the CEO also play that role. Consider having the CEO be secretary as well. There is no power in these roles when properly construed, so the board loses nothing but ambiguity.

Committees. With the single exception of a nominating committee, all committee descriptions can be omitted from the bylaws and covered in board policy. The only time the nominating committee is included is when the bylaws provide the method by which the membership chooses board members.

Staff. Bylaws are for the membership and board, not for staff. All material relating to staff can be omitted.

Legal Review. The bylaws constitute a legal document. Legal counsel should review any substantive changes. It is best that legal counsel not *write* bylaws, but only review the board's product. Attorneys are qualified to opine on the legality and risk exposure of bylaws, but are not qualified to determine how the board wishes *to be.*

⚗ Resource C ⚗

POLICY CONTRIBUTORS

Several board policies have been presented to illustrate portions of the text. The policies are not reproduced as examples of ideal language, content, or specificity. They are, however, actual products of the boards, councils, or commissions cited. Board policies are subject to amendment, so the policies here are represented to have been in effect only as worded at their original development. Policies from the various sources have been converted to a common format for convenience of reading, but language and organization have been preserved.

Hundreds of policies were made available to me by organizations using the policy governance model or some adaptation thereof. Of these only a few have been used in this text, here listed by policy title.

> "Administrative Clarity." An Executive Limitations policy of Southwest Counseling Service, Rock Springs, Wyoming. *Chapter Five, Exhibit 10.*
> "Board Job Contributions." A Board Process policy of Ramsey Action Programs, St. Paul, Minnesota. *Chapter Seven, Exhibit 17.*
> "Board Meetings." A Board Process policy of the Cincinnati-Hamilton County Community Action Agency, Cincinnati, Ohio. *Chapter Seven, Exhibit 16.*
> "Budgeting." An Executive Limitations policy of the Milwaukee Association for Jewish Education, Milwaukee, Wisconsin. *Chapter Five, Exhibit 6.*
> "Commissioner Responsibilities." A Board–Executive

Relationship policy of the Rhode Island Board of Regents, Providence. *Chapter Six, Exhibit 12.*

"Committee Principles." A Board Process policy of the Bissell Centre, Edmonton, Alberta. *Chapter Eight, Exhibit 19.*

"Communication and Counsel to the Commission." An Executive Limitations policy of the Metropolitan Waste Control Commission, St. Paul, Minnesota. *Chapter Five, Exhibit 8.*

"Delegation to the Executive Director." A Board–Executive Relationship policy of the Naperville Park District, Naperville, Illinois. *Chapter Six, Exhibit 11.*

"Employee Protection." An Executive Limitations policy of Social Advocates for Youth, Santa Rosa, California. *Chapter Five, Exhibit 7.*

"Financial Condition." An Executive Limitations policy of the Voyageur Outward Bound School, Minnetonka, Minnesota. *Chapter Five, Exhibit 5.*

"Governing Manner." A Board Process policy of Loudoun Hospital Center, Leesburg, Virginia. *Chapter Seven, Exhibit 15.*

"International Food and Development." An Ends policy of Lutheran World Relief, New York. *Chapter Four, Exhibit 3.*

"Mission." An Ends policy of the Ohio State Board of Education, Columbus. *Chapter Four, Exhibit 1.*

"Monitoring Executive Performance." A Board–Executive Relationship policy of the Washington County Developmental Learning Center, Cottage Grove, Minnesota. *Chapter Six, Exhibit 13.*

"Officer Responsibilities." A Board Process policy of Planned Parenthood of Metropolitan Washington, Washington, D.C. *Chapter Eight, Exhibit 18.*

"Protection of Assets." An Executive Limitations policy of Southeast Georgia Planning and Development Commission (subsequently renamed Southeast Georgia Regional Development Center), Waycross, Georgia. *Chapter Five, Exhibit 9.*

"Purpose of MIBOR." An Ends policy of the Metropolitan Indianapolis Board of Realtors, Indianapolis, Indiana. *Chapter Four, Exhibit 2.*

"Relationship of Board to Moral Ownership." A Board Process policy of The Eastway Corporation, Dayton, Ohio. *Chapter Seven, Exhibit 14.*

"Service Priorities." An Ends policy of the El Paso Center for Mental Health and Mental Retardation (subsequently renamed the Life Management Center), El Paso, Texas. *Chapter Four, Exhibit 4.*

REFERENCES

Ackoff, R. *Creating the Corporate Future.* New York: Wiley, 1981.

Albee, E. *Who's Afraid of Virginia Woolf?* New York: Atheneum, 1962.

Anthony, R. N. "Can Nonprofit Organizations Be Well Managed?" In D. Borst and P. J. Montana (Eds.), *Managing Nonprofit Organizations.* New York: AMACOM, 1977.

Baker, H. H., Jr. "Replace Congress with a 'Citizen Legislature.'" *The Chicago Tribune,* June 16, 1989, Sec. 1, p. 27.

Blumenthal, L. "Nonprofits Awakening to Need for Effective Boards." *Nonprofit Times,* 1988, *2,* 5–20.

Carver, J. "The Director's Employment Contract as a Tool for Improved Governance." *Journal of Mental Health Administration,* 1979a, *6,* 14–25.

Carver, J. "Profitability: Useful Fiction for Nonprofit Enterprise." *Administration in Mental Health,* 1979b, 7 (1), 3–20.

Carver, J. *Business Leadership on Nonprofit Boards.* Board Monograph Series, No. 12. Washington, D.C.: National Association of Corporate Directors, 1980a.

Carver, J. "Toward a Technology of Governance." Unpublished paper, 1980b.

229

Carver, J. "Is America Ready for Self-Governance: The Third Sector." In D. Nachmias and A. Greer (Eds.), *The Crisis of Authority: Citizen Boards and the Governance of Public and Private Agencies.* Milwaukee: Urban Research Center, University of Wisconsin, 1981a.

Carver, J. "The Market Surrogate Obligation of Public Sector Boards." *Journal of Mental Health Administration,* 1981b, *8,* 42–45.

Carver, J. "Toward More Effective Library Boards." *Focus on Indiana Libraries,* 1981c, *35* (7/8), 8–11.

Carver, J. "Improving Board Control and Effectiveness: The Problems of Non-profit Governance." Three-part series. *The Non-profit Administrator's Guide,* 1982, *1* (2) 14–16, (3) 9–16, (4) 7–11.

Carver, J. "Leadership Through Boards, Councils and Commissions: Creating the Future Through Better Governance." Paper presented at the annual meeting of the National Association of Community Leadership Organizations, Cleveland, Sept. 19, 1983.

Carver, J. "Consulting with Boards of Human Service Agencies: Leverage for Organizational Effectiveness." *Consultation,* 1984a, *3* (3), 27–39.

Carver, J. "Professional Challenges for an Emerging Community: The Challenge to Nonprofit Governance." Paper presented at the annual meeting of the Nonprofit Management Association, San Francisco, June 6–10, 1984b.

Carver, J. "Redesigning Governance in the Cities." *Florida Municipal Record,* 1984c, *58,* 2–4.

Carver, J. *A Tested, Fresh Approach to Designing the Board's Job.* Audiotape set. Milwaukee, Wis.: Family Service America, 1985a.

Carver, J. *Strategic Leadership: New Principles for Boards, Councils and Commissions.* Audiotape set. San Francisco: Public Management Institute, 1985b.

Carver, J. "Women on Governing Boards." Unpublished paper, 1985c.

Carver, J. "Boards as Cost Centers." Unpublished paper, 1986a.

Carver, J. *Eighteen Principles for Effective Leadership by the Board of Directors: An Introduction to the Technology of Governance for Nonprofit Organizations.* Untitled monograph series. Berkeley, Calif.: Center for Community Futures, 1986b.

Carver, J. *Nonprofit and Governmental Boards: New Design for Leadership.* Videotape set. Atlanta: Georgia Power Company, 1986c.

Carver, J. *Governing Parks and Recreation: Board Strategic Leadership in a New Light.* Videotape set. Alexandria, Va.: National Recreation and Park Association, 1987.

Carver, J. "Re-inventing the Governing Board." *Access,* 1988a, *1* (1), 4–8.

Carver, J. "Vision, Values and the Trivia Trap." *Florida Focus,* 1988b, *1* (2), 1–5.

Carver, J. "A Model for Strategic Leadership." *Hospital Trustee,* 1989a, *13* (4), 10–12.

Carver, J. "Economic Development and Inter-Board Leadership." Submitted for publication, 1989b.

Carver, J. "Governing Parks and Recreation." Submitted for publication, 1989c.

Carver, J. *Re-inventing the Board: Strategic Leadership for Public and Nonprofit Governance.* A national video teleconference. Athens: University of Georgia, 1989d.

Carver, J., and Clemow, T. "Redeeming the Church Board." Submitted for publication, 1990.

Chait, R. P., and Taylor, B. E. "Charting the Territory of Nonprofit Boards." *Harvard Business Review,* 1989, *89,* 44–54.

Crosby, P. B. *Quality Is Free.* New York: McGraw-Hill, 1979.

Crosby, P. B. *Quality Without Tears.* New York: McGraw-Hill, 1984.

Davis, S. M. *Managing Corporate Culture.* Cambridge, Mass.: Ballinger, 1984.

Deming, W. E. *Out of Crisis.* Cambridge: Center for Advanced Engineering Study, Massachusetts Institute of Technology, 1986.

Drucker, P. F. *The Effective Executive.* New York: Harper & Row, 1967.

Drucker, P. F. *Management: Tasks, Responsibilities, Practices.* New York: Harper & Row, 1974.

Drucker, P. F. "Managing the Public Service Institution." In Diane Borst and Patrick J. Montana (Eds.), *Managing Nonprofit Organizations.* New York: AMACOM, 1977.

Drucker, P. F. "Managing the 'Third Sector.' " *The Wall Street Journal,* October 3, 1978, p. 26.

Drucker, P. F. "What Business Can Learn from Nonprofits." *Harvard Business Review,* 1989, *89* (4), (July–Aug.), 88–93.

Ewell, C. M. "How Hospital Governing Boards Differ from Their Corporate Counterparts." *Trustee,* 1986, Dec., 24–25.

Felton, E. "The Politics of Influence Peddling." *Insight,* September 18, 1989, 22–23.

Ferguson, M. Untitled presentation to the World Future Society, Toronto, July 1980.

Fram, E. H. "Nonprofit Boards: They're Going Corporate." *Nonprofit World,* 1986, *4* (6), 20–36.

Fram, E. H. *Policy vs. Paper Clips: Selling the Corporate Model to Your Nonprofit Board.* Milwaukee, Wis.: Family Service America, 1988.

Gale, R. Letter to author, 1989.

Geneen, H. S. "Why Directors Can't Protect the Shareholders." *Fortune,* 1984, *110,* 28–29.

Haskins, C. P. "A Foundation Board Looks at Itself." *Foundation News,* 1972, *13* (2), (Mar.–Apr.).

Houle, C. O. *Governing Boards: Their Nature and Nurture.* San Francisco: Jossey-Bass, 1989.

Imai, M. *Kaizen.* New York: Random House, 1986.

Juran, J. M., and Louden, J. K. *The Corporate Director.* New York: American Management Association, 1966.

Kiernan, M. "Your Guy in Washington: Members of Congress May Be More Useful than You Think." *U.S. News & World Report,* 1989, *107* (6), 54–56.

Kirk, W. A. *Nonprofit Organization Governance: A Challenge in Turbulent Times.* New York: Carlton Press, 1986.

Koontz, H. *The Board of Directors and Effective Management.* New York: McGraw-Hill, 1967.

Louden, J. K. *The Effective Director in Action.* New York: AMACOM, 1975.

McConkey, D. *MBO for Nonprofit Organizations.* New York: AMACOM, 1975.

McGowan, R. A. "An Integrated Approach to Board Development." *Health Care Management Review,* 1987, *12* (3), 29–30.

Mueller, R. K. *Board Life: Realities of Being a Corporate Director.* New York: AMACOM, 1974.

Mueller, R. K. *The Incompleat Board: The Unfolding of Corporate Governance.* Lexington, Mass.: D. C. Heath, 1981.

Nader, R. Cited in Kiernan, M. "Your Guy in Washington: Members of Congress May Be More Useful than You Think." *U.S. News & World Report,* 1989, *107* (6), 54.

Nason, J. W. *Foundation Trusteeship: Service in the Public Interest.* New York: The Foundation Center, 1989.

National School Boards Association. Untitled advertising flyer. Alexandria, Va.: National School Boards Association, undated.

Neu, C. H., Jr., and Sumek, L. J. "Municipal Governance Challenge of the 1980s." *Florida Municipal Record,* 1983, *56,* 11–22.

O'Connell, B. *The Board Member's Book.* New York: The Foundation Center, 1985.

Odiorne, G. S. *Management and the Activity Trap.* New York: Harper & Row, 1974.

Peters,, T. J. *Thriving on Chaos: Handbook for a Management Revolution.* New York: Alfred A. Knopf, 1988.

Peters, T. J., and Waterman, R. H. *In Search of Excellence: Lessons from America's Best-Run Companies.* New York: Harper & Row, 1982.

Price, W. S. *Manual on Governance and Policy Planning for Board Members.* Silver Spring, Md.: Wolfgang S. Price Associates, 1977.

Reddin, W. J. *Effective Management by Objectives: The 3-D Method of MBO.* New York: McGraw-Hill, 1971.

Skinner, W. "The Productivity Paradox." *Harvard Business Review,* 1986, *64,* 55–59.

Smith, E. E. "Management's Least-Used Asset: The Board of Directors." In *The Dynamics of Management*. AMA Management Report No. 14. New York: American Management Association, 1958. Cited by Koontz, H. *The Board of Directors and Effective Management*. New York: McGraw-Hill, 1967.

Swanson, A. "Who's in Charge Here? Board of Directors and Staff—The Division of Responsibility." *Nonprofit World*, 1986, *4* (4), 14–18.

Waterman, R. H., Jr. *The Renewal Factor: How the Best Get and Keep the Competitive Edge*. New York: Bantam, 1988.

Witt, J. A. *Building a Better Hospital Board*. Ann Arbor, Mich.: Health Administration Press, 1987.

INDEX

A

Able, E., 201
Accountability: CEO, 51, 112–117, 150, 156; as cumulative responsibility, 114–117; problems of, 11; staff, 51; to constituencies, 20, 130–133, 174, 195–196
Accounting activities, 84
Accreditation, 207–208
Ackoff, R., 3
Action taking (board): reactive stance of, 11; short-term bias of, 11
Activities: commendable, 59–61; as means, 64
Activity levels (board), 12–13, 48–49
Advisory boards, 2–3, 216, 218
Advisory functions (board), 14, 158
Agendas: automatic approval, 175–176, 207–208; initiation of, 33, 174, 176–177, 179; perpetual, 177–179, 192, 209–211; planning content of the, 176–177; screening criteria for, 170–172. See also Meetings

Albee, E. F., 137
Alberta Ministry of Parks and Recreation, 12
Amendments, policy, 43, 52, 76
American Association of Museums, 201
Anthony, R. N., 7
Approval process: approval syndrome and, 50–53, 89–90, 94, 99–100, 103, 217; traditional reactive, 11, 86–87, 90–91
Asset protection, 97
Association boards, 207, 216–217
Audit, external, 122
Authority, problems of, 11–12

B

Baker, G. C., 103
Baker, H. H., Jr., 219
Barth, N., 90
Beneficiaries: mission, 69–70, 131, 193–196. See also Ownership interest
Blumenthal, L., 201
Board Process (policy), 37–39, 48,

138, 143-144, 201-202; core products, 69, 140-141, 143, 177-178;
on meetings, 170-171, 182; moral
ownership and, 130-133; optional products, 141-143
Board-CEO-staff relationship, 116-
117, 128-129, 157-159
Board-employee relationship, 115-
116, 176
Board-Executive Relationship (policy), 37, 39, 48, 143-144; accountability and, 114-117, 176; importance of, 109-110
Board-Executive relationship (policy), role distinction and, 125-
129, 150-152
Board-Executive Relationship (policy), structure of, 112-116
Board-staff relationship, 115-116,
176; policy, 37; prescribed, 13-14
Boards: classifications of, 1-6;
common shortcomings of, 10-
12; diversity and dynamics of,
135-139, 186-191, 211-212; economic classifications of, 4-6;
holism of, 152-155, 159-162, 202;
officers of, 149-155; organizational positions of, 2-4; as ownership subsets, 146; ownership-staff
bridge role of, 139-144; roles
articulation of, 20; self-governance obligation of, 132-135; as
special managers, 17-19; as trustees, 17, 131-133, 145, 197-198
Bowers, R., 54
Bryn Mawr Associates, 22
Budgets, policy and, 13, 32, 51,
99-104, 119
Business boards, 218

C

Carver, J., 182
CEO: board delegation to the, 48,
174-176; defining a, 110-117; freedom of action of, 89-93, 107-108,
116-117, 127-128; job contribution of, 116-117, 181; monitoring
of the, 118-125, 186; positional

accountability of, 51, 112-117,
150, 156; qualifications of, 116;
recommendations, 126
Chain of command, 127-128, 157-
158
Chairperson function, 138, 152-155,
204; CEO separation from the,
112-114, 150-151
Chait, R. P., 22, 108
Chavez, D., 193-194
Cheerleader functions (board), 14
Church boards, 216
Cincinnati-Hamilton County Com-
munity Action Agency, 138-139
City councils, 214
Civic club boards, 218
Clients (consultant), xiv
Collegial board-CEO relationship,
116-117
Commendable aspects vs. ends,
59-63
Committees, board, 137, 146, 155-
163; CEO relationship to, 113,
156-157; legitimate, 162-163;
policy job product of, 161-162;
staff relationship to, 158-159;
traditional, 164-166
Communication (board), 15
Communication, internal: down-
ward, 88-89. See also Executive
Limitations
Compensation management, 84, 97
Computerization, 62
Conformity and innovation, 205-
209
Confrontations, board member, 135-
139
Congressional boards, 219-220
Consent agenda, 175-176, 207-208
Constituencies: accountability to,
20, 130-133, 174, 195-196. See
also Ownership interest
Consultants, board, xiv-xv, 208-209
Consumers, board. See Beneficiaries
Context, 202; external world, 57-59;
with other boards, 66, 96-97, 147,
180-181, 196. See also Ownership
interest
Control, 21

Conventional wisdom, 205-209
Cost: control, 97, 197; effectiveness, 77, 205; mission statement on, 70-73
Credentials, staff, 61
Criteria, evaluation, 119-121, 124-125
Crosby, P. B., 197
Current policy, 42-43

D

Davis, S. M., 25
Decision making: CEO, 125-128, 176; concrete, 30-33, 51; decentralization of, 36; information for board, 118; staff-level, 127-128, 198
Delegation, 36, 46, 198, 203, 218; rubber stamping and, 173-174; solidarity and, 53; unitary, to the CEO, 110-112, 125-128, 150-152, *See also* Executive Limitations (policy)
Deming, W. E., 197
Disagreement, 186-189
Discipline, common, 20
Discrimination, policy on, 104-105
Discussions, meetings, 186-192
Distance factors, 13, 18, 115-116, 158-159, 204-205
Documentation: centralized, 43; consumer records, 84; language, 42-43, 54; minutes and, 40, 154-155, 190-191; policy, 42-43, 49-50, 189-191; procedures manuals, 43; staff-submitted, 40, 50-53, 89-90, 206; written, 42-43, 51, 183, 198-200
Drucker, P. F., 2, 8, 27

E

Eastway Corporation, 132-133
Efficiency. *See* Time management
El Paso Center for Mental Health and Mental Retardation, 71-72
Employees. *See* CEO; Staff-board relationship
Encompassment (policy), 44

Ends and means confusion, 35-36, 59-64
Ends (policy), 35-37, 47-48, 218; articulation of, 67-73, 179-181, 195-196; attainment of, 85-86, 185, 193-194; as a board product, 73, 179-181; evaluation compared to, 76-80; long-range, 74-75, 177-179; mission statement of, 64-67. *See also* Executive Limitations (policy)
Environmental Protection Agency (EPA), 62-63
Ethics and prudence (organizational): approval process and, 87; moral obligation of, 87, 88, 92; policy areas, 95-96; staff, 37. *See also* Executive Limitations (policy); Values, organizational
Evaluation: approaches to, 79-80; of the CEO, 124-125; consumer-based, lack of, 7, 66-67, 76, 218; difficulty of, 76-77; productivity and, 59-60; shortcomings, 77-78
Ewell, C. M., 145
Excellence: commitment to, 92, 210-212; of the means, 85-86
Executive Limitations (policy), 35-37, 39, 47-48, 143-144; performance criteria and, 119-121; proactive constraint by, 87-91; range of, 105-108, 209; staff action and, 91-96; typical topics of, 96-97. *See also* Ends (policy)
Executive means. *See* Means, staff
Expertise, board member, 29, 83
External responsiveness, 19, 84, 169, 174-175

F

Facilities management, 84
Federal government boards, 219-220
Fees (subsidized), 31
Felton, E., 219
Ferguson, M., 209
Fiduciary responsibility: budget policy and, 99-104. *See also* Ownership interest

Field, P., 46
Finance committees, 165
Financial condition policy, 98-100, 122, 151-152
Financial reports, 13, 119
For-profit boards, 4, 217-218
Fortune 500 companies, 8-9
Foundation boards, 215
Fram, E. H., 89, 113
Frameworks, conceptual, 26-27
Frantzreb, A., 201
Fund-raising responsibility, 141-143
Funding, public, 132, 169, 207, 216
Future thinking, 20, 210. *See also* Planning functions (board)

G

Gale, R., 10, 22
Geneen, H. S., 8, 112, 218
Goals, 58, 70-72. *See also* Ends (policy)
Goethe, J. W., 212
Governance, ineffectiveness of, 8-12, 205-208
Governance, policy: hallmarks of, 12, 29, 74, 178; implementation of, 182-186; management *vs.*, 18-19; process, 37-38; pursuit of excellence and, 209-212. *See also* Management functions (board); Policy making
Governing boards, 2
Governmental boards, 5-6, 207, 214; state, 215, 219
Grantors, 132
Group dynamics, 135-139

H

Harriet Tubman Women's Shelter, 162-163
Haskins, C. P., 164
Hierarchy, organizational, 61-62
Holding company boards, 217
Holism, 152-155, 159-162, 202
Horizontal integration. *See* Integration
Hospital boards, 8-9, 197, 207, 216

Houle, C. O., 2, 207
Houser, R. V., 214

I

Imai, M., 211
Impact. *See* Ends (policy)
Incidental information, 118-119
Independent Sector, 189
Ineffectiveness: of boards, 8-12, 205-208, 215; problem-based solutions to, 5
Information: for the board, 20-21, 106; classes of, 118-119; judgment of, 118-119; on owner's concerns, 145
Inspection, direct board, 122-123
Integration, horizontal *vs.* vertical, 66-67
International development goals, 70
Involvement level (board), 12-13
Issues: nested levels of, 48-49, 71, 73, 126-128, 171-172, 177; screening meeting, 170-172, 176-177; sizes of, 20, 48-49

J

Jackson, J., 191
Jenkins, P. T., 22
Job description (board), 20, 38, 149-155, 204-205; basic contributions, 143-144; group process governance, 136-139; policy development emphasis of, 53-55, 202-203; products, 139-144; staff *vs.*, 46-49, 176-177
Job description (CEO), 116-117
Job descriptions (board officer), 152-155
Job descriptions (organizational), topic level, 47-48
Juran, J. M., 9

K

Kiernan, M., 219
Kirk, W. A., 59
Koontz, H., 189

L

Language: of meetings, 169–170; mission statement, 64–67, 194–195; policy, 42–46, 50, 107–108, 122, 183–184, 197–200
Leadership: CEO, 116, 128–129; job design for, 9, 128–129; policy-focused, 28–30, 181, 211–212
LeFevre, R. J., 75
Legal requirements, 104, 214–215
Legislative action, 142
Life Management Center, 90
Line board, 3
Linkage. *See* Ownership interest
Logical containment principle, 44–46
Louden, J. K., 9, 22
Loudoun Hospital Center, 135
Lutheran World Relief, 70, 90
Lyon, G. T., 90–91

M

McConkey, D., 21
McGowan, R. A., 202
Management activities (staff): complexity of, 83–85; management perogatives and, 175
Management documents. *See* Documentation
Management functions (board), 14–15, 17–19; governance *vs.*, 18–19. *See also* Governance
Management literature, 9, 208
Market evaluation, lack of, 6–8, 66–67, 76, 218
Means, board: Ends separation from, 35–36. *See also* Ends (policy)
Means, organizational: ends confusion with, 59–63, 85; evaluation of, 77–80
Means, staff: the board's stake in, 85–87; complexity of, 83–85; proactive constraint of, 87–91. *See also* Executive Limitations (policy)
Meetings: achieving consensus in, 187–189; language of, 167–170; minutes of, 40, 154–155, 190–191; process criteria for, 170–171, 194–195; pursuing diversity in, 186–187, 195–196, 203. *See also* Agendas
Members of boards: orientation of, 203–205; process and dynamics of, 135–139, 186–191; responsibilities of, 133–134, 149–155; selection of, xii, 146, 201–204. *See also* Boards
Memory, institutional, 189–191, 210
Mental health service goals, 71–72
Metropolitan Indianapolis Board of Realtors, 69
Metropolitan Waste Control Commission, 105–106
Milwaukee Association for Jewish Education, 103–104
Minutes, the. *See* Meetings
Misconduct, 134
Mission statement: articulation of, 67–69, 179, 194–195, 202; on beneficiaries, 69–70; characteristics of, 64–67; on cost, 70–73; on product, 69
Model of governance: applications of, 213–220; criteria for a, 19–22, 213; implementation of, 182–186. *See also* Governance, policy
Monitoring, performance, 211; criteria for, 119–121, 166; information for, 118–119; methods of, 121–123
Moral obligations (board). *See* Ethics and prudence (organizational)
Moral ownership, 17–18, 130–133, 184, 197, 202
Morale, staff, 61
Mueller, R. K., 18, 181
Myers, R. P., 205

N

Nader, R., 219
Naperville Park District Commissioners, 33, 110–111, 193
Neu, C. H., Jr., 8

Nomination committees, 165–166
Nonprofit boards, 4–5, 169, 197, 201, 213, 215; muted market of, 6–8, 218
Nonprofit organizations, types of, xv–xvi

O

Objectives. *See* Ends (policy)
O'Connell, B., 189, 195, 203
Odiorne, G. S., 60
Officers, board, 149–155
Ohio State Board of Education, 68
Operations, organizational, 84, 97, 127; technology-driven, 62–63. *See also* Staff operations
Orchard Country Day School, 104
Ordinances, 214
Organization: history and, 189–191, 210; transcending the, 57–59
Organizational means. *See* Means, organizational
Other boards. *See* Context
Outcome-driven organization, 19–20, 58. *See also* Ends (policy); Values, organizational
Oversight (board): of staff, 13–14, 82–85. *See also* Executive Limitations (policy)
Oversight (public), 5, 80, 195, 197–198, 207–208
Ownership interest: board, 16–17; board linkage with, 144–147, 179–180, 196–198, 207–208; moral, 17–18, 130–133, 184, 197, 202

P

Parent-subsidiary boards, 216–217
Peckham, R. J., 10, 193
Performance: the board's own, 132–135; evaluation of, 116; monitoring, 76, 79–80, 118, 121–123; preestablished criteria for, 119–121
Perpetual agenda. *See* Agendas, perpetual
Personnel committees, 164

Personnel management, 84
Personnel protection policies, 32, 103–105, 107
Peters, T. J., 28–29, 43, 211
Philosophy. *See* Ends (policy); Values, organizational
Planned Parenthood of Metropolitan Washington, 67, 75, 90, 154–155
Planning functions (board), 14, 20; long-range, xix, 74–75, 177–179
Policies: budget, 13, 32, 51, 99–104, 119; financial condition, 98–100; monitoring of, 121–123; staff action limitation, 91–97; traditional or familiar, 84, 183–184, 189–190, 205–210. *See also* Documentation
Policy: amendments to, 43, 52, 76; areas of, 28, 95–97; board *vs.* staff-originated, 33, 46–49, 94–95; categories of, 34–39, 97, 163, 183–184; horizontal *vs.* vertical, 48–49, 52; sizes, 44–50; values and perspective and, 25–28, 71, 73, 94–95
Policy architecture, 49–50, 52
Policy making: characteristics of, 42–44; concrete decisions and, 30–33, 51; justifications for, 95–96; leadership focus on, 28–30; levels of, 49–50, 52, 73, 125–129, 170–172; perpetual, 177–179, 192–194; proactive, 33, 53–54; proscription *vs.* prescription in, 12–15, 88–91; sequence of, 182–183; speed of, 172–173, 185, 190; unity of voice and, 186–191; value issues focus of, 71, 73, 170–172. *See also* Governance, policy
Power of the board, 21–22, 164; ownership, 16–17, 130–133, 196–198, 207–208
Preboard *vs.* subboard work, 159–162
Prescription. *See* Policy making
Price, W. S., xix
Proactivity, 20, 87–91
Procedures. *See* Board Process (policy)

Product. *See* Mission statement
Productivity, 59–60
Program committees, 165
Program evaluation, 76–77
Program policy. *See* Ends (policy)
Prudence. *See* Ethics and prudence (organizational)
Public organizations, xv–xvi, 214–220
Public scrutiny, 5, 80, 195–196, 206–208
Putnam, G., 11, 210

Q

Quantification of activities, 60
Quinco Consulting Center, xix–xx

R

Ramsey Action Programs, 143–144
Reactivity, 11, 50–51
Recommendations: by the executive, 125–126, 137; policy options *vs.* committee, 159–162; staff-level, 127–128, 158–159
Record keeping. *See* Documentation
Recruitment, board, 146, 201–204
Reddin, W. J., 140
Reports: executive, 121–122; externally required, 84; financial, 13, 119. *See also* Documentation
Representation of specific groups, 146
Research on boards, 9
Responsibility, accountability *vs.* personal, 114
Results. *See* Ends (policy)
"Return on CEO," 128
Review of staff work, 11
Rhode Island Board of Regents, 46, 115, 195
Risk management, 84, 106, 198
Romanko, B., 12
Rubber stamping, board, 173–176, 206–208

S

Saunier, A., 90
School boards, 40, 169, 173–174, 199, 207, 214–215

Secretary, board, 154–155
Services. *See* Ends (policy)
Shea, J. G., 90
"Size of issue" matrix, 48–49
Skinner, W., 197
Smith, E. E., 9
Social Advocates for Youth, 104–105
Southeast Georgia Area Planning and Development Commission, 105–106
Southeast Georgia Regional Development Center, 204
Southwest Counseling Service, 107
Staff operations: board distance from, 13, 18, 115–116, 158–159, 204–205; board stake in, 85–87, 198; complexity of, 83–85; job description, 47; policies limiting, 91–96
Staff-board relationship: board committees and, 158–159; board meetings and, 168–169, 187; policy distinctions and, 46–49. *See also* Executive Limitations (policy)
Staff-level issues, 46–49, 74–75
Stakeholders, linkage with, 130–132, 144–147, 206–207
Stewardship, 133
Strategy, organizational, 58, 75
Structure, organizational: board-CEO, 112–116; commendable, 61–62; minimalist, 149–150, 156; policy architecture and, 49–50, 52
Sumek, L. J., 8
Swanson, A., 127
Systems thinking, 202, 211

T

Talk, managing. *See* Meetings
Taylor, B. E., 22, 108
Teamwork, board-CEO, 128–129
Technology, commendable, 62–63
Third World development, 70
Time management: approval fragmentation and, 52–53; efficient, 21, 29; of meetings, 167–173; short-term focus and, 11, 52; trivia and, 10–11, 43, 118–119, 137, 214–216

Titles, CEO, 112
Topic documents, 49
Trade association goals, 69
Training: board member, 204–205;
    staff, 61
Treasurer of the board, 151–152, 155
Tri-county Mental Health Services,
    90
Trivia, time wasting on, 10–11, 22,
    168, 174
Trusteeship, 17, 131–133, 145, 197–
    198
Turnover, board, 189–190, 204–205

U

Unanimity, 189
Unit cost and productivity, 60
Unity from diversity, 20, 186–191,
    195–196
Unwritten policy, 41–42, 191

V

Vacuums, policy, 92–93
Values, organizational, 19, 202–203;
    arena and fabric of, 93–95; choos-
    ing among, 71, 73, 102, 170–172;
    explicit, 42–43; financial data and,
    99, 102; policy based on, 25–28,
    30–33, 172–173, 189–191, 208–210;
    sizes and levels of, 44–46, 71, 73
Vendors policy, 97
Vertical integration. See Integration

Vice President, board, 154–155
Vision, board, 19, 29, 202–203,
    211–212; long-range, 74–75, 177–
    181, 194–196
Voluntarism: CEO directed, 142; con-
    notations of, 16–17, 134
Voyageur Outward Bound, 99–100

W

Washington County Developmental
    Learning Centers, 122–123
Watchdog functions. See Oversight
    (board)
Waterman, R. H., Jr., xix, 28–29, 43,
    75, 89
Weeks, J. P., 33
Weisman, H. G., 220
Williams, N., 204
Witt, J. A., 9
Work (board): committee, 159–162;
    hands-on, 144–148; prescriptions
    on, 14–15; staff-based division of,
    34, 157–159
Workgroup boards, 3–4, 147–148, 218
Worries as policy topics, 95–96,
    101–102, 184, 191
Writing: policy, 42–43, 54. See also
    Language

Y

Young Women's Christian Associa-
    tion (YWCA), 103, 210

ISBN 1-55542-231-4